AI for Good

AI for Good

Applications in Sustainability, Humanitarian Action, and Health

Edited by

Juan M. Lavista Ferres, PhD, MS

William B. Weeks, MD, PhD, MBA

WILEY

To my wife, Veronica, and our children, Antonia, Valentin, and Lucas: thank you for always being there and for the incredible family we've built together.

—Juan

To my wonderful children—Tanner, Atticus, Savannah, Scout, Joplin, and Hoke—their partners, and the delightful grandchildren they've produced (Isla, Momo, Elsie, and Hilton, so far). I am hopeful because the world's future is in your hands.

—Bill

100% of the author royalties from this book go to support humanitarian relief efforts.

Contents

Contents

Contents

Foreword

—*Brad Smith, Vice Chair and President of Microsoft*

In 2018, when we launched Microsoft's AI for Good Lab, our goal was ambitious yet clear: to harness the transformative power of AI to tackle global challenges and enhance lives worldwide. In just five years, I've watched Juan and his team of researchers, subject matter experts, and data scientists do just that as they formulate and advance that mission into inspiring results. Every day, they bring a sense of wonder and optimism to their work, solving our most pressing problems and improving lives at scale across society.

This book begins with a useful primer on what AI is and how it's used in a variety of applications, followed by a series of applied scientific studies. It explores how AI helps today's leading experts take on global challenges in health, human rights, and climate change. At Microsoft, we talk about the many ways AI offers more potential for the good of humanity than any invention that has preceded it. After reading this book, I hope you'll share my optimism for the possibilities of this powerful new technology.

An example of this collaboration is the lab's work on retinopathy of prematurity (ROP), a condition in children who are born prematurely. ROP occurs when premature birth disrupts the normal eye development of blood vessels in the retina, often leading to injury of the eye. As more premature babies survive, thanks to neonatal care, the prevalence of ROP has increased. However, if detected early, laser surgery can save a baby's vision. The challenge is that there are not enough ophthalmologists trained to diagnose and treat ROP, especially in the Global South, where the trend in premature births is rising, but healthcare infrastructure is lagging.

By combining the expertise of ophthalmologists with AI, we've developed an app that replaces expensive diagnostic machinery with a smartphone camera powered by AI. This innovation enables healthcare workers in remote areas to swiftly diagnose ROP, increasing access to essential interventions. This simple app not only improves access to important healthcare services, but also eases pressure on a system overwhelmed by an increase in demand.

When disasters strike, AI can help save lives. In 2023, the world faced fires, earthquakes, and flooding. The AI for Good Lab and its partners used geospatial tools that combined satellite images with AI models to map where buildings had been damaged or destroyed. These tools put real-time, actionable data into the hands of rescue teams, significantly enhancing their life-saving efforts.

When speed is critical, AI can aggregate, analyze, and share information with local authorities, but it cannot substitute the work of responders who are conducting rescue efforts on the ground. It's this joint effort between technology and decision-makers that reduces the time needed for making life-saving choices and boosts their capacity to act quickly and efficiently.

As these examples show, AI can play a critical role in addressing global challenges. They also reflect our dedication to ensuring that technology's benefits are available to all.

AI's potential reminds me of electricity, another world-changing invention from more than a century ago. In 1882, Thomas Edison's Pearl Street Station generator lit up homes and businesses in

New York City. Yet today, more than 150 years later, access to reliable electricity is still out of reach for more than 700 million people around the world. We must avoid creating a similar gap with AI and ensure that it is available to everyone, everywhere.

The responsibility now falls on us to guide AI's evolution responsibly. I am grateful for the innovative, compassionate individuals at the forefront of using AI for good.

Introduction

—*William B. Weeks, MD, PhD, MBA*

Writing is a lonely endeavor that, to be honest, is draining. Authors put a lot of themselves into writing. Picking the right next word, getting the phrasing correct, and accurately conveying the material all take effort. To be sure, spell-check helps, as do grammatical suggestions. However, writing about technical processes and research findings requires a lot of second-guessing and ego oversight. It is not enough just to get words on paper: someone reading them might follow your suggestions, and if the words are misleading or inaccurate, they could be more harmful than helpful. There is an ethical imperative to get the work right, to revise and check and confirm the work and the words so that they accurately depict what you did as a researcher, what you found, and what the limitations of your findings are.

Nonetheless, I love to write about and conduct research. Because of its challenges, I find the research process and the conveyance thereof to be highly intellectually stimulating and engaging. But more importantly, good research, when shared, can improve the world.

After a 30-year career at Dartmouth Medical School as a professor, teacher, and health services researcher who studied health systems and how people used them, I joined Microsoft. I love working at Microsoft and have had wonderful managers here—Dr. Jim Weinstein during my time at Microsoft Research, and now Dr. Juan M. Lavista Ferres, the co-editor of this book and the leader of the AI for Good Lab, the work of which fills this book. But, further, I think that Microsoft's top leadership—Satya Nadella and Brad Smith, who fund the AI for Good Lab—seek to use their positions to do good in the world.

In teaching classes on the financial and strategic management of healthcare organizations at Dartmouth, I often contrasted the two Latin phrases that express the ethics of business and medicine: "caveat emptor" and "primum non nocere," respectively. Caveat emptor means "let the buyer beware." If an organization produces something and sells it and it does not work out for the customer, too bad—the customer should have done due diligence and might even have anticipated that the product was not going to be useful. Medicine has an antithetical ethic: first do no harm. Healthcare providers have a fiduciary responsibility to their patients: they have an ethical obligation to share the risks and benefits of treatment decisions and collaboratively work with patients to tailor care pathways to achieve patients' goals in a way that is consistent with their values.

With a mission "to empower every person and every organization on the planet to do more," Microsoft's ethic aligns more with the medical one than the business one, which is why I like working there. Much like that of a provider and a patient, Microsoft seeks to have long-term and helpful relationships with its customers, ones in which customers benefit from Microsoft products in ways that are consistent with their goals and values.

Perhaps Microsoft's ethic of empowerment is most evident within Microsoft's AI for Good Lab. Considered part of Microsoft's philanthropic efforts, the Lab seeks to engage largely not-for-profit organizations in one of two ways. First, by providing Azure Cloud credits so those with data science expertise can use those credits to begin work on a particular project without incurring cloud storage and compute expenses. Second, by providing time-limited and project-specific data science expertise to those organizations that have data but do not have the advanced analytic skills to use the data to improve the world. The Lab also engages in work that addresses social problems that may not have a specific not-for-profit collaborator, like rapidly assessing damage from natural disasters or war, or providing tools that can help researchers and policymakers identify where broadband access or health inequities exist in the United States.

That work is presented in this book. By writing the book, we seek to help readers who are interested in how artificial intelligence and advanced data science techniques can be used to solve world problems by providing examples of the Lab's efforts to do so. So, part of the reason to write this book is to share knowledge with others who are interested, might learn about the approaches that the Lab has used, and, hopefully, apply those methods in a propagative way to address more problems. The world is complex, and we need as many thoughtful, curious, and motivated people who want to spend time addressing its problems as possible. We hope this book reaches them.

Moreover, I worry. As a physician, I worry about the world's health and the massive inequities in care access, quality, and outcomes that drive health disparities, within countries and across countries. As an economist, I worry that, unless efficient and effective solutions to some of the most pressing issues in the world (like climate change, humanitarian action, and health equity) are addressed, incentives that drive market behavior will worsen the plight of the disenfranchised. As a father of six and grandfather of four, I worry that the world I leave to my kids and theirs will be a worse one than the one I inherited.

So, my primary reason for writing a book that demonstrates how artificial intelligence and sophisticated data analytics can be used to solve the world's most pressing problems is because I have hope that these technologies can help, and hope assuages worry. The tools that are described herein are not panaceas—just as with a medical intervention, the choice of the tool, the approach, and the target must be clearly described, cautiously applied, and carefully interpreted.

But I am hopeful that these tools, when judiciously, rigorously, and ethically applied, can empower the world's populations to live in more just societies, avoid unnecessary harms that might otherwise befall them, and live healthier, more fruitful, and more fulfilling lives.

A Call to Action

—Juan M. Lavista Ferres, PhD, MS

Jeffrey Hammerbacher, one of the first data scientists at Facebook, once said, "The best minds of my generation are thinking about how to make people click ads."

When I first came across Hammerbacher's quote, I was leading the metrics team for Bing. Although I wasn't working directly on ads, part of my job was to understand the trade-offs between ads and relevance, so this statement resonated deeply with me.

To be clear, search engines like Bing and Google have immensely enriched society by granting unparalleled access to information and empowering individuals in novel ways. Yet, while recognizing these contributions, the pressing challenges of our times necessitate collective innovation, creative application of new tools and methods, and solutions that attempt to solve those challenges and not just provide information access.

The problems that we seek to address within the AI for Good Lab are foundational to societal improvement. For example, each year, millions of children die before they reach the age of five, with a significant majority of these deaths being entirely preventable. The climate crisis affects hundreds of millions of people, a staggering 1.6 billion people live with severe disabilities, and half of the world's population has inadequate access to high-quality healthcare. The world needs all the help it can get.

Over the past five years, I've had the opportunity to see the remarkable ways in which artificial intelligence and technology can address some of those challenges. While they aren't silver bullets, artificial intelligence and technology can be instrumental in solving specific issues. However, one challenge is that non-profit organizations and governments, which are at the forefront of addressing these problems, often do not have the capacity to attract or retain the artificial intelligence experts that they need to solve them.

Some might find it surprising, but even though predicting which person will click on your ad and which child has a higher chance of infant mortality are vastly different in societal terms, from a pure data science standpoint, they are essentially the same problem. If we can apply AI algorithms to optimize ad clicks, why can't we direct some of our best minds and most advanced technologies toward optimizing human life, well-being, and the health of our planet?

I am optimistic and strive to leave the world better than I found it—a goal I believe is more widespread than commonly perceived. I'm profoundly grateful to Microsoft for the chance to lead our AI for Good Lab that embraces this very mission.

I'm not going to lie: demonstrating an impact in this complex world is not easy. Over the years, my successes have taught me a lot, but my failures have taught me even more about making a tangible impact. And I've learned a few lessons.

I learned that there is a huge difference between solving a problem on paper and solving one in a real-world setting. One profound realization I had was that, as humans, we are addicted to complexity: we like complex problems and complex projects. This is the reason we sent a person to the moon before we added wheels to our luggage. However, seeking complexity is the wrong approach. If we want to try to impress people and look smart, our solutions will be complex. But if we want to measurably improve the world, our solutions must be simple. And building simple solutions is much harder.

I've learned that, when working on a problem, it is critical to collaborate with subject matter experts. No matter how much we data scientists think we understand a problem, it is crucial to work with those who fundamentally understand the problems we seek to address. Without insight from these experts, we might not understand potential issues with the data, we might focus our efforts on solutions that are not meaningful, are not pragmatic, or are unlikely to be implemented.

There is a difference between applied and pure research. In applied research, we focus on a problem and seek the best hammer to solve it. In basic research, we aim to create a new hammer. While both are essential for scientific advancement, one of my most significant realizations is that there's an imbalance between the two: it's not that the world needs fewer hammers, but it certainly needs more people looking to solve real world problems.

> *Don't try to make the problem fit your tools; get yourself the tools that fit the problem.*
>
> —*Toby Berger*

Academia brims with brilliant individuals. But if the currencies of academia—like publications, citations, or the h-index—are the sole objectives of academic work, they might hinder genuine impact. I strongly believe that, even if it is much harder to measure, the impact that our work has on improving society is the right measure.

My career path differs significantly from that of many of my lab colleagues and academic peers. I did not intend to spend a career in research: with a background in computer science, I spent my early years developing software solutions. But the combination of the two disciplines, which occurred during my tenure at Microsoft, gave me insight into the importance of combining the rigor of research with the utility of creating simple, practical, implementable, and scalable solutions.

In my position as the Director of Microsoft's philanthropic AI for Good Lab, I have been able to recruit some of the brightest minds I've ever experienced. I am profoundly grateful to them: they have taught me nearly everything I know about artificial intelligence.

The intent of this book is different from the many texts that aim to teach the fundamentals of artificial intelligence. By sharing real-world examples of how artificial intelligence and advanced data science methods can be applied for good, we seek to inspire the reader to envision new possibilities for impactful change. We want our work to engage readers by exploring pressing questions, igniting a broader conversation about ethically redirecting our technological capabilities for the greater good, and showing that it can be done.

The smartphones we carry in our pockets surpass the computing power that once sent astronauts to the moon.

With artificial intelligence and data at our fingertips, we now have the tools to address the world's most pressing problems.

We no longer have excuses.

Part I

Primer on Artificial Intelligence and Machine Learning

We intend for this book to be available to a broad audience, in particular, those without expertise in artificial intelligence or machine learning.

To make the book more accessible to that audience, we have purposely avoided including too many technical details of the studies. We have avoided the use of mathematical formulae and equations. Interested readers can find those in the references at the end of each chapter.

Nonetheless, artificial intelligence and machine learning tools have their own language and applications and limitations; studies applying artificial intelligence and machine learning have common processes, practices, and terms. Therefore, in the following chapters,

1

we provide a primer that defines artificial intelligence in lay terms, describes the applications and limitations of artificial intelligence, provides a brief glossary of commonly used practices and terms used in the application of artificial intelligence, and presents an overview of the structure that we applied to each of the chapters.

Those versed in artificial intelligence and machine learning should feel free to skip this part and jump right into the meat of the studies that we present (each of which is independent and not reliant on knowledge in any of the other chapters). Those wanting an introduction to or a light refresher on artificial intelligence, its application, and its evaluation should probably read this part before reading the studies.

Chapter 1
What Is Artificial Intelligence and How Can It Be Used for Good?

—*William B. Weeks*

Defining artificial intelligence begs the question of how one defines intelligence. It's a sticky and complex wicket because whole philosophical arguments and schools hang on the definition of intelligence. But, for the purposes of this book, we define intelligence as the ability to learn.

Learning entails acquisition of knowledge and application of that knowledge. Acquisition of knowledge without application is simply data. As humans, we are constantly obtaining data; however, much of the data that we obtain is filtered out. While our brains are purportedly the most complex entities in the universe, were we not able to filter out data, we would become overwhelmed by it. Imagine driving or taking the subway to work, and capturing and cataloguing every sight, smell, innuendo, look, and feeling that you experienced. I would bet that most readers—if thinking back to their last commute to work—would be hard-pressed to remember any details of it. Perhaps if something out of the ordinary happened, that would stand out. Or maybe if you heard your favorite song being sung by a busker in the metro station, that might penetrate your natural filtering system and persist for a while. But we filter out a lot, in large part to maintain the efficiency of our brains.

As humans have evolved, we have increasingly moved from a true/false, good/bad categorization mechanism for data inputs. Such categorizations might have even become embedded in our thinking process, possibly in an inefficient manner: most people shy away from snakes, even though most snakes are not dangerous. Nonetheless, because some snakes are dangerous, for efficiency, we may categorize all snakes as dangerous. And it really doesn't do us much harm, assuming that humans have very little or no use for snakes. The depiction of snakes as evil in biblical or mythological stories only reinforces our bias toward snakes.

But what if some snakes were useful to humans? Given humans' propensity to disregard or abhor snakes, that would be a challenging question to answer. Only a few humans become herpetologists and can, perhaps, achieve the objectivity necessary to study that question. Counter to being inculcated by natural training and belief systems that have persisted over millennia, these herpetologists might be able to apply their brains in a very focused manner to determine, without filters and bias, which snakes might be useful to humans and why.

Humans can apply their brains to try to avoid filtering and natural propensities to think in impartial ways. The entire scientific process is designed to be impartial. One considers an answerable question ("Might some snakes be useful to humans?"), designs a study to answer the question ("Let's objectively examine and document the potential harms and benefits of human–snake encounters for 100 randomly selected snake species."), collects data in a formalized manner ("Here is the list of those harms and benefits, with harms and benefits evaluated on a scale of 1 to 5, for each snake."), analyzes the data ("We conducted a regression analysis that evaluated the anticipated severity of harms and extent of benefits of 100 snakes based on their color, length, species, and whether they were venomous."), reports the findings ("Ninety-five percent of the snakes we studied were not dangerous to humans; many species of snakes were indirectly useful to humans by reducing populations of harmful rodents and insects, serving as a food source, and inspiring medical treatments."), and makes overall and policy conclusions ("A minority of snake species are harmful and many snake species are helpful to humans. Let's not categorically kill or be fearful of snakes.")

The work described is learning. Our herpetologist acquired data, analyzed it, and applied it in a new way that might change behavior and lead to more fruitful encounters with snakes in the future—not to mention generating less anxiety and a sea change toward snake-related biases. That learning took a lot of human effort and was limited by the requirements of research. Our herpetologist crafted the question, informed by the literature, on how to classify snakes. They might have been limited by linear analytic techniques that ignored more nuanced interactions between the variables they collected and the relationships between snakes and humans. They might have wanted to inform their study with more data on snakes (which are nocturnal, and which are tree-dwelling?) and human behaviors (what are the characteristics of humans who are harmed by snakes?). But, until recently, models that could be used to facilitate such complex data analytics have not been available.

What Is Artificial Intelligence?

That brings us to artificial intelligence. Artificial intelligence is intelligence—the ability to learn and apply knowledge—that is conducted by machines.

The term *artificial intelligence* was coined at a summer research project that was held at Dartmouth College in 1956 and attended by researchers from Dartmouth, Harvard, IBM, and Bell Telephone Laboratories. Organized by John McCarthy, a Dartmouth mathematics professor, the objective of the conference was "to proceed on the basis of the conjecture that every aspect of learning or any other feature of intelligence can, in principle, be so precisely described that a machine can be made to simulate it."

Over the last 65 years, the field of artificial intelligence can be categorized as having had cycles of intense interest (known as "AI summers"), followed by periods of reduced funding and disillusionment (known as "AI winters"). While the lay public might be under the impression that large language models like ChatGPT formed the nidus of the artificial intelligence revolution, today, we are surrounded by artificial intelligence algorithms that collect data, analyze it, and learn from it.

Consider your Amazon, or Walmart, or Netflix account. You buy an item. Based on your purchase—and, likely, your age, sex, and your history of other purchases—algorithms might suggest several other items that you might like. By aggregating data on behaviors that include what you buy, what you watch on YouTube, what you like on Facebook, and what others who have similar interests and characteristics buy and watch, these companies can steer you toward purchases or activities that, indeed, you are likely to enjoy. And with each new purchase or view, the algorithms can better learn your preferences and the preferences of those like you and further enhance your interactive experiences.

Artificial intelligence is behind the development, improvement, and maintenance of these algorithms. When automated, the process requires much less human involvement than our herpetologist's effort. Because of its effectiveness in driving sales, artificial intelligence has been largely used in commercial endeavors—collecting data, learning patterns, and deploying that learning to drive sales.

What If Artificial Intelligence Were Used to Improve Societal Good?

That is the premise of Microsoft's philanthropic AI for Good Lab— that these tools that are very effective at driving commercial behavior, can be used to attain social good through objectively conducted research. They can do so in three ways:

- *First, the tools can be used to facilitate data collection.* While we are more awash in data than at any other time in humanity, sometimes data is challenging to collect in timely, consistent, and objective ways. In this book, we provide examples of how, when trained, artificial intelligence algorithms can use satellite data to identify whales, or poultry farms, or building damage following an earthquake. Without satellite data or acoustic data or the ability to perform identification tasks in an automated way, it would take an inordinate amount of time for humans to collect data or images, classify them, and enter them into data-sets, with each step potentially being complicated by human error. Artificial intelligence can expedite data collation, classification, and analysis in a replicable and consistent way, thereby reducing costs and allowing insights from such data to be generated much more rapidly.

- *Second, artificial intelligence can be used to classify images so that scarce human resources are used more efficiently and effectively.* For example, among children, chronic otitis media is the most common cause of deafness and retinopathy of prematurity is the most common cause of blindness. For both conditions, timely treatment could prevent deafness and blindness, but treatment requires scarce medical specialists: otolaryngologists and ophthalmologists, respectively. Trained on images of normal and abnormal tympanic membranes or normal and abnormal retinae, artificial intelligence algorithms can be applied to videos obtained by unskilled community health workers to identify which frames in the video are of adequate quality for assessment, and then determine the probability that the child has chronic otitis media or retinopathy of prematurity. By doing so, only those children likely to benefit from treatment can be referred to the scarce medical resources for intervention: specialists then spend less time screening and more time treating, and more patients get care that prevents lifelong adverse consequences associated with lack of appropriate and timely treatment.

- *Finally, artificial intelligence can analyze data in novel ways that explore non-linear relationships among a multitude of variables to develop new insights regarding relationships between those variables and outcomes of interest.* In part constricted by data availability and in part restricted by computer power limitations, statistical methods used to analyze data have focused on examining linear and discrete relationships between variables and outcomes of interest. There is inherent bias in those traditional approaches: researchers like our herpetologist need to identify the limited variables that they need to collect to conduct their studies and then assume relationships between particular snake characteristics and their potential harms or benefits. However, just like humans' interactions with one another, relationships are complex, non-linear, highly interrelated, contextually determined, and time-dependent. Artificial intelligence algorithms can incorporate a virtually infinite number of variables to identify their individual and collective relationships to outcomes of interest.

Make no mistake—artificial intelligence is no panacea. As the following chapter suggests, there are rules that must be followed in its application and there are limits to how it can be used.

Nonetheless, artificial intelligence holds great promise for addressing the world's most pressing social problems. In this book, we give examples of how Microsoft's philanthropic AI for Good Lab uses artificial intelligence and other advanced data science techniques to conduct research in the areas of sustainability, humanitarian action, and health to generate innovative uses of existing data, novel insights, and new diagnostic pathways that can be used to improve life and address the world's biggest problems.

Chapter 2
Artificial Intelligence: Its Application and Limitations

—Juan M. Lavista Ferres

In many ways, "artificial intelligence" is a marketing term that has evolved over time. Even back in the 1970s, some applications that had a few rules were considered artificial intelligence. Today, there are many debates about what qualifies as artificial intelligence. In practical terms, most of the time when we talk about artificial intelligence, we are referring to machine learning.

So, what is machine learning? It is a technique involving algorithms that transform data into rules. In conventional programming, humans use their intelligence and knowledge to create rules expressed in software code. In contrast, machine learning relies on data and success criteria, using this data to generate rules while optimizing that criteria.

Many say that data is the new oil. In reality, data has nothing to do with oil; data is the new code.

Machine learning methods are not new: they are older than computers. We didn't refer to them as machine learning in the past, but as statistical methods. This includes techniques such as linear regression, logistic regression, and linear discriminant analysis (LDA). Some of these methods, like linear regression, date back to the early 19th century.

As an example, imagine you want to predict the price of a house. A basic model might use just square footage. By collecting data on square footage and sale prices, you can plot them on a chart (see Figure 2.1). The machine learning model then attempts to fit a curve that best describes the relationship between the two, while minimizing errors.

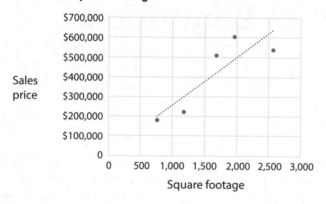

Figure 2.1 A scatterplot of home sales price and square footage, with a trend line.

It is important to understand that no matter how sophisticated a machine learning model becomes, its primary objective is to fit a curve. You might ask, "Isn't this something humans can do?" While it's true that humans can conceptualize problems with a small number of dimensions, doing so becomes impossible when dealing with thousands or millions of dimensions: our brains simply cannot handle it. However, given the right data, sufficient computing power, and time, machine learning algorithms can try to find a solution.

In this book, we often use *AI algorithms* and *machine learning* interchangeably, although it's worth noting that machine learning is a specific subset of AI focused on data-driven learning and prediction. A *model* in machine learning is the outcome of training an algorithm on data, where the algorithm learns and encapsulates this knowledge in its parameters. For instance, in a linear model y=ax+b, a and b are parameters that the algorithm learns from the data. Once these parameters are determined, they define the actual model.

Why Now?

Despite the fact that the term was coined almost 70 years ago, only recently has artificial intelligence become a universal topic. So, the pivotal question is:

Why now?

Two critical ingredients for machine learning and artificial intelligence are data and processing power. The accessibility and cost-effectiveness of both have changed dramatically over the years. *Moore's Law* anticipated the dramatic increase in processing power per dollar and the decrease in data storage per dollar (see Figure 2.2). The impact of greater processing power and cheaper data storage on the capacity to use artificial intelligence is profound.

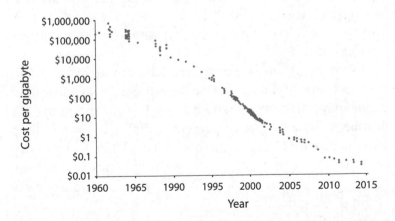

Figure 2.2 The drop in the cost of a hard disk per gigabyte, 1960 to 2015.

In the 1990s, storing 1 gigabyte of data—roughly equivalent to one minute of 4K video—cost about $10,000. Storing a two-hour movie that we casually watch at home today would have required a

$1.2 million investment. In 2023, a 10-terabyte hard disk (which is 10,000 gigabytes) costs about $118, reducing the storage cost of that same movie to $1.20.

Processing power has had a parallel evolution. Since Gordon Moore's initial observations in 1965, computational capacities have doubled roughly every 18 months. Comprehending the impact of this exponential growth can be challenging. For perspective, in 2004, the most powerful supercomputer was the NEC Earth Simulator; it cost $750 million. By 2023, a NVIDIA GPU card with three times the processing power of the Earth Simulator costs around $3,000.

The Power of Artificial Intelligence

The power of artificial intelligence stems from its ability to use data to solve problems, allowing us to address challenges that were once too intricate for traditional computer programs. In the 1990s, teams of software developers dedicated years to building systems that could understand handwriting. Yet today, with open datasets like MNIST and artificial intelligence libraries like PyTorch, a software developer can build a system to recognize handwritten numbers using just ten lines of code.

Moreover, there are problems wherein artificial intelligence is the only viable solution. Worldwide, over 450 million people have diabetes, and with changing dietary habits, this number will rise. Up to 21 percent of diabetics have retinopathy—a disease of the retina that impairs vision—when they are first diagnosed; over time, most diabetics will develop retinopathy. And diabetic retinopathy is the primary cause of blindness globally.

Early detection and treatment of diabetic retinopathy can prevent vision loss; however, with only about 200,000 ophthalmologists available in the world to diagnose and treat this growing number of diabetics, it is logistically impossible for every diabetic to be screened for timely treatment.

The good news is that researchers, including those in our Microsoft's AI for Good Lab, have developed artificial intelligence models that can detect diabetic retinopathy as accurately as top-tier ophthalmologists. In situations like these, where there simply are not enough medical professionals to screen patients, artificial intelligence isn't merely beneficial—it's the only viable solution. Its potential isn't limited to this condition; artificial intelligence algorithms can also help identify patients at risk for other diseases, improving the efficiency of healthcare providers around the world.

Artificial intelligence enables us to tackle problems that traditional programming couldn't solve and promises worldwide scalability.

The Challenges and Lessons Learned from Using Artificial Intelligence

While the power of artificial intelligence lies in its ability to learn from data, the quality and integrity of the data are paramount to its ethical and effective application. Here, I discuss nine lessons and challenges of applying artificial intelligence to real-world problems.

Models Can Be Fooled by Bias

Just as faulty code can produce inaccurate study results, biased or erroneous data can distort artificial intelligence applications.

In 1991, Halpern and Coren analyzed a random sample of individuals who had died and asked their family members whether the deceased were left- or right-handed. The researchers uncovered a concerning finding: on average, left-handed people died nine years earlier than their right-handed counterparts. This study was published in the *New England Journal of Medicine,* one of the world's most prestigious medical journals. However, Halpern and Coren failed to consider changes in social norms with regard to left-handedness. In the early 1900s, many parents forced their left-handed children to use their right hands. This social norm artificially reduced the percentage of left-handed people in the population. From 1920 to 1950, parents stopped this practice (see Figure 2.3), so the proportion of the population that reported themselves as being left-handed individuals rose considerably. This artificial increase in the left-handed population gave the illusion that left-handed individuals died younger, when in reality that was not the case.

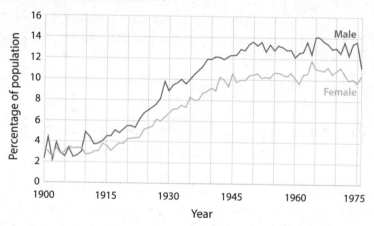

Figure 2.3   Proportion of left-handed people in the population.

Our findings have social ramifications: if a life insurance company uses handedness as a feature in their actuarial models, it could erroneously conclude that left-handed people are more likely to die younger and might unjustly charge them more for life insurance policies.

The point is that models trained on data are only as good as the data they use, and using data without questioning and understanding it can lead to flawed analytical output; output that can harm people. A significant portion of the data we collect has some bias; if we don't understand these potential biases, our models will not be correct.

Predictive Power Does Not Imply Causation

People often say, "Correlation does not imply causation." This means that just because two things *correlate*—consistently move in the same or opposite directions—doesn't mean one causes the other. In machine learning, it is important to understand that predictive power also does not imply causation. Simply because a machine learning model can predict outcomes based on certain data doesn't indicate that those data cause the predicted outcome.

Consider this analogy: imagine you are inside a windowless building. If people come in carrying umbrellas, you might predict that it's raining outside. However, the presence of umbrellas does not *cause* the rain.

Supervised machine learning is the process of mapping inputs to outputs using pairs of input and output data. This approach's predictive power is crucial in many scenarios. For instance, when you're driving and running late for a meeting, the ability of an algorithm to accurately predict traffic congestion is crucial. In such cases, the underlying cause of the traffic—whether it's a baseball game or road construction—is irrelevant. However, in other contexts, like cancer research, it's vital not only to predict whether a person will develop cancer but also to understand the causes of cancer.

It is important to note that machine learning, by itself, does not uncover causality. While it can help us identify potential clues, causality cannot be directly inferred from the data alone. Being able to predict an outcome does not automatically grant us insight into the factors that cause it.

Unfortunately, many people fail to understand the difference between causality and predictive power. A few years ago, Gallup conducted a survey with a simple question: "Do you believe correlation implies causation?" Surprisingly, 64 percent of Americans answered "yes."

For example, in constructing a machine learning model to predict drownings, variables such as season, day temperature, and the number of people swimming possess predictive power. At the same time, ice cream sales, which depend on day temperature, also show a high correlation with both day temperature and drownings, thus demonstrating predictive capability. However, it is important to recognize that not all these correlations imply a causal relationship with drownings (see Figure 2.4).

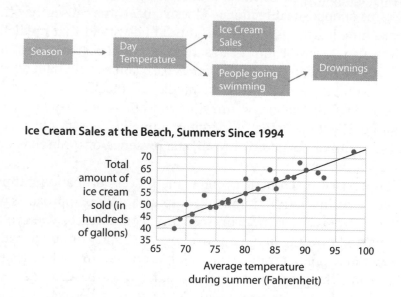

Figure 2.4   The relationship between day temperature and ice cream sales.

This relationship demonstrates that, in the absence of direct information, if our objective is to predict drownings, we can build a model based on ice cream sales, which will show predictive power. Of course, this doesn't imply causation; banning ice cream sales would merely disrupt this relationship, rendering it ineffective in prediction.

In summary, it is critical to understand that correlation and predictive power do not necessarily imply causation. This does not mean that such information is not useful; rather, predicting an event is distinctly different from understanding its causes.

A common misconception, particularly prevalent in the computer science community, is the belief that sophisticated machine learning techniques can directly reveal cause-and-effect relationships. However, no matter the level of sophistication in data analysis or machine learning models, data itself does not inherently encode causality, thus hindering the direct extraction of causal relation-ships. For example, Figure 2.5 illustrates a directed acyclic graph in three distinct scenarios, each resulting in the same data output for variables A and B.

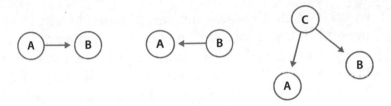

Figure 2.5 Directed acyclic graph for three different scenarios with the same data output for A and B.

This doesn't mean that AI cannot aid in understanding cau-sality. While we cannot directly infer causality from the data, AI can significantly assist in the process of formulating hypotheses for causality. We can then use this information, which will require combining AI with human expertise, domain knowledge, and a rig-orous scientific approach.

AI Algorithms Can Discriminate

When AI learns from historical data, it is susceptible to the same biases and prejudices that might have existed in the past. In the 1980s, St. George's Hospital Medical School in London experienced this firsthand when an algorithm used to recommend hospital admission was found to be biased against women and racial minori-ties. The algorithm didn't introduce new biases, it merely mirrored existing ones. It is important to scrutinize and test algorithms for biases, especially when they can cause harm.

While a model can be predictive, it can still be unfair. The like-lihood of a person repaying a loan is heavily influenced by their disposable income. It is well understood that, regardless of race or ethnicity, individuals with the same disposable income tend to have similar default rates. However, in countries like the United States, the distribution of disposable income varies based on race or ethnicity. Measuring disposable income is complex, as it requires individuals to disclose details about their spending habits. In contrast, determining someone's race or ethnicity is typically straightforward.

If we account for disposable income, race or ethnicity does not affect the probability of loan repayment. Thus, adding race or ethnicity to a predictive model would not improve its accuracy. Yet, in situations where a bank cannot ascertain disposable income, given the differing distributions of disposable income across races or ethnicities, a model based solely on race or ethnicity can still have predictive power. Such a model would be deeply unjust, as we know that race and ethnicity don't inherently affect an individual's likelihood of repayment.

Models Can Cheat (the Problem with Shortcut Learning)

AI models can sometimes take unexpected shortcuts in their learning process. In a 2017 study focused on diagnosing skin cancer, researchers used images provided by dermatologists. Unknown to the researchers, pictures more likely to be of cancerous lesions often contained fragments of a ruler shown beneath the lesion, a standard practice among doctors because lesion size can be associated with outcome. In contrast, images of non-cancerous lesions typically did not include a ruler. As a result, the model associated the presence of a ruler with a positive cancer diagnosis. Despite its seemingly impressive predictive capability, the model was essentially trained to recognize rulers rather than malignancies.

Models Do Not Generalize to Out-of-Distribution Cases

When training an artificial intelligence model, the dataset is typically split into multiple hold-out sets. This is done to ensure that the model can generalize without overfitting, which means memorizing solutions found in the training set. The model's accuracy is then evaluated on these hold-out sets, comprising data that the model has not been trained on. However, the metrics used to evaluate accuracy assume that real-world data distributions are similar to those in the dataset. If the actual distribution of data differs, the model's results may not generalize well.

For example, a skin cancer model trained predominantly on Caucasian skin tones may not perform effectively on data from African Americans, Hispanics, or Asians. Therefore, it is important for model developers to clearly disclose the characteristics of the training data and for users to understand the limitations of the model's applicability to different contexts. Using diverse and inclusive datasets broadens generalizability.

Models Can Be Gamed

In the world of machine learning, models are increasingly being deployed to make significant decisions, ranging from credit scoring to personalized marketing. However, these models, as sophisticated as they are, can be gamed by those who understand their underlying mechanics.

There is an anecdote that during the 1800s, the British government in colonial India was concerned about the high number of people bitten by cobra snakes in Delhi. To address this problem, the government decided to pay a bounty for every dead cobra. Initially, the policy was a success: cobra killings increased, and the number of cobras on the streets declined. The policy was a metric-driven success.

However, a few months after the policy's introduction, something unexpected happened. The number of dead cobras continued to increase, but so did the number of people bitten by cobras. Killing cobras had become a business, leading people to breed cobras for income. Not only was the public policy ineffective, but it also exacerbated the problem it was intended to solve.

In the 1970s, Charles Goodhart, a former advisor to the Bank of England and Professor Emeritus at the London School of Economics, described this exact problem when he wrote, "When a measure becomes a target, it ceases to be a good measure."

The *cobra effect* can also occur in machine learning. By understanding how a model works, users can game the system.

For example, some insurance companies offer discounted health insurance premiums to individuals who consistently reach a certain daily step count. To measure these steps, companies use phones or devices like Fitbits. Before incentives were introduced, these measures correlated highly with actual daily steps. However, after introducing incentives, people quickly found ways to manipulate the system. A common method is using phone rockers, devices specifically designed to simulate daily steps and exploit the system (see Figure 2.6).

Figure 2.6 A phone rocker device (Amazon.com, Inc.).

Some Tools Can Be Used as Weapons

Every year, thousands of individuals lose their voices due to diseases like amyotrophic lateral sclerosis (ALS). One's voice isn't merely a sound, it often defines our identity. With today's generative AI models, it is possible to replicate someone's voice using only a few minutes of recording. For those afflicted by debilitating conditions like ALS, this technology can be life-changing.

However, the same voice-cloning technology has its dark side. Instinctively, we tend to trust familiar voices and often use them as a means of authentication. When we receive a call from an unrecognizable number but hear a familiar voice—be it a relative, friend, or coworker—we're inclined to trust the caller. This reliance on voice as a verifier of identity can be exploited. For instance, cybercriminals have already begun to misuse this technology. In a recent incident, criminals used generative AI to clone the voice of a company director in the United Arab Emirates in an elaborate heist that resulted in a theft of approximately $35 million.

This example underscores the dual nature of AI technology—it can serve as both a tool and a weapon. When developing artificial intelligence models, it is imperative for researchers to consider the potential misuse of their creations.

Models Can Create an Illusion of Certainty

George Box, a renowned British statistician, once remarked, "all models are wrong, but some are useful." When building models that decision-makers will rely on, it is important to recognize the limitations and risks of those models should they be used for critical decision-making.

Before the 2008–2009 housing crisis, many financial institutions, regulators, and investors relied heavily on sophisticated financial models to assess risk. These models often included assumptions about housing prices, interest rates, and default probabilities. One key tool was the use of ratings provided by credit rating agencies, which assigned grades (like AAA, AA, etc.) to various financial instruments, including mortgage-backed securities (MBS) and collateralized debt obligations (CDOs).

> "Deciding under uncertainty is bad enough, but deciding under an illusion of certainty is catastrophic."
> —Kenneth E. Boulding

These ratings were perceived as a gold standard of risk assessment. Investors and financial institutions often took these ratings as near-certain indicators of the risk level, underestimating the uncertainty and complexity inherent in these financial products.

Many of the risk models used at the time were based on historical data that reflected a period of rising housing prices and low default rates. These models failed to adequately account for the possibility of a significant downturn in the housing market or a systemic increase in defaults.

The 2007–2008 financial crisis is a stark example of the dangers of overreliance on seemingly precise forecasts and models. It illustrates how the illusion of certainty can lead to widespread systemic risks, highlighting the importance of considering uncertainty and potential model limitations in financial decision-making and regulation.

AI Expertise Alone Cannot Solve World Problems

AI expertise alone cannot solve global problems; collaboration with subject matter experts (SMEs) is imperative to achieving those solutions. One of the most significant and vital lessons from working on AI for Good projects is the critical need to collaborate with subject matter experts. The lessons previously described underscore a fundamental issue for data scientists: domain knowledge is essential for solving complex problems. While data scientists may be experts in AI and modeling, it is likely impossible to have a meaningful impact without the appropriate subject matter experts' input on the problem they are attempting to solve.

For every successful project in AI for Good, there are many failures. Some are due to data scientists thinking they can solve these problems without a subject matter expert.

For example, in the initial stages of the COVID-19 pandemic, data scientists globally acted swiftly and with the best of intentions to assist through data analysis. While some of these efforts might have been somewhat effective, a significant number either failed to make a substantial impact or, in some cases, inadvertently introduced new challenges. This was largely attributable to a lack of comprehensive understanding of the data, gaps in knowledge about data collection methodologies, and insufficient expertise in virology. A common issue encountered, particularly in projects aimed at detecting COVID-19 through CT scans, was the prevalence of *shortcut learning*, which hindered the reliability and effectiveness of their findings.

Another example is in the context of analyzing infant mortality. My journey in AI for Good began by collaborating with Seattle Children's Hospital on infant mortality and Sudden Infant Death Syndrome (SIDS). This was my first AI for Good project, and thanks to the amazing CDC open dataset, we were able to work with colleagues to find new hypotheses for SIDS and infant mortality.

While trying to predict the survival rate of premature babies (one of the main causes of infant mortality worldwide), the models trained on the CDC dataset uncovered maternal smoking as one of the main predictive features. Maternal smoking being a predictor made sense to us, but the direction of the predictor was puzzling. The model indicated that among premature babies, if the mother smoked, the chances of the child surviving were higher. This finding was counterintuitive, and we were hesitant to even mention it to the doctors, fearing a problem with the data.

After much deliberation and nearly losing faith in our data, we decided to share our findings with the doctors. It turned out to be true that among premature babies, those with mothers who smoked had a higher survival rate. But this wasn't because smoking was beneficial; rather, it is quite the opposite. The reason for this phenomenon is that smoking is a cause of prematurity, but among the causes of prematurity, it is less severe than others.

Conclusion

The examples discussed in this book illustrate that while AI offers great potential to address global challenges, it also has inherent limitations. The principle of "garbage in, garbage out" is a well-known adage in statistics that underscores the necessity for high-quality, accurate data in the development of AI algorithms. For these algorithms to be effective, they need to be trained on data that is both reliable and representative. Additionally, it is crucial to validate these models using datasets that are randomly selected and held out from the training process.

AI models are typically designed to perform optimally on data that shares the statistical characteristics of the dataset used in their development, as well as on the specific population to which the models are applied. It is essential that these models are developed ethically and responsibly, with a clear logical basis, and their limitations must be explicitly acknowledged.

It is important to recognize that data alone may not capture all critical information. Data collection processes are often imperfect and can be subject to biases. Moreover, while AI models excel at making predictions, discerning causality from these predictions necessitates expert knowledge. This is why collaboration with subject matter experts is vital when data scientists tackle problems using AI.

As a key takeaway from this book, remember that collaborating with SMEs is not merely optional or a "nice to have"; it is a crucial component of effectively applying AI for social good.

Large Language Models

In November 2022, the world of artificial intelligence (AI) witnessed a significant shift. OpenAI, a frontrunner in AI, launched ChatGPT, a groundbreaking platform built on GPT-3.5, an exceptionally advanced AI model. ChatGPT was more than just a remarkable technological achievement; it provided people globally with an unprecedented, direct experience of AI. This development represented not merely a minor enhancement in AI technology, but a monumental leap forward.

We're still figuring out all the effects of these advanced AI models. But one thing is clear: GPT (Generative Pre-trained Transformer) model technology has greatly changed how we understand and use AI. People became much more interested in AI, with a 900 percent increase in online searches about it (see Figure 2.7).

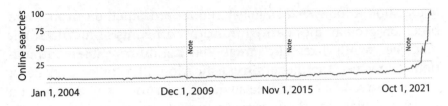

Figure 2.7   Trends in public interest: the surge of AI curiosity.

This interest wasn't just casual. Countries started serious discussions about AI's many effects. Governments and regulators rushed to understand the risks and opportunities of this new technology. They talked about setting priorities and making rules, showing that they understood AI's big impact.

The financial markets reacted too. The stock prices of companies making GPUs (the key hardware for training these models) jumped by over 300 percent. This shows how much confidence and expectation there is in the AI industry.

Right now, we're in the early stages of an "AI hype cycle." Large Language Models like GPT are a big achievement in AI, and a turning point for society. They've sparked a new wave of AI research and applications, marking the start of a new era.

However, in all this excitement, we should remember that these systems are still machine learning models. They're an advancement of algorithms and techniques developed over the last 20 years. What's really new is their size, complexity, and abilities.

As we keep exploring AI's potential, it's important to keep a balanced view. We should recognize these developments as groundbreaking, but also see them as part of the ongoing evolution in AI.

In this section, I provide a straightforward explanation of what these models are, outlining both their limitations and their potential for positive impact.

Understanding Language Models

At the core of today's linguistic technologies, such as GPT, lies the concept of a language model. Imagine you begin a sentence with "This morning I woke up and saw a beautiful blue _____."

What should follow? A language model predicts the continuation based on probabilities derived from vast amounts of text data. For instance, words like "sky" might be highly probable continuations. However, the model's sophistication allows it to consider a diverse range of possibilities, such as "bird" or "car," each with a specific probability, showcasing its nuanced understanding of different contexts.

The Training Process: Learning Language Through Data

These models are developed using a substantial corpus of diverse data, involving books, websites, dialogues, and more. By deliberately excluding certain words or phrases from this dataset, the model learns to predict these gaps with increasing accuracy. This training is crucial for the model to capture the complexities and subtleties of language and context.

Historical Perspective: Two Decades of Evolution

Although it may not be immediately apparent, large language models (LLMs) have been evolving for over two decades. Throughout a significant portion of this time, people have been using them in various applications, ranging from the autocorrect features in word processors to predictive typing on smartphones. These models significantly enhance our digital experiences by facilitating more efficient and accurate communication.

The Generative Aspect of GPT

Once trained, these models do more than just interpret language—they can actively generate it. When presented with a sequence of words, the model selects the most probable next word. By iteratively incorporating each new word into the existing context, it constructs coherent and contextually relevant text. This generative capability is what the *G* in GPT stands for, emphasizing its ability to produce original content. Unlike simple predictive models that only suggest individual words or phrases, GPT can create entire passages, ranging from simple sentences to complex paragraphs.

Pre-training: The P in GPT and Beyond

Traditionally, machine learning models were specifically tailored for distinct problems, requiring unique datasets. However, models like GPT represent a paradigm shift. pre-training on a general task, such as predicting the next word in a sentence, allows these models to be fine-tuned for a wide range of applications. For instance, GPT, initially trained on a vast corpus from the open web, can be specialized for tasks like medical record analysis, even if it wasn't exposed to such data initially. This pre-training approach, denoted by the *P* in GPT, underlines its adaptability and broad applicability.

Transformers: The T in GPT and Its Revolutionary Impact

The *T* in GPT stands for "Transformer," a groundbreaking architecture introduced in 2017 with the paper "Attention Is All You Need" by Vaswani and colleagues. Transformers revolutionized the training of large-scale language models, enabling them to handle extensive datasets and develop unprecedented complexity and capability. This architecture has since become fundamental in natural language processing, allowing for more efficient and accurate models.

In conclusion, LLMs like GPT are the result of decades of research and development in natural language processing. They represent sophisticated tools that have evolved to interpret and generate human language with remarkable accuracy. These models are reshaping our interaction with technology, making it more intuitive and seamless, and opening new avenues for AI applications across various fields.

Limitations of LLMs

In the fascinating world of LLMs, where breakthroughs often appear shrouded in mystery and wonder, it's vital for us to grasp the real essence of these sophisticated technologies. The smart responses and seemingly human conversations generated by these LLMs are not products of true understanding, but rather the result of intricate mathematical processes.

Demystifying AI's Intelligence

Although LLM models can be incredibly advanced, they do not actually understand or possess consciousness. Their capabilities hinge on performing complex mathematical computations. The appearance of human-like behavior is a result of their training, where they are fed enormous quantities of data created by humans. This training enables them to imitate human speech and thought patterns, but it's important to realize that this imitation is not the same as real comprehension.

Understanding Truth

A major challenge in developing LLM models is their inability to differentiate truth from fiction. These models learn from the data they receive, but they cannot judge the truthfulness or accuracy of that information. The quality and characteristics of the training data are crucial in determining the outputs of the model. If the data is biased or flawed, the responses from the LLMs will reflect these issues. Therefore, carefully selecting and curating training data is essential for building a trustworthy and ethical large language model.

The Phenomenon of LLM Hallucinations

One fascinating aspect of LLMs is their tendency to *hallucinate*. Because of their generative nature, they pick words based on probabilities, leading to outputs that may not be anchored in reality and could be completely fabricated. The LLMs, lacking real awareness, can't tell the difference between responses based in reality and these fictional creations, which poses a unique challenge in using these models.

The Impact of LLMs

Despite their limitations, the influence of LLMs has been remarkable, especially in the latter part of 2023. For instance, GPT-4 has achieved significant milestones, such as passing both the multiple-choice and written sections of the bar exam. The true strength of these models lies in their ability to learn from a vast source of information: the World Wide Web. This immense resource contains a significant portion of our collective human knowledge and is by far the most important dataset in the world. By training on this enormous dataset, LLMs can build a representation of the world that replicates the complex relationships found within human understanding.

In summary, while these advanced LLMs don't possess real understanding or consciousness, their capacity to process and emulate human language and thought is immensely powerful. As we continue to evolve and refine these technologies, it's crucial to understand their abilities, limitations, and the ethical implications they bring.

LLMs and the Power for Good

LLMs are already making a significant impact on the world in various ways. In this discussion, I outline three key areas where their influence is particularly notable.

LLMs as a Language Aid

When we discuss LLMs, the majority of discussions happen about the power that AI has in areas like healthcare diagnostics, but an area that's not often discussed is the power that LLMs have as a language aid in assisting non-native speakers to write fluently.

This opportunity deeply resonates with me. I am a non-native English speaker who leads a research lab in which over 70 percent of members hail from the Global South and are also non-native speakers. Approximately 95 percent of research is published in English, yet only 4.7 percent of the global population are native English speakers. When I give talks in Uruguay, my homeland, I always emphasize the importance of mastering both coding and English. I was fortunate; my parents ensured I learned English from a young age. However, many brilliant minds have not had that opportunity.

Throughout my career, I've observed that intelligence, innovative ideas, and hard work are uniformly distributed globally, but opportunities are not. One such opportunity is being able to proficiently communicate in English. English is a native language for fewer than 400 million people, but there are roughly 1.5 billion English speakers in the world. And all 100 of the world's most influential science journals publish in English. Often, the merit of one's ideas or research becomes secondary if it's not communicated clearly and effectively in English. And this isn't limited to academia; it's a reality in many spheres of life. English accounts for 60 percent of world Internet content and while a *lingua franca* simplifies global communication, proficiency remains elusive for many.

Recently, the journal *Nature* published an article highlighting the challenges non-English speakers face when trying to publish in scientific journals. As Mariana Lenharo observed, many journals lack clear policies that separate the quality of science from the quality of English writing.

The article, based on a study by Dr. Henry Arenas-Castro, revealed that non-native English speakers experienced paper rejections due to writing issues at least 2.5 times more often than their native-speaking counterparts. Many journals recommend that non-native English speakers use professional editing services before submitting, an expense many can't afford, especially in the Global South.

Many of us in global academia and corporate careers work in roles where impeccable English is a prerequisite. As non-native speakers, we must not only excel in our work but also master a second language, a task that often feels daunting and sometimes impossible to achieve.

With GPT, the ability to write confidently in English is now within reach for everyone.

LLMs, like GPT, are not a panacea, but they have the potential to bridge language gaps in remarkable ways. A good translation tool doesn't just provide a literal translation of words between two languages. It must also convey the meaning, tone, cultural connotation, and context.

LLMs work by refining text that may not be well structured, converting it into expressions akin to those of a native speaker. This is especially vital for non-native speakers who often grapple with the nuances of English grammar and syntax. The model assists not just by ensuring grammatical accuracy, but also by enhancing vocabulary to match the quality of native English publications.

Importantly, it aids in establishing a logical flow of content, a critical element for any publication, ensuring ideas transition seamlessly from one section to the next. There are also cultural and idiomatic nuances that may not resonate universally, and the model is adept at identifying and substituting these with more globally understood terms.

Great ideas are distributed equally around the world, but our language skills are not. In a world that faces significant challenges, we need everyone who can contribute to be able to do so. This reminds us of the democratizing impact Gutenberg aimed for when he invented movable type, which was a significant stride in the spread of literacy and knowledge.

LLMs for Democratizing Coding

I consider myself fortunate in many aspects of my life, particularly because my parents gave my brothers and me a computer when I was eight years old. This early exposure provided me with the invaluable opportunity to learn coding. The profound impact of coding on my life is undeniable. However, among my friends and classmates, I was the only one with this privilege. More than three decades later, less than 0.5 percent of the world's population knows how to code.

Learning to code is akin to mastering a new language, serving as our interface to programming computers. Although there has been a significant positive impact from more people learning to code, it's challenging to foresee a radical increase in the number of coders in the coming decades.

However, the advent of LLMs could bring about a substantial shift. Advanced systems like GPT-4 have the capability to translate natural language into actual programming languages. These models empower people to write programs and automate processes in their native tongues, be it English, Spanish, Mandarin, or others. This technology has the potential to democratize programming, extending its reach to hundreds of millions worldwide and bridging the gap between those who can code and those who cannot.

LLMs in Areas Like Medicine

In April 2023, John W. Ayers and colleagues published a study in *JAMA Internal Medicine* that compared the responses of physicians to those of GPT-4 when answering patient queries. The study found that GPT-4 not only provided more accurate answers than the doctors, but also demonstrated greater empathy.

It's noteworthy that GPT-4 has not been extensively trained on a significant portion of medical knowledge, much of which remains behind paywalls. Additionally, the model was not specifically trained for medical scenarios. Despite these limitations, its impressive performance highlights the potential impact of such models.

Currently, approximately 4 billion people—nearly half of the world's population—lack access to medical doctors. While medical access has improved over the past few decades, particularly in the Global South, the challenges remain significant.

These AI models are not poised to replace doctors. However, if they can provide accurate responses to human inquiries, they could enable doctors to concentrate on areas where they excel. While we have yet to see these models deployed in production environments for medical consultation, the promising results from this study suggest a path forward in addressing global healthcare disparities.

The full article on the impact of left-handedness is available at:

Lavista JML, Nasir M, Bijral A, Subramanian SV, Weeks WB, "Modeling to explore and challenge inherent assumptions when cultural norms have changed: a case study on left-handedness and life expectancy." *Archives of Public Health* 2023; 81(1):137. doi: 10.1186/s13690-023-01156-6.

Ferres, Juan M. Lavista, Elliot K. Fishman, Steven P. Rowe, Linda C. Chu, and Elias Lugo-Fagundo. 2023. "Artificial Intelligence as a Public Service." Journal of the American College of Radiology.

Lavista Ferres, Juan Miguel. 2023. "AI Methods and Their Application to Health and Prevention Using Open Data." PhD-Thesis-Research and graduation internal. https://doi.org/10.5463/thesis.172.

Chapter 3

Commonly Used
Processes and Terms

—William B. Weeks and Juan M. Lavista Ferres

Common Processes

Machine learning is a discipline within the field of artificial intelligence that uses particular methodological processes to develop statistical methods to evaluate the models that its application generates. This section describes the processes that are generally used to analyze a dataset.

First, researchers obtain appropriate permissions to use a dataset. Depending on the type of data to be used, this might include verification that the publicly accessible dataset can be used for the purposes of the study or that an institutional review board has reviewed the use of the data.

Next, researchers evaluate the quality and volume of the dataset and perform some initial assessment of the dataset's variables (which might include information obtained from satellite imagery, audio recordings, photographs, videos, geolocators, or medical records, for instance). This data might be *cross-sectional*, collected at a single point in time, or *longitudinal*, repeatedly collected over time. Methods that use artificial intelligence or machine learning are very *data hungry*. If there is inadequate data volume or quality, the study might not be able to be completed or, perhaps, less sophisticated analytic approaches will be required.

Then, researchers randomly split the dataset into a training dataset, a validation dataset, and a testing dataset. Most of the data would be used for training, while some is used for validation and some is held out and used for training. Because the datasets they use are very large, the characteristics of each of the three randomly split subsets should be similar. The researchers might test this hypothesis to ensure that they are.

The training dataset is used to train the model. Training entails supervised or unsupervised learning. *Supervised learning* trains models on labeled data (for instance, pictures that have been pre-specified to be a cat or contain melanoma); *unsupervised learning* does not use labeled data but instead identifies patterns or classes of objects of interest—essentially labeling them—as part of the learning process. The training process requires many iterations and experiments, in which variables used to predict model outcomes are introduced or excluded and permutations of the data inputs (for instance, the number of pixels per inch in an x-ray) may be examined. The goal of this process is to try to arrive at a model that accurately predicts the outcome of interest, within the training dataset.

Once a model is trained, the researchers turn their attention to validation. Here, the model's performance is tested on the validation dataset. The researchers may change weights or importance of certain variables and may drop variables that do not substantially contribute to the model. Models with more variables use more space, require more compute power, and take longer to run; therefore, they are more expensive to implement. By paring the model to its most efficient and effective form on the validation dataset, researchers optimize the trade-off between the model's inputs and its accuracy.

Finally, researchers test the model. Here, they no longer change the model's structure, input variables, or variable weights. On data to which the model has not been exposed, they objectively test its ability to predict the outcome of interest (for instance, does the photograph of the skin indicate that the patient has leprosy or not). And they use the following commonly used measures to evaluate the model's performance.

Commonly Used Measures

Researchers use commonly defined measures to evaluate the model's quality and accuracy.

There are four possible prediction outcomes for a model:

- *True positives*. Here the model *correctly* classifies a picture of skin that *does* demonstrate leprosy (it has been labeled by a physician as a picture of a leprous lesion).
- *True negatives*. The model *correctly* classifies a picture of skin that *does not* demonstrate leprosy (again, it was labeled by a physician as not containing a leprous lesion).
- *False positives*. The model *incorrectly* classifies a picture that *does not* demonstrate leprosy as including a leprous lesion.
- *False negatives*. The model *incorrectly* classifies a picture that *does* demonstrate leprosy as *not* including a leprous lesion.

In aggregate, the performance of the model is defined by the following:

- The *true positive rate* (also known as *recall* or *sensitivity*) is the number of true positives divided by the sum of true positives and false negatives. This captures the proportion of all positively labeled objects (pictures with leprosy) that the model correctly classifies as positive.
- The *true negative rate* (also known as *specificity*) is the number of true negatives divided by the sum of true negatives and false positives. This captures the proportion of all negatively labeled objects (pictures without leprosy) that the model correctly classifies as negative.

- *Precision* is the number of true positives divided by the number of true positives plus false positives. Precision calculates how accurate a classifier model is by measuring how often the model correctly predicts a particular class (the degree to which pictures that the model indicates show leprosy are of patients who actually do have leprosy).
- *Accuracy* is the sum of true positives and true negatives divided by all the cases examined (which is the sum of true positives, true negatives, false positives, and false negatives). Accuracy calculates how well the algorithm has classified truly positive and truly negative cases among all cases examined.
- The *area under the receiver operating curve* (or *area under the curve, AUC*) is commonly presented as a graphic that displays two parameters: the true positive rate and the false positive rate. While displayed as a graphic, the AUC value is an aggregate measure of performance that is the proportion of the space when plotting true positives against false positives. AUC varies from 0 (none of that space is captured) to 1 (all of that space is captured). A higher AUC is preferable; a value of 0.5 means that the model is operating at the same performance level of a coin toss.
- *F1*, also known as the *harmonic mean of precision and recall*, is calculated as two times the equation (precision times recall) divided by (precision plus recall). The F1 score ranges from 0 to 1, with 1 indicating perfect precision and recall.
- *Intersection over union (IoU)* is a metric for measuring the accuracy of an object detection model. The greater the IoU, the greater the region of overlap between the object as defined by the model and the object as defined by "ground truth," or as labeled by experts.
- A *correlation coefficient* captures the statistical relationship between two variables—the way that they change in relationship to one another. Ranging from -1 to 1, a value closer to -1 or 1 indicates that the variables change in either an opposite direction (as variable A increases, variable B decreases, and, if perfectly so, the correlation coefficient is -1) or in the same direction (as variable C increases, variable D also increases, and, if perfectly so, the correlation coefficient is 1).

- A *Dice similarity coefficient* is a measure comparing human segmentation to automated segmentation that ranges from 0 to 1, with higher numbers indicating greater alignment. It is essentially the correlation of the identification of an area (like a human organ or a building footprint) as predicted by a model with the ground truth, or classified by a human.
- *N-fold cross-validation* is a process wherein pooled data is divided into N separate groups (or "folds"), for the purposes of testing the model's generalizability by validating it on one fold and testing it on the remaining ones.
- *Shapley Additive Explanations (SHAP)* is a method to explain the output of any machine learning model by computing the contribution of each variable (or feature) used in the model to its predictive output. Usually presented visually, SHAP can demonstrate the strength and direction of each variable on the model's output.
- *Fréchet Distance* is a measure of similarity between curves that takes into account the location and ordering of the points along the curves. A shorter distance means that the curves track more similarly to one another.

The Structure of the Book

In the following chapters, we provide examples of the research that the AI for Good Lab conducted. The work uses artificial intelligence and advanced data science techniques. We provide the examples as summaries of academic articles that Lab members have contributed to writing. To expand readership and interpretability, we purposely avoid detailed technical descriptions of the methods used in the projects and try to avoid jargon. Further, the summaries that we provide do not include every finding uncovered in the academic papers.

We organize our collective work into three categories:

- *Sustainability*, having to do with topics related to climate change
- *Humanitarian action,* having to do with humanitarian relief efforts and accessibility

- *Health*, having to do with diagnosis and treatment of health conditions

For ease of reading, we summarize our work using the first person, active voice: we invariably use "we" to refer to work that was done. That is purposeful: the work was done collaboratively, often with multiple internal and external partners. We list those partners and their primary affiliations at the time the work was completed in the acknowledgments section, but additional details about the individual collaborators can be found in the referenced papers.

Finally, we follow a similar structure for each chapter:

- We start with an executive summary that summarizes the work.
- We then provide the reader with an overview of why this work is important, to provide context for the work and an understanding of why the Lab sought to complete that particular project.
- We then provide a summary of the methods used and the research findings before engaging in a discussion that articulates the key insights, the limitations, and the implications for the work.
- Finally, we provide a "what we learned" section that highlights how insights into aspects of the work that might have been peripheral to that particular research project and its findings might apply to other projects and areas.

Throughout, we provide figures and tables. These are easier to ingest than text that tries to describe numbers or trends. Importantly, these figures and tables help summarize the work and demonstrate how the graphics generated by artificial intelligence and sophisticated data analytic techniques can summarize information and inform decision-makers.

We hope that these examples provide insights into potential objects of, approaches to, and applications of artificial intelligence in the service of social good. The world is increasingly complex; fortunately, it is also increasingly inundated with data that can be used by artificial intelligence models to improve the life across the planet. Best of luck to our readers in extending this work.

Part II

Sustainability

Human-fueled climate change is transforming the planet. Climate change has created more frequent and more violent storms, altered natural environments (thereby threatening the existence of certain species), and highlighted human activities and innovations that promote—or could curtail—climate change.

In concert with satellites and sensors, artificial intelligence can be used to study and mitigate the effects of climate change. While humans are extremely good at recognizing patterns, we can get led astray. We bring with us biases that can limit our ability to see subtle patterns, and our eyes and brains simply cannot process gargantuan volumes of data available at the pixel level.

Computers can remedy those pattern-recognizing deficits. By processing data at a sub-optical (and sometimes sub-aural) level, comparing a multitude of targeted data elements that are longitudinally captured, and calculating relationships, machines can use artificial intelligence to recognize patterns and potentially anticipate future states.

In this section, we highlight how Microsoft's AI for Good Lab has used machine learning and artificial intelligence to study climate change using visual and auditory sensors, images, and satellite data to identify and measure places on Earth that might contribute to or mitigate climate change, understand animal behavior, and even forecast degradation of solar panels: each of the examples can help policymakers understand and make informed decisions regarding how to address climate change.

Chapter 4

Deep Learning with Geospatial Data

—*Caleb Robinson, Anthony Ortiz, Simone Fobi, Amrita Gupta, Girmaw Abebe Tadesse, Akram Zaytar, and Gilles Hacheme*

Executive Summary

The availability of satellite data has radically transformed how we can monitor and influence numerous activities on Earth, including agriculture, urban planning, disaster monitoring and response, and climate change research. However, different satellites have different data collection methodologies and resolutions, which makes the application of deep learning methodologies challenging. Here, to realize the potential of deep learning for remote sensing applications like satellite imagery, we developed a library of processing code called *TorchGeo* that provides ways to load data from a variety of benchmark datasets, allows for sampling of geospatial data, and provides transformers that can be used with *multispectral imagery*—that is, imagery with channels beyond red, green, and blue—which can be used to reveal the presence of gas, biological activity, water quality, and pollution, for instance. *TorchGeo* is the first library that released pre-trained models for multispectral satellite imagery that can be used in downstream sensing tasks when there is limited labeled data. To promote further research, we used existing datasets and benchmarks to create reproducible benchmark results that can be used to accelerate satellite imagery–based research efforts.

Why Is This Important?

While human activity is contributing to climate change, until recently, we were not able to monitor its impact very efficiently or effectively. However, the deployment of numerous satellite systems allows us to continuously monitor climate change and—importantly—the influence of numerous human activities (like the use of land for agriculture, urban development, and climate change mitigation—such as monitoring the location, size, and efficiency of solar panel farms) on climate change. Such monitoring allows us to respond quickly to non-human and human disasters by identifying the location, extent, and degree of damage from tsunamis, hurricanes, and war, for example.

However, a multiplicity of satellite systems exist: some are older and some are newer. They collect and process data in different ways. They collect data across different spectra—from the human visual spectrum of red, green, and blue to infrared and ultraviolet spectra that can capture information on biological activity, water depth and quality, and air pollution. Further, they collect data at different spatial resolutions—some monitor huge areas for large events (tracking hurricanes across the Atlantic Ocean, for instance), while others can identify objects as small as cars over relatively small swaths.

The problem with this abundance of data and data sources is that it is challenging to integrate that data in a useful and reproducible way so that researchers, city planners, environmental regulators, and agriculturalists can use that information comprehensively to understand the current state of a particular geography, inform their choices about future actions, and monitor the impact of those choices. Without such data aggregation and integration, information would be lost, decisions would not be as informed, and monitoring would be limited.

Here, we used deep learning techniques to integrate data from a variety of satellite data sources across multiple spectra. Through data processing, we were able to generate improved projections and levels of spatial resolution, standardize that process, and publish a Python code package that allows interested parties around the world to do the same.

Methods Used

In this work we used publicly available datasets from multiple sources that examine multiple areas across the world, including:

- Landsat 8 imagery and Cropland Data Layer masks that are used to create a benchmarking dataset
- The So2Sat dataset, which uses Sentinel-1 and Sentinel-2 data to classify over 400,000 image patches, with one of 42 local climate zone labels collected from different urban areas across the globe
- The LandCover.ai dataset, which includes high-resolution red, blue, and green imagery over Poland and has land cover masks
- The Chesapeake Land Cover dataset, which consists of imagery and land cover masks for parts of six states in the Northeastern United States
- The RESISC45 dataset, which consists of red, green, and blue image patches of varying spatial resolutions, each of which is classified as one of 45 classes
- The ETCI 2021 dataset, generated for a flood detection competition
- The EuroSAT dataset, which consists of Sentinel-2 images that are classified into ten target classes
- The UC Merced dataset, which consists of red, green, and blue image patches from the United States, classified into 21 categories
- The COWC Counting dataset, which consists of aerial imagery labeled with the number of cars in the image

After optimizing the data loading process, we created simple, reproducible benchmark results for eight of the aforementioned datasets. We tested and confirmed the accuracy and reproducibility of benchmark generation, and we tested the performance of our models across multiple parameters.

Findings

We articulated the challenges inherent in using multiple satellite-sourced, multispectral imaging, and classification datasets. This finding is perhaps best demonstrated in Figure 4.1, which shows an example of heterogenous geospatial layers collected from different sources (A and B in Figure 4.1) from which a user might want to sample data. Because those layers have different coordinate reference systems, patches of imagery (C and D in Figure 4.1) sampled from layers that cover the same area will not be pixel-aligned. The software packages that we developed transparently perform the appropriate alignment steps by reprojecting and resampling during data loading so that users can train deep learning models without having to manually align data layers.

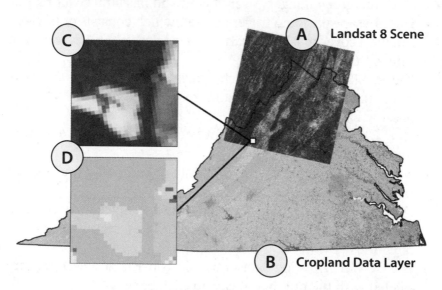

Figure 4.1   An example of heterogenous geospatial layers collected from different sources (A and B) and using different coordinate reference systems (C and D).

We also resolved the issue wherein different layers of geospatial data have different coordinate reference systems and spatial resolutions (see Figure 4.2, top). This means that data from different sources is not pixel-aligned and cannot be used in modeling pipelines. After reprojecting data into the same coordinate system and resampling into the highest spatial resolution, data can serve as inputs or masks to deep neural networks (see Figure 4.2, bottom).

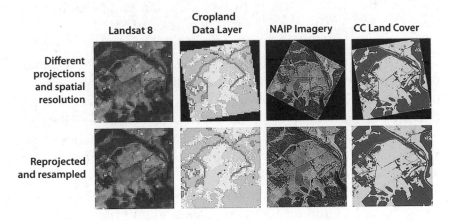

Figure 4.2 Examples of geospatial data that have different projections and spatial resolutions (top) and those same data reprojected and resampled so that they can serve as inputs or masks to deep neural networks (bottom).

The TorchGeo Python package that this work developed generated code for five commonly used functions needed to explore geospatial data:

- Data loaders for geospatial datasets common in the literature
- Data loaders for combining uncurated geospatial raster and vector data layers with the ability to sample pixel-aligned patches
- Augmentations appropriate for multispectral imagery
- Data samplers appropriate for geospatial data
- Pre-trained models for many common remotely sensed imagery sources

Discussion

Through data processing, model testing, model optimization, replicability testing, and efficient code development, we were able to address and remedy challenges that researchers and users commonly encounter when working with geospatial data from multiple sources. We published that code as TorchGeo, a Python package that allows users to bypass common preprocessing steps necessary to align geospatial imagery with labels.

Our work contributes to the satellite imagery–using community in a second way: the software package we developed serves as a platform for performing geospatial machine learning research. The platform can be scaled over large volumes of geospatial imagery that are currently underexplored but now can easily be integrated. Further, the software package provides a catalog of benchmark geospatial datasets that are now available through a common interface, making it easier for researchers to explore new ideas with existing work without having to repeat expensive computations. Future work includes building inductive biases appropriate for geospatial imagery into deep learning models and exploring data fusion techniques.

What We Learned

We found that a unified, consistent, objectively tested, and multidisciplinary approach to solving a common set of problems that users encounter when processing and analyzing geospatial data can lead to effective, efficient, and reproducible solutions. Further, consistent with Microsoft's AI for Good mission, we found that leveraging publicly available datasets and making our solution to these common challenges publicly available is an effective way to support the broader research community.

Data processing and employing large computing models consumes energy, generates heat, and contributes to climate change. By helping to minimize the need for unnecessary and redundant data processing, model development, and computer usage, this work helps mitigate climate change. In addition, part of responsible use of artificial intelligence entails efficient use of scarce resources and ensuring that those resources are widely available, particularly in areas where resources are constrained and, in the case of resources needed to mitigate climate change, where climate change impact is likely to be greatest.

The publicly available code that we generated can minimize preprocessing requirements, expedite the use of publicly available datasets, contribute to the generation of insights from these datasets to monitor and mitigate climate change, and allow humanitarian action efforts to more expeditiously respond to natural disasters. It can also help put land to its best use in a way that minimizes resource needs, curtails unnecessary energy use, and makes publicly available geospatial datasets more accessible.

The full article on which this summary is based is:

Stewart AJ, Robinaon C, Corley IA, Ortiz A, Lavista JM, Banerjee A. "TorchGeo: Deep Learning with Geospatial Data." *arXiv*: 2111.08872. doi: 10.48550/arXiv.2111.08872.

Chapter 5
Nature-Dependent Tourism

—Darren Tanner and Mark Spalding

Executive Summary

Climate change and a dependence on tourism have led island countries to consider sustainable ways to manage their natural resources, often by embracing the concept of the *Blue Economy*: a sustainable use of ocean resources for economic growth that preserves the health of the ocean ecosystem. Here, we used machine learning and artificial intelligence tools to leverage user-generated content in an effort to understand tourist activities and preferences, as well as to model and map multiple nature-dependent sectors of the tourism industry in five small island nations in the Eastern Caribbean. We additionally boosted the accuracy of these models by further incorporating input from local governments and tourism experts.

The approach that our research team developed is scalable and practical. It can be used by a number of countries that want to transform the role of tourism in their economies so that they improve the sustainable use of their natural resources in a way that preserves them, to the country's long-term economic advantage.

Why Is This Important?

Climate change is greatly impacting the planet. Unfortunately, current economic interests preserve that destructive process: vested interests that profit from climate change are unlikely to change unless motivated to do so through ecological policy and financial penalties.

One way to limit unsustainable consumption of natural resources is to articulate the source and value that is—or could be—generated from tourism that is dependent on preservation of natural resources, by shifting the focus of tourism toward the principles of ecotourism. Ecotourism is defined by the International Ecotourism Society as "responsible travel to natural environments that conserves the environment, sustains the well-being of the local people, and involves interpretation and education." Ecotourism generates revenues for countries that engage in it. While this market-focused approach may be most immediately impactful in locations where ecotourism already flourishes, it may be helpful in providing an economic rationale for investing in the preservation of natural resources for sustainable use more generally.

By using artificial intelligence to demonstrate the art of the possible, we show how countries interested in sustainable tourism development could use publicly available data posted by past tourists who have engaged in nature-dependent tourism activities to determine what such tourists seek and where they seek it. Further, by incorporating local expertise from government officials and tourism operators, such models can be modified so that they influence local economic development and natural resource development.

Methods Used

We used a three-pronged method to develop an artificial intelligence–informed model that was designed to help five island nations in the Eastern Caribbean identify where many tourists already recognized natural values and where nature-dependent tourism value was high at a national level.

After using an assessment process to identify the best data resources, we focused on user-generated data that could be reviewed using artificial intelligence and machine learning: specifically, we used image and text data posted on user content–collecting websites. While we considered a variety of activities that were nature dependent, we selected seven to model:

- On-reef activities (like snorkeling and diving)
- Nature-dependent beaches
- Paddle sports
- Recreational fishing
- Eating at seafood restaurants
- Wildlife viewing, which was modeled differently for birdwatching and boat-based whale and dolphin watching

We obtained user-generated content from tourist-generated posts on several platforms: specifically, from Flickr images, eBird, Diveboard, and Tripadvisor reviews and pictures. We then used these posts to identify locations where nature-dependent activities occurred. Next, we used local expertise from industry and government partners to guide model building and to locate additional data sources. Finally, our team enhanced or modified user-generated data with locally sourced datasets, such as information on dive sites and dive shops, key fishing locations, cruise ship visitor destinations, and key birdwatching sites.

Our team used the additional data to generate weighted tourism locations, which were mapped using national statistics to highlight the locations of the different activities. The process of data collection, processing, modeling, and mapping is shown in Figure 5.1.

Process of Modeling and Mapping Values of Ecosystem to Tourism

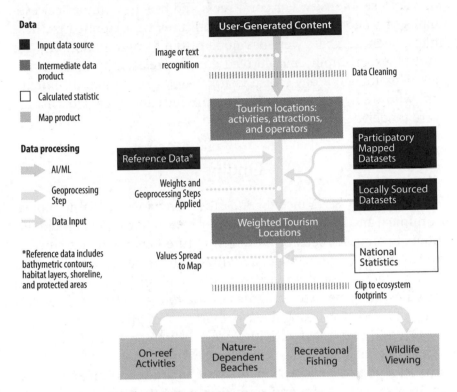

Figure 5.1 The data collection, processing, modeling, and mapping process (From Spalding et al., 2023 / with permission of Elsevier).

The user-generated content and additional data sources provided information on location and use intensity. This information is dependent on the diversity of natural resources, with some being confined to distinct habitats (like beaches or coral reefs) and others being spread across multiple ecosystems. For distinct habitats, use intensity values were linked to high-resolution maps of those ecosystems and then spread across the relevant habitat. For fishing and whale watching, intensity was modeled using a decay function based on the distance to the fishing or whale watching operator, spreading those scores across fishing or whale watching areas.

To calculate "value," our research team generated modeled maps of use intensity. For coral reefs and beaches, numerical estimates of visitor numbers and expenditures were applied to these maps. Such numbers were developed from a combination of prior studies, expert input, and derived datasets relating to these activities. The impact of day cruise visitors (not all of whom disembark and whose stays are generally time-limited) and overnight visitors were modeled separately.

Findings

For Grenada, St. Vincent and the Grenadines, Saint Lucia, Dominica, and St. Kitts and Nevis, our research team generated use intensity maps for each of the seven nature-dependent activities as well as the nature-dependent activities in aggregate (see Figure 5.2).

Further, for each country, for coral reef and beach–associated activities, we generated estimates of the tourism expenditures and numbers of visitors using those activities (see Table 5.1).

Overall, reef-based activities were estimated to account for 8 percent of all tourism expenditures, while beach activities were estimated to account for 22 percent of such expenditures. Further analysis suggested that cruise tourism generates very different patterns of use of beach and reef-dependent activities. Cruise visitors represent 70 percent of all visitors to these countries. However, after correcting for their much shorter average lengths of stay, cruise visitors represent only 14 percent and 7 percent of time invested in those activities, respectively. Further, cruise visitors' expenditures are even lower, and were estimated to represent only 5 percent and 2.3 percent of total beach and reef activity expenditures.

Discussion

In five Eastern Caribbean countries, this project leveraged user-generated content, expert opinions, and operator information to identify the location of seven nature-dependent activities, the intensity of the use of those activities, and—for two of those activities—estimates of the annual numbers of users and expenditures.

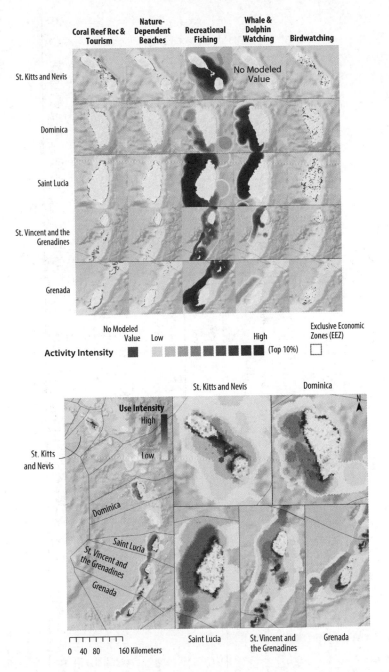

Figure 5.2 For five Eastern Caribbean countries, specific use intensity maps for five nature-dependent activities (top) and aggregate use intensity maps for seven nature-dependent activities (bottom). (Spalding et al., 2023 / with permission from ELSEVIER)

Table 5.1 Tourism expenditure and visit estimates for beach and coral reef–dependent activities.

Numerical values for expenditure and visitation derived from the reef and beach models. For reefs, the numbers represent all associated expenditure or visitation. For beaches, the numbers represent the likely drop in expenditure or visitor returns expected from limited environmental degradation. Visitor values are not corrected by length of stay, hence, for example, the apparently high numbers for St. Kitts and Nevis, in terms of visitors, do not show up in expenditure as almost 90% are short-stay cruise passengers. Monetary values are expressed in 2019 US dollars.

	Dominica	Grenada	St. Kitts and Nevis	Saint Lucia	St. Vincent & the Grenadines	TOTAL
Total tourism expenditure	$100,874,168	$162,811,879	$165,229,932	$870,950,990	$105,298,900	$1,405,165,869
Total nature dep. beach expenditure	$8,971,862	$39,634,719	$35,589,482	$207,227,645	$26,670,739	$318,094,447
Total on-reef expenditure	$11,382,075	$13,097,875	$6,667,569	$76,963,697	$10,206,966	$118,318,182
Total visitors	313,670	468,527	1,099,944	1,125,962	282,952	3,291,055
Total nature dep. beach visitors	27,945	85,092	180,406	211,423	60,198	565,064
Total on-reef visitors	19,389	22,732	22,444	59,536	18,999	143,100

To be sure, these countries are aware of the value of tourism to their economies. But the maps that this project generated provided additional information as to the location and diffusion of nature-dependent tourist activities across their geographies and into the ocean space beyond their shores. Such information not only highlights where there is particularly high value but also where additional value might be created. For example, nature-dependent beach values are concentrated on a small number of beaches, with 5 percent of beaches generating 68 percent of all nature-dependent beach expenditures and 5 percent of coral reefs generating 80 percent of expenditures on nature-dependent coral reef expenditures. Expansion of access to a larger proportion of beaches and coral reefs might preserve those resources, overall, by augmenting receipts from visiting them.

Further, our ability to differentiate use patterns when comparing overnight to cruise ship visitors underscores the variation in the true potential use, intensity of use, and location of use across these two groups.

Importantly, in the context of climate change, other work has suggested that modest changes in water quality—or some similar environmental change—could markedly reduce tourism receipts from beach or coral reef activities. This suggests that our modeling efforts have practical application as governments consider their long-term ecological sustainability practices. By demonstrating multiple components of nature-dependent activities, maps like those produced in this project can be used in marine spatial planning, an important activity in the development of Blue Economies in these countries and elsewhere. These methods can be replicated in other settings to enable future visioning, understand current patterns of use intensity, and generate realistic inferences about the costs and benefits of development—or the potential impact of investments and interventions.

What We Learned

We learned that activity use models can be generated from user-generated content and that the usefulness of those models can be improved upon by incorporating local knowledge and information. This project also showed that generating estimates of relative use across a number of nature-dependent activities is possible and need not be tied to a metric that has units; however, we can incorporate other data sources and elements to convert relative use data to data with units—such as visitors or dollars. An easy-to-understand and non-controversial model of relative activities can be used as the basis for further, more specific model development.

In addition, while our static model is useful, we learned that a longitudinal effort would potentially be able to divine changes in user patterns for particular segments of nature-dependent activities, changes in relative intensity of use across those segments, the impact of efforts to redirect use or numbers of visitors, and—should the economic activity analytic be expanded to other nature-dependent categories—their economic impact.

The full article on which this summary is based is:

Spalding MD, Longley-Wood K, McNulty VP, Constantine S, Acosta-Morel M, Anthony V, Cole AD, Hall G, Nickel BA, Schill SR, Schuhmann PW, Tanner D. "Nature dependent tourism – combining big data and local knowledge." *Journal of Environmental Management* 2023; 337: 117696. doi: 10.1016/j.jenvman.2023.117696

Chapter 6
Wildlife
Bioacoustics Detection

—Zhongqi Miao

Executive Summary

Automatically detecting sound events with artificial intelligence has become increasingly popular in the field of bioacoustics, particularly for wildlife monitoring and conservation. Conventional methods predominantly use supervised learning techniques, which depend on substantial amounts of manually annotated bioacoustics data. However, manual annotation in bioacoustics is tremendously resource-intensive, both in terms of human labor and financial resources; further, manual annotation requires considerable domain expertise. This requirement for domain expertise consequently undermines the validity of crowdsourcing annotation methods, such as Amazon Mechanical Turk. Additionally, the supervised learning framework restricts application scope to predefined categories within closed settings.

To address these challenges, we developed an approach that leverages a multi-modal contrastive learning technique called Contrastive Language-Audio Pre-training (CLAP). CLAP allows for flexible class definition during inference by using descriptive text prompts and can perform Zero-Shot Transfer on previously unencountered datasets. Here, we found that without specific fine-tuning or additional training, an out-of-the-box CLAP model could effectively generalize across nine bioacoustics benchmarks, covering a wide variety of sounds that were unfamiliar to the model. We showed that CLAP achieved comparable, if not superior, recognition performance compared to supervised learning baselines that are fine-tuned on the training data of these benchmarks.

Our experiments also found that CLAP holds the potential to perform tasks previously unachievable in supervised bioacoustics approaches, such as foreground/background sound separation and the discovery of unknown animals. Consequently, CLAP offers a promising foundational alternative to traditional supervised learning methods for bioacoustics tasks, facilitating more versatile applications within the field.

Why Is This Important?

Exacerbated by habitat loss and climate change, the decline in global biodiversity is a pressing global concern. To measure changes in biodiversity, ecologists use advanced technologies like camera traps, acoustic recorders, and satellites for extensive and nuanced data collection. Autonomous Recording Units are particularly useful for monitoring sound-producing animals like birds, frogs, and marine mammals. These devices generate enormous datasets that are difficult to analyze manually. Traditional analytic methods require human annotators to identify animal sounds, a process that is both laborious and requires specialized knowledge. Consequently, crowdsourced platforms like Amazon Mechanical Turk have not significantly contributed to the task of bioacoustics data analysis.

Artificial intelligence techniques are increasingly being adopted to automate bioacoustics data analysis. A common approach uses convolutional neural networks (CNNs) or visual transformers that are based on supervised learning. However, these methods face significant limitations: they require copious amounts of annotated data and are constrained by predefined labels, which restricts their ability to identify novel species. Challenges in data annotation include ambiguity in identifying sound events, overlapping sounds, and the need for expertise in bioacoustics annotation.

Here, we introduce a bioacoustics recognition framework called CLAP. This framework addresses the limitations of supervised learning methods by employing a multimodal contrastive learning approach that circumvents the need for large, annotated datasets and fixed categories. Multimodal contrastive learning approaches take advantage of the associations across multiple modalities (like text, images, and audio) by comparing the output of those different modalities (for instance, in identifying a particular bird species) and contrasts those outputs to maximize similarities of observed pairs of text and audio, for instance, and minimizing similarities of artificially paired data. CLAP uses large sets of audio–text pairs to correlate audio samples with semantic concepts. This enables the model to identify and categorize sounds based on learned semantic relationships rather than rigidly defined labels.

A key advantage of CLAP is its ability for *Zero-Shot Transfer,* meaning it can identify sounds from species that were not present during training. For instance, when trained on a range of bird calls, the model can later recognize almost any bird species by assigning them to a post-training category like "bird." This is enabled by the model's grounding in semantic understanding, which allows it to generalize to sounds with similar semantic contexts.

Methods Used

In conventional supervised learning frameworks, artificial intelligence models are constrained by predefined categories, limiting their flexibility and practical applicability. We developed a multi-modal contrastive learning approach designed to expand the capabilities of artificial intelligence in audio recognition, wherein audio features and text features are integrated in a singular model (see Figure 6.1).

The central concept behind multi-modal contrastive learning is its ability to maximize the similarity between the feature embeddings derived from raw audio samples and corresponding textual descriptions. These embeddings are typically obtained through convolutional neural networks or Transformer-based encoders for the audio samples and large language models for the text samples. This technique frees the model from the requirement of fixed categorical labels; instead, labels can be defined post-training for specific project needs.

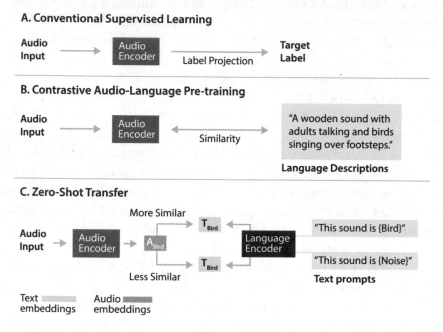

A. Conventional Supervised Learning

Audio Input → Audio Encoder → Label Projection → Target Label

B. Contrastive Audio-Language Pre-training

Audio Input → Audio Encoder ← Similarity → "A wooden sound with adults talking and birds singing over footsteps."

Language Descriptions

C. Zero-Shot Transfer

Audio Input → Audio Encoder → A_{Bird} → More Similar T_{Bird} / Less Similar T_{Bird} ← Language Encoder ← "This sound is {Bird}" / "This sound is {Noise}"

Text prompts

Text embeddings   Audio embeddings

Figure 6.1 Contrasting conventional supervised learning, contrastive audio-language pre-training, and Zero-Shot Transfer approaches (Zongqi M et al., 2023 / Zhongqi Miao / CC BY 4.0).

A significant innovation introduced by multi-modal contrastive learning is the Zero-Shot Transfer, wherein categories can be defined in natural language terms during the inference stage. For example, categories like "bird songs" or "noise" can be instantiated after the model has been trained, offering unparalleled flexibility compared to traditional machine learning approaches. These categories are not confined to single definitions. They can be complex descriptive phrases that allow for nuanced tasks like foreground/background separation in bioacoustics or the discovery of novel animal species through sound.

We sought to demonstrate CLAP's generalizability across multiple bioacoustics sources, with a focus on group-level recognition (e.g., birds, whales, and frogs) rather than species-specific identification. We also examined the use of *timestamp-based sound event existence classification,* a technique that mitigates challenges associated with pinpointing the exact timing of sound events in lengthy audio recordings. To assess its robustness, we evaluated CLAP on nine unfamiliar bioacoustics benchmark datasets.

We used two different audio feature extractors to evaluate performance:

- A convolutional neural network-based encoder (Pre-trained Audio Neural Networks, PANN)
- A Transformer-based encoder (Hierarchical Token-Semantic Audio Transformer, HTS-AT)

We compared these to a supervised learning baseline model, ResNet-18, which was selected due to its wide applicability and effectiveness on smaller datasets. We used Average Precision to evaluate model performance.

We prepared three versions of the CLAP model, each differing in the scale of the pre-training data used. The diversity of these training datasets allowed us to evaluate CLAP's ability to adapt to a broad range of bioacoustics tasks, even when the model had not encountered similar data during training.

To validate CLAP's generalizability, we used eight public bioacoustics datasets and one dataset that detects gunshot sounds in rainforests. These datasets were selected to encompass a wide array of sound sources, from birds and whales to gunshots in tropical areas (this sound was chosen, in part, to assess CLAP's applicability in anti-poaching efforts). Notably, none of these datasets were part of the CLAP training data, making them novel and unfamiliar to the model.

Findings

When compared to fully supervised ResNet-18 baselines generated from several bioacoustics benchmarks, CLAP models had comparable average precisions. Notably, the Transformer-based CLAP model that was trained on 2.1 million audio–text pairs outperformed or matched the performance of supervised baselines in six of the benchmarks. The convolutional neural network-based CLAP model, on the other hand, demonstrated weaker performance, which we attributed to its smaller model size and fewer pre-training pairs.

We found that window size emerged as an important factor in audio segment classification. In the *BirdVox* benchmark (a collaboration between the Cornell Lab of Ornithology and NYU's Music and Audio Research Lab that aims to investigate machine listening techniques for the automatic detection and classification of free-flying bird species from their vocalizations), a seven-second window size for the CLAP-HTS-AT 2.1M model was associated with performance degradation. This finding is likely because Transformer models require a constant input audio length, and the Bird-Vox dataset, with its default two-second audio segments, had to be manipulated to fit that parameter. The stretched audio segments led to the inclusion of unnatural sounds, impacting model accuracy. However, in general, longer window sizes seemed to improve the performance of Transformer-based CLAP models (see Figure 6.2).

We also found that detailed text prompts significantly improved model accuracy (see Table 6.1).

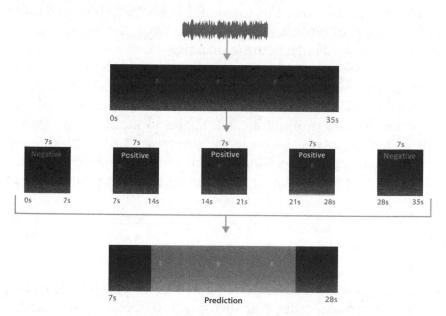

Figure 6.2 Illustration of fixed window sound event existence classification. By using a visual classification model, the presence or absence of the sound event of interest is predicted for each segment. Using these predictions, we can obtain approximate timestamps for the localization of sound events.

Table 6.1 Text prompts to perform zero-shot classification for each benchmark

#	Benchmarks	Text Prompts
1	BirdVox	*Is this a sound of birds chirping in the background or noise?*
2	Jackdaw	*Is this a sound of birds chirping or noise?*
3	Freefield	*Is this a sound of birds chirping or noise?*
4	Wablr	*Is this a sound of birds chirping or noise?*
5	Rfcx	*Is this a sound of birds singing far in the background or frogs?*
6	Hiceas	*Is this a sound of whale vocalizations or noise?*
7	Enabirds	*Is this a sound of birds chirping or noise?*
8	Meerkat	*Is this a sound of meerkats clucking or non-animal noise?*
9	Tropical-Gunshots	*Is this a sound of gunshots in the distance or broken branches and noise?*

Source: Zongqi M et al., 2023 / Zhongqi Miao / CC BY 4.0.

For example, in the BirdVox and Tropical-Gunshots datasets, including descriptive words in the text prompts substantially improved average precision scores. Interestingly, CLAP was capable of distinguishing between foreground and background noises simply by using appropriate text prompting, a notable achievement given the challenge in bioacoustics training data (see Table 6.2).

Table 6.2 Experiment Results on Text Prompts

(a) CLAP-HTS-AT 2.1M performance of recognizing birds in the background. Higher is better.

Is this a sound of {} or frogs?	AP
birds	0.54
birds singing	0.63
birds singing in the background	0.73
birds singing *far* in the background	0.79
Supervised baseline AP:	0.88

(b) CLAP-HTS-AT 2.1M performance of recognizing gunshot sounds in tropical rainforest. Higher is better.

Is this a sound of {A} or {B}?	AP
A: Gunshots B: Noise	0.36
A: Gunshots in the distance B: Noise	0.57
A: Gunshots in the distance B: Broken branches or noise	0.67
Supervised baseline AP:	0.64

(continues)

Table 6.2   *(continued)*

(c) CLAP-PANN (128K) performance of recognizing meerkat sounds
    using two-second window. Higher is better.
Is this a sound of *{}* or non-animal noise?

AP meerkats	0.56
meerkats growling	0.68
meerkats clucking	0.80
meerkats clucking or growling	0.79
growling	0.63
clucking	0.82
clucking or growling	0.78
animals	0.85
animals growling	0.82
animals clucking	0.86
animals clucking or growling	0.88
Supervised baseline AP:	0.94

Source: Zongqi M et al., 2023 / Zhongqi Miao / CC BY 4.0.

We also found that, despite not having been trained on Meerkat-related audio or text, the CLAP-PANN model performed impressively on the Meerkat dataset when descriptive text prompts like "clucking" were used. This suggests that there is potential for Zero-Shot Learning to recognize previously unencountered sounds when prompted effectively.

Discussion

This work highlighted CLAP's efficacy in achieving competitive results compared to fully supervised baselines in identifying animal sounds. CLAP excelled in six out of nine bioacoustics benchmarks that were novel to the system through Zero-Shot Transfer. Moreover, the use of semantic-based inference allowed for identification of previously unknown animals when descriptive text prompts were used. Traditional supervised or unsupervised methods fall short in this regard, as they either limit models to predefined label sets or fail to associate learned audio features with any semantic meaning.

CLAP is an innovative solution to the challenges of automated bioacoustics analysis. It overcomes the constraints of supervised learning by eliminating the need for large, manually annotated datasets and the limitations of fixed categories. Through semantic understanding and Zero-Shot Transfer capabilities, CLAP shows promise in making significant contributions to the monitoring and preservation of global biodiversity.

However, our study has limitations. First, the dataset used to train CLAP was limited to daily life and standard audio, which suggests the need for incorporating bioacoustics-specific data for improved performance. Second, our methods did not include automated ways to generate high-quality text prompts; generating automated high-quality text prompts will be important to future research and extended model application. Finally, the model's inability to differentiate between fine-grained categories of animal sounds is a significant hindrance to its broader, real-world application.

Nonetheless, we found the CLAP models to potentially be useful in bioacoustics sound recognition while underscoring the critical roles of text prompts, window size, and training data. Future research should further explore these roles, include more comprehensive datasets, and use new prompt engineering techniques.

What We Learned

In the context of climate change, monitoring changes in global biodiversity will become increasingly important. Traditional ways to do so require labor-intensive labeling and specialized knowledge and training on the part of the human labeler. We found that developing a multi-modal artificial intelligence model that builds on previous work can—by integrating text and audio with the appropriate prompts—generate labels with much less human involvement.

While the model needs further refinement for real-world application, our efforts underscore how artificial intelligence might be used to reduce human labor input and expertise requirements to improve the scope, scale, and speed of biodiversity monitoring. We could imagine using this model as well as remote sensors to identify, catalogue, and monitor any number of animals that produce auditory output, across the globe.

The full article on which this summary is based is:

Zongqi M, Elizalde B, Deshmukh S, Kitzes J, Wang H, Dodhia R, Lavista J. Zero-Shot transfer for wildlife bioacoustics detection. DOI: 10.21203/rs.3.rs-3180218/v1.

Chapter 7
Using Satellites to Monitor Whales from Space

—*Caleb Robinson, Kim Goetz, and Christin Khan*

Executive Summary

Climate change and other human impacts challenge biodiversity and put many species at risk of extinction. Some of the most influential of those animals are large marine mammals, like whales, that act as a kind of canary-in-a-coal-mine for the health of the ocean, the quality of its waters, and the impact of human activities such as overfishing. However, because many whale species have large home ranges and can migrate long distances across vast oceans, monitoring these animals is challenging. Technological innovation is increasing the utility of satellite imagery, with very high-resolution satellites holding the promise of identifying species and better understating their presence and distribution in remote locations that are challenging for vessels and aircraft to reach. Here, we describe the development of the collaborative Geospatial Artificial Intelligence for Animals (GAIA) initiative and share challenges faced, lessons learned, and a vision for monitoring the abundance and distribution of whales in the future.

Why Is This Important?

This work is important for three reasons. First, while humans have become adept at monitoring easily accessible indicators of environmental change—like temperature, molecular volumes in the atmosphere, and rates of glacial melt—it has been more difficult to monitor the presence and location of larger, top predators, particularly ones that live in the oceans, often far offshore in difficult-to-reach locations. Second, current sampling methodologies based on visual sightings (vessels, planes) or acoustic detections (hydrophone arrays, moored buoys, gliders) are concentrated in a relatively narrow area of the coast close to shore. The increased spatial resolution of satellite imagery, advancements in artificial intelligence, and expansion in compute power provide an opportunity to analyze such high-resolution satellite data at scale. Finally, this work provides an example of how collaborative, multidisciplinary, public–private partnerships can share a common aim, contribute from their relative strengths, and learn from one another to provide solutions that can be useful to the community around the world. In our highly complex world, such collaborative partnerships will be foundational for future work in conservation biology.

Methods Used

The initiative for Geospatial Artificial Intelligence for Animals (GAIA) was founded to leverage such partnerships. Crafted to design a large-scale operational platform capable of detecting marine mammals from satellite data, GAIA is composed of government agencies, independent research organizations, academia, and the private sector. This initiative was spawned, in part, by the need for the U.S. government to provide Stock Assessment Reports to report on the abundance of whales, and in part by the need for the U.S. Navy to protect the environment and have situational awareness around whale aggregations. The initiative leveraged academics and private sector organizations that had technological expertise in satellite imagery processing and analysis. GAIA focuses on two endangered species with a high risk of extinction: the North Atlantic right whale and the Cook Inlet beluga whale. The population of both is estimated at less than 500 animals and has experienced population declines. Additionally, both species have distinct body characteristics and behaviors that might influence detectability by very high-resolution satellite imagery.

Over recent years, an increasing number of satellites have been able to capture higher-resolution images over the entire Earth (see Figure 7.1). Since 2010, about 75 satellites have been launched each year on average and mean spatial resolution has dropped to 30 centimeters, or about 1 foot.

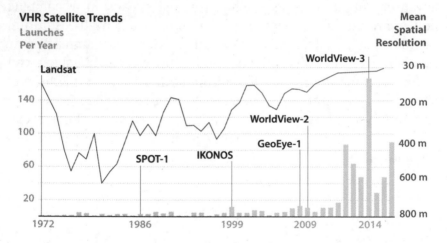

Figure 7.1 Trends in the type, number, and mean spatial resolution of satellites (Khan CB et al., 2023 / MDPI / CC BY 4.0).

Satellite imagery has improved from being able to identify animal habitats in the mid-1970s, to being able to identify individual animals in 2002. With the incorporation of artificial intelligence, since 2019, multiple species have been identified, density estimates have been calculated, and small cetaceans have been recognized.

Metadata is associated with each satellite image, which includes information on sensor type, acquisition date and time, pixel resolution, spectral bands, and nadir angle from which the image was obtained. The nadir angle is particularly important, as the image becomes distorted the farther the satellite is tilted from a direct overhead pass.

Because satellite sensors are typically programmed to go dormant unless being specifically tasked, archived imagery over the open ocean is sparse. Therefore, the GAIA initiative tasked Very High Resolution satellite imagery to collect information over known seasonal hotspots for North Atlantic right whales and Cook Inlet beluga whales beginning in 2020. We developed a preprocessed workflow to take those raw images and prepare them for inspection by a human analyst:

- Downloaded imagery and stored the files in Microsoft Azure
- Matched the multispectral and panchromatic files and then for all matching pairs:
  - Transformed the coordinate system from a sphere to a flat surface (UTM projection)
  - Resampled the multispectral file to match the spatial resolution of the panchromatic file
  - Merged the lower-resolution color image with the higher-resolution monochromatic image (pansharpening)
  - In all of these steps, ensured that files were saved as Cloud Optimized GeoTIFFs (COGs)

Figure 7.2 shows examples of how high-resolution panchromatic imagery, and lower-resolution multispectral red, green, and blue imagery can be processed to generate a pansharpened image of two right whales in Massachusetts's Cape Cod Bay and three beluga whales in Alaska's Cook Inlet.

Findings

As shown in Figure 7.2, even in the processed images, the presence of whales does not recognizably jump out to the naked eye; we could imagine that there could be confusion around whether the identified figures are, indeed, whales. To differentiate whales from non-whales, we annotated the images with labels, manually, using expert validation by National Oceanic and Atmospheric Administration scientists. The labeling process incorporated a "human-in-the-loop" approach that uses machine learning to identify image patches that *might* contain whales. Those labeled images were then used to improve algorithms identifying those chips in an iterative way—known as *active learning* in the machine learning community—which then results in a more efficient annotation process.

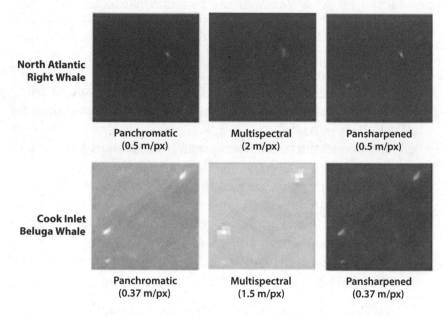

North Atlantic Right Whale

| Panchromatic (0.5 m/px) | Multispectral (2 m/px) | Pansharpened (0.5 m/px) |

Cook Inlet Beluga Whale

| Panchromatic (0.37 m/px) | Multispectral (1.5 m/px) | Pansharpened (0.37 m/px) |

Figure 7.2 Examples of how high-resolution panchromatic imagery and lower-resolution multispectral imagery can be combined to generate a pansharpened image of two right whales in Massachusetts's Cape Cod Bay and three beluga whales in Alaska's Cook Inlet.

Discussion

We found that we could use high-resolution satellite imagery, and a human-in-the-loop active learning workflow to annotate images of North Atlantic right whales and Cook Inlet beluga whales. This work demonstrated that it is possible to process very high-resolution imagery at an operational scale with the potential for real-time insights.

Our findings have broader applications beyond monitoring whales. For instance, such data could be ingested into existing maritime domain awareness platforms such as WhaleMap, Whale Alert, OBIS-SEAMAP, and EarthRanger to increase mariner awareness and allow them to avoid areas of whale aggregations.

While promising, there are several limitations to the use of Very High Resolution satellite imagery in identifying large sea creatures:

- First, access to such imagery is expensive, and data sharing is limited by strict licensing agreements. Long-lasting solutions—like partnerships and limited data sharing agreements that are supported by third parties (like governments) that have a vested interest in such analyses—as well as time (since technological innovation costs tend to drop over time) might overcome those financial barriers.
- Second, because satellite sensors do not continuously collect imagery over open water, archival imagery is limited. This limits retrospective comparisons but is solvable going forward.
- Third, manual downloading of imagery is time-consuming; however, with programmatic access to Very High Resolution satellite imagery, much of that downloading and processing could be automated.
- Fourth, environmental conditions like cloud cover and wind conditions may pose a challenge for image processing and the ability to identify animals, especially to the species level.

Future research can leverage artificial intelligence to address some of these limitations. Updating and iterative validation of models will be necessary.

What We Learned

First, we learned that Very High Resolution satellite imagery can be processed and annotated to identify particular species of whales. As image resolution, artificial intelligence, and workflows improve, we can likely expand the use of this tool to other species.

Second, we learned that an iterative active-learning process that leverages machines and humans is an efficient and effective way to label data. While there is a plethora of data in the world, labeled data is much rarer, and the labeling process is expensive and time-consuming. The process described here can be broadly applied to other data labeling problems in satellite image analysis.

Finally—and most importantly—we learned that a coalition of collaborators, from different sectors and industries, and all with their own areas of expertise is necessary to solve the world's problems. Further, we demonstrated that such coalitions can tackle challenging problems where the conservation community can benefit from cutting-edge solutions.

The full article on which this summary is based is:

Khan CB, Goetz KT, Cubaynes HC, Robinson C, Murnane E, Aldrich T, Sackett M, Clarke PJ, LaRue MA, White T, Leonard K, Ortiz A, Lavista JM. "A biologist's guide to the galaxy: leveraging artificial intelligence and very high-resolution satellite imagery to monitor marine mammals from space." *Journal of Marine Science and Engineering,* 2023; 11(3): 595. doi: 10.3390/jmse11030595.

Chapter 8
Social Networks of Giraffes

—*Juan M. Lavista Ferres, Derek Lee, and Monica Bond*

Executive Summary

Climate change impacts the natural habitat of animals and may, therefore, change their behaviors which may, in turn, impact their ability to reproduce. To understand that potential impact, it is important to analyze behaviors in a reproducible way and track behavioral changes over time. Here, we used a dataset of 1,081 giraffes (species *Giraffa camelopardalis*) that researchers created, having used artificial intelligence to individually identify them. This dataset allowed us to study their social behaviors within and across distinct social communities in a larger population over a five-year period.

Giraffes are not territorial. Males mate with multiple females, and they differ in size based on gender and age. While they form distinct social groups, they can move between these groups. Therefore, believing that sex- and age-class differences might mediate social connectedness and transitions among communities, we hypothesized that adult males—and the youth of both sexes—would show greater degrees of social connectedness and movement across groups (betweenness) than adult females, which form stronger and more stable relationships. We also expected that young animals would be more socially connected than adults (see Figure 8.1).

Figure 8.1   Giraffe in Tanzania, August 2023 (A, V, L Lavista-Guzman).

Using static and dynamic network clustering techniques, we identified four distinct mixed-sex social communities, which we termed "super-communities" to differentiate higher-level social organization from intermediate-level female-only communities. We found that about 70 percent of giraffes remained within their same super-community, and those (usually adult males) that visited different super-communities often returned to their original one. Further, we found that males—both adults and calves—had higher social centrality scores than females, and adult males were closer to all other individuals in the network and transitioned among super-communities twice as often as females and calves, reflecting their roaming reproductive strategy of seeking females in oestrus.

Of all age and sex classes, young males had the most social ties and moved most often among groups, which we attributed to social exploration prior to natal dispersal (movement from the group into which one is born to another group). Overall, female giraffes demonstrated stronger social associations than males, but males demonstrated more social connectedness, reflecting differences in reproductive and life-history profiles. Our findings suggest that giraffe translocations that do not consider sociality are likely to disrupt established social associations, potentially reduce fitness, and possibly impact species' reproductive habits.

Why Is This Important?

Climate change impacts the natural environment of animals, often limiting their habitats and range. Those changes might influence the social behaviors of those animals, potentially having an impact on their ability to successfully reproduce. To be able to understand that potential impact, it is important to understand the social dynamics that exist within animal groups.

When considering the social behaviors of mammals, others have found differences in life-history strategies between male and female mammals. For example, in *polygynous* (a one male to multi-female breeding pattern) species where males provide no care for offspring, males maximize their fitness by defending groups of females or territories rich in resources. Females, on the other hand, are primarily motivated by mate selection and offspring-rearing responsibilities. This divergent set of life-history requirements, mediated by age and sex, likely governs variations in social behavior.

Further, mammalian social groups often exhibit a fission–fusion dynamic, wherein the group composition is variable but still governed by stable community structures. These dynamics may vary by age and sex due to differences in life history. However, data on this topic is scant for long-lived species because studying them requires extensive, lengthy, and large-scale research efforts to evaluate the complexities of their social networks.

Here, we examine the social networks of giraffes, a species chosen for their size-dimorphic nature and fission–fusion social organization. Giraffes are especially compelling subjects because their social groupings are non-random clusters with distinct social structures, often covering extensive areas. They live in fluctuating social groups influenced by multiple factors such as kinship, sex, age, and ecological conditions. While females tend to maintain long-term bonds with other females, males typically have fewer stable associations; adult males are more inclined to solitude than are females and younger males.

In addition, giraffe society has a hierarchical organization: their social groupings can be divided into cliques, subcommunities, and spatially separated communities. This complex social fabric is further complicated by sex and age variations. For instance, female-only associations in a giraffe metapopulation have been found to be organized into more than a dozen communities, each with 60–90 females, that are spatially overlapping but socially distinct.

Importantly, Masai giraffes (*G. c. tippelskirchi*) that we studied are categorized as an endangered subspecies on the International Union for Conservation of Nature Red List and reside in a multilayered complex social system. Preserving giraffe habitats and promoting their coexistence with people are both likely to be more productive for conservation than translocating a limited number of individuals to new areas, which would destabilize social relationships and potentially reduce fitness.

Mixed-sex associations among giraffes are, however, less understood. Reproduction appears to influence social relationships: females tend to form nursery groups when calves are born around the same time, and younger males often band together in bachelor groups or follow older males. Older males generally roam solo, covering large areas in search of receptive females. This roaming behavior may link female communities. Little is known about how social associations evolve as giraffes transition from calves to young adults, although some studies indicate that social connectedness varies with age.

Seeking to resolve gaps in the literature, we focused on two objectives. First, we sought to explore the structure of super-communities in a metapopulation of free-roaming Masai giraffes, comprising multiple age and sex classes. Second, we wanted to compare the social connectedness and movements of male and female juveniles and adults. In our social network study, a node is a giraffe, and two giraffes are connected in the social network if they have been seen together in a group formation on any given day. We used three measures to quantify connectedness:

- Degree (number of associates or edges)
- Closeness (geodesic distance to other associates)
- Betweenness (number of shortest paths passing through the individual)

We hypothesized that, due to their roaming reproductive strategy, adult males would have higher social connectedness, move more often among super-communities, and travel greater distances than adult females. Further, given that adult females form long-term bonds while males roam and younger animals explore, we expected younger males and females to have higher social connectedness than adult females but not adult males. Finally, as both are in a phase of social exploration, we anticipated that younger males and females have similar levels of social connectedness.

Methods Used

We used data collected from giraffes that were living in the Tarangire Ecosystem in northern Tanzania, which lies in the eastern branch of the Great Rift Valley, covers approximately 30,000 km², is home to various vegetation types, and has three distinct seasons. Our work focused on an area that spans 1,500 km² and includes five administrative units with different levels of wildlife protection: Tarangire and Lake Manyara National Parks, Manyara Ranch Conservancy, and Lolkisale and Mto wa Mbu Game Controlled Areas. None of these units is fenced, facilitating giraffe movement across them. However, the Rift Valley escarpment forms a natural western boundary, limiting giraffe movements. Human influence, including increasing population density and agriculture, have created restrictions for these animals to move in the other directions.

Our study used fixed route transect surveys along all dirt tracks in the study area. Photographic identification data was collected between May 2011 and October 2016. We used an artificial intelligence algorithm that leveraged the unique coat patterns of each giraffe to identify them. Data collection followed Pollack's robust design, with two secondary sampling periods within one seasonal primary sampling period. Animals were sampled multiple times during the study, and by the second year of the study, most adults were identified and therefore subsequent surveys subsampled from the known population. Surveys were conducted at a constant speed, with the same team of two observers and a driver and the same camera type. When giraffes were encountered, photographs were taken for individual identification from a distance of no more than 150 meters.

"Giraffe group" definitions were based on coordinated movement and activity; we rejected using distance-based definitions of "groupness" because of the variability of inter-individual distances. Based on various physical characteristics, giraffes were classified into one of three age categories:

- Calves (less than one year old)
- Sub-adults (one to three years old)
- Adults (more than three years old)

For each encounter, the team recorded age, sex, and GPS coordinates. Identification of individuals from photographs was facilitated by WildID, an artificial intelligence software package.

In our social network analysis, individual giraffes were treated as nodes and their associations as edges. We measured the *degree* (number of associates), *closeness* (geodesic distance to other associates), and *betweenness* (number of shortest paths passing through the individual) of social behaviors.

Further, *centrality* (the clustering of nodes in a network), *closeness centrality* (how close a node is to all other nodes in a network), and *betweenness centrality* (an indicator of the node's influence across a network) were calculated to assess social connectedness within giraffe populations.

Sex and age were included in the analysis. Metrics were normalized to allow for meaningful comparisons across different classes. We differentiated between a community of adult female-only associates and a mixed-sex super-community, with individuals in the same community showing stronger associations with each other than with members of other communities. Social networks were visualized using geolocation layouts based on average latitude and longitude coordinates for each giraffe. To account for variations in sample sizes, all metrics were normalized.

Our dataset consisted of 1,081 giraffes that had been observed at least six times in the five-year observation period; demographically, 65 percent of the giraffe population were females, and 73 percent were adults.

Field research permission was obtained from multiple Tanzanian agencies, including the Tanzania Commission for Science and Technology, the Tanzania Wildlife Research Institute, and the Tanzania National Parks.

Findings

We identified four super-communities that had stable community structures with high community assertiveness values. Both static and dynamic algorithmic approaches confirmed these four distinct super-communities, surprisingly mirroring geographic delineations despite not taking geographic location into account (see Figure 8.2).

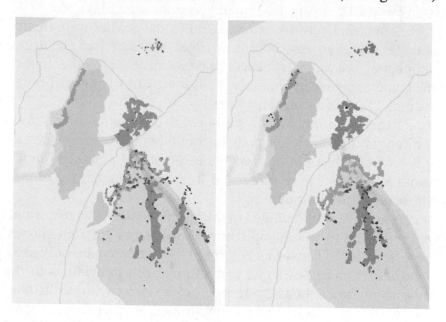

Figure 8.2 Both static (left) and dynamic (right) network clustering demonstrated four super-communities of giraffes (Lavista JM, et al., 2021 / With permission of Elsevier).

We eliminated the west super-community from analysis, as its members showed virtually no transitions to other super-communities, leaving three super-communities for analysis.

On average, a giraffe was connected to 65 others. Male giraffes exhibited a higher degree of social interaction, especially among calves. Throughout the study's five-year period, 70 percent of giraffes remained within their original super-community, 27 percent ventured into one new super-community, and three percent visited all three examined super-communities (see Figure 8.3).

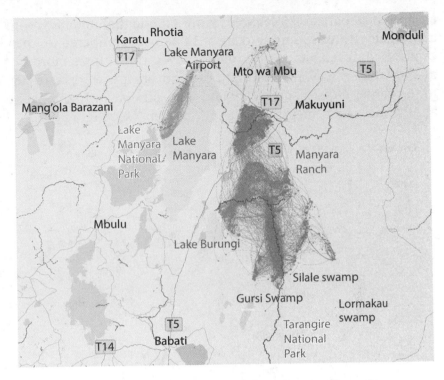

Figure 8.3   All observations and connections for Masai giraffes in the Tarangire Ecosystem, Tanzania during 2011-2016 (Derek E. Lee et al. 2022 / Springer Nature).

Only 1.3 percent of adult females visited all three super-communities while 11 percent of adult males did; and while adult males made up only 23 percent of the overall giraffe population, they constituted 74 percent of giraffes that transitioned among all three super-communities.

Over any given four-month observation period, approximately 90 percent of giraffes stayed within their super-community and about 10 percent moved. Most transitions occurred between the center and north super-communities, despite a tarmac road acting as a physical barrier. Males were more mobile than females, with adult males transitioning at a rate of 14 percent compared to 7 percent for adult females. Adult males moved three times more frequently than calves. Interestingly, calf movements were restricted to the center super-community and were similar in frequency to adult female movements, both at 6–7 percent (see Figure 8.4).

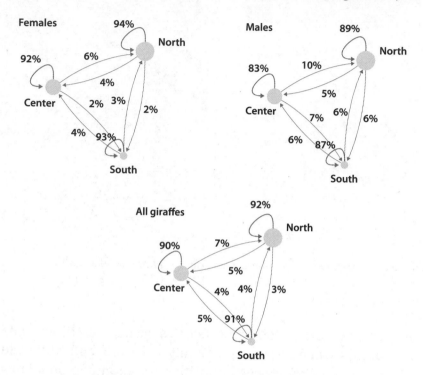

Figure 8.4   Transition rates among super-communities for all giraffes, male giraffes, and female giraffes (Lavista JM, et al., 2021 / With permission of Elsevier).

We also found that the observed transitions did not follow Markovian properties, meaning they were not purely dependent on the current state. Specifically, 90 percent of transitions resulted in a return to the original super-community, while 10 percent of transitions remained in the new super-community.

Males demonstrated a higher *closeness centrality*—how close a node is to all other nodes in a network—than did females. Further, male adults had greater closeness centrality than male calves, which had closeness centrality measures no different from those for female adults and calves.

Calves demonstrated a higher *betweenness centrality*—which indicates a node's influence over the flow of information in a network—than adults, and male calves had a higher betweenness centrality than female calves.

We were able to construct a social network graph that revealed two distinct subgraphs connected by a single female giraffe. The graph had a diameter of 6 and a radius of 2, with an average path length of 2.6, suggesting a tightly knit community.

We discovered multiple adult female-only social communities within the giraffe population. These female communities were found to be contained within one of the four identified super-communities, implying that they did not cross super-community boundaries.

The areas of each super-community varied substantially. Adult males traveled 1.5 times as far as adult females and calves (see Figure 8.5).

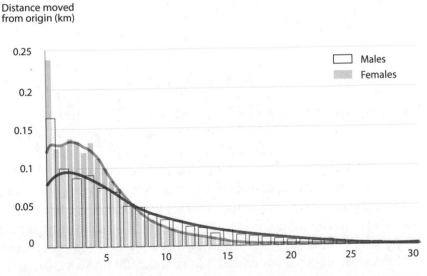

Figure 8.5 Mean distances moved from first detection (km) for male and female giraffe adults and calves (Lavista JM, et al., 2021 / With permission of Elsevier).

Spatial analysis also indicated that male movements were less constrained and covered a more diffuse area than that of females; male calves' movements were dependent on their previous locations (see Figure 8.6).

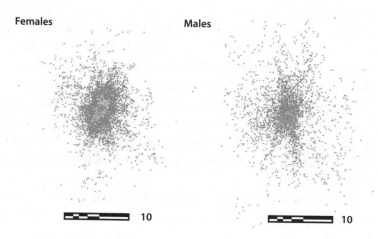

Figure 8.6 Spatial distribution of movements from the first position for every sequential pair of observations of female and male giraffe adults and calves (Lavista JM, et al., 2021 / With permission of Elsevier).

Discussion

We used a five-year dataset of 1,081 giraffes in the Tarangire Ecosystem to study the relationship between giraffes' age and sex and their social networks and social interactivity. We found that adult male giraffes displayed unique roaming reproductive strategies that led to their high social connectivity and increased travel between super-communities. Consistent with our hypothesis, we found that adult male giraffes exhibited the highest closeness centrality across all age and sex classes, implying that they maintained closer connections with all other individuals in their social network. In addition, male giraffes traveled greater distances and more frequently switched between super-communities than females, likely reflecting their pursuit of females in oestrus.

Contrary to expectations, we found that immature male giraffes have greater social connectedness than their female counterparts. Particularly intriguing was the observation that male calves moved more frequently among groups and had more social ties than any other class. This increased social activity among young males was attributed to their explorations of their social and ecological environment before they leave their natal group, also known as *natal dispersal*, which is more common in male than female mammals.

Our study found a previously unknown metapopulation structure of giraffes in the region: we found four super-communities of mixed sexes and ages, three of which consisted of approximately 300 individuals and one (the isolated west super-community) with about 100 individuals. These super-communities are themselves composed of multiple adult female social communities, which can range in size from 60 to 90 individuals. Likely, the social fabric of these communities is based on fission–fusion dynamics, leading to fluid and continually changing group formations.

We found that adult female giraffes have smaller home ranges than males and maintain more stable and closer social bonds within their subset of females. In contrast, adult males often roam alone, continually seeking females in oestrus across various groups, thereby increasing the number of social connections for both males and females. Additionally, dispersing subadult and young adult males also occasionally form bachelor herds, thus increasing their number of ties even further compared to females.

Finally, we found remarkable social fidelity across age and sex classes. Over 90 percent of giraffes remained in the same super-community throughout the five-year study, and 70 percent never switched at all. Nonetheless, adult males transitioned between super-communities twice as often as females and calves. Such behavioral nuances amplify the multilayered nature of giraffe society, illustrating how differences in movement patterns and reproductive strategies among sexes serve to knit these complex social structures together.

The mating behavior of male giraffes is dictated by the need to find and mate with females who are receptive only for a brief period during their approximately two-week cycle. In a landscape where females are widely dispersed and where their home ranges rarely overlap, adult males must adopt a roaming strategy to maximize their reproductive success. This behavior is not unlike that observed in African elephants.

Energetically, the roaming reproductive strategy and mate guarding can be demanding. However, unlike other species that accumulate fat reserves for the mating season, giraffes do not exhibit this "fattening phenomenon," potentially because they are unique among browsers in their ability to ruminate while walking.

Finally, our findings contribute to a broader understanding of multilevel social organization in animals. Giraffes exhibit a complex social structure characterized by core units of ever-changing groups based on kinship, sex, and age, which then form larger nested social units up to the level of super-communities. The multilevel organization and complex social dynamics evident in giraffes point to similar evolutionary trajectories of sociality across diverse animal species.

What We Learned

We drew on existing theories of mammalian dispersal patterns, which usually show a male-biased tendency to disperse and a female-biased tendency to stay close to their place of birth. Males improve their dispersal success by learning about female distribution and social dynamics in these exploratory sorties. Our observations confirmed that young male giraffes in our study entered non-natal adult female social communities and returned to their original communities before final natal dispersal.

We also learned that super-communities—large social structures—are influenced by various landscape features. For instance, physical landmarks like Lake Manyara and the town of Mto wa Mbu demarcate the boundaries of some super-communities. Interestingly, anthropogenic elements like roads and farmlands did not completely inhibit movement between communities; however, such features might limit males' roaming strategies, potentially affecting genetic diversity.

We speculate that one particularly small super-community in Lake Manyara National Park is at risk for stochastic events like disease outbreaks due to its limited size and lack of interactivity with other super-communities. This underlines the importance of male giraffes' periodic movements between super-communities to mitigate inbreeding risks. The consistency in population sizes across various super-communities, regardless of their geographical extent, suggested that there might be an optimal population size regulated by factors such as habitat availability and social dynamics.

Earlier reports that giraffes have fluid and constantly shifting social structures were superficially correct but failed to understand that the root of the flexibility is nonrandom social associations between individual giraffes. Giraffes live in a complex, structured society with a foundation composed of fission–fusion groups mediated by social, ecological, reproductive, temporal, and anthropogenic factors operating in tandem, not independently. Adult male roaming reproductive strategies connect adult female communities and occasionally connect mixed-sex super-communities, which should maximize genetic diversity of the metapopulation. Given that the Masai giraffe is categorized as an endangered subspecies, our analysis should be reevaluated over time. Changes in the behaviors and patterns that we found might indicate destabilized social relationships and potentially reduce reproductive fitness.

The full article on which this summary is based is:

Lavista JM, Lee DE, Nasir M, Chen Y, Bijral AS, Bercovich FB, Bond ML. "Social connectedness and movements among communities of giraffes vary by sex and age class." *Animal Behavior* 2021; 180: 315-318. doi: 10.1016/j.anbehav.2021.08.008

Chapter 9

Data-driven Approaches to Wildlife Conflict Mitigation in the Maasai Mara

—*Akram Zaytar, Gilles Hacheme, Girmaw Abebe Tadesse, Caleb Robinson, Rahul Dodhia, and Juan M. Lavista Ferres*

Executive Summary

In Kenya's Maasai Mara, a growing human population and competition for scarce resources are intensifying conflicts between pastoralists and wildlife. This escalation poses severe threats to endangered species and jeopardizes the livelihoods of local communities. A common source of conflict arises when wildlife, such as lions, cheetahs, and wild dogs, prey on livestock traditionally secured in *bomas*—enclosures used by pastoralists to keep their livestock. In response to the loss of their cattle, pastoralists sometimes resort to indiscriminately poisoning wildlife. This reactionary measure leads to a vicious cycle of loss, impacting both the wildlife population and the pastoralists' cattle.

Non-profit organizations, such as the Kenya Wildlife Trust (KWT) and the Smithsonian Institution, have been working to address similar problems. However, implementing conservation initiatives in this context is complex, as there is a need to account for the diverse dimensions of the problem, such as the uncapped population expansion, competition over scarce resources, and the community's economic demands, alongside the urgent need to protect endangered animals exposed to climate change effects. These complexities manifest in the continuous struggle to make operational decisions for allocating monetary and human resources to the most vulnerable communities and species.

To address this intricate issue, we collaborated with our partners, the KWT and the Smithsonian Institution, to develop a data-driven solution. This solution leverages high-resolution satellite imagery with guidance from domain experts to pinpoint potential conflict zones. Specifically, we trained convolutional neural network models on sub-meter solution images provided by DigitalGlobe. These models were adept at identifying boma settlements, including cattle enclosures and buildings, as well as detecting the presence of cattle throughout the Maasai Mara. By integrating these boma settlement maps with incident reports and animal tracking data, we can generate conflict risk indicators. These indicators are instrumental in directing focused interventions, such as building predator-proof bomas and launching educational campaigns against the use of poisons. Such proactive measures not only safeguard livestock but also foster a harmonious coexistence between wildlife and human communities. Furthermore, the insights gained from this work have the potential to inform wildlife conflict mitigation strategies beyond the Maasai Mara, contributing to broader sustainability efforts in Kenya and beyond.

Why Is This Important?

The Maasai Mara region in Kenya is a keystone in the world of biodiversity, a unique ecosystem teeming with an array of species, including many large carnivores. It therefore represents a significant component of the country's tourism industry. This delicate balance of nature, however, is increasingly under threat due to the intersection of population settlement expansion and resource scarcity, partly due to climate change. For the indigenous Maasai Mara communities, which have coexisted with these majestic creatures for generations, the challenges are multifaceted. Livestock, the backbone of their economy, often falls prey to large predators. This conflict, primarily stemming from livestock depredation, not only threatens the livelihoods of these pastoralists but also leads to retaliatory measures such as the indiscriminate killing of predators. Such actions, while a response to immediate threats, perpetuate a destructive cycle, jeopardizing both the local ecology and the community's well-being.

Understanding and addressing this conflict requires a comprehensive, multifaceted strategy that encompasses hotspot identification, resource allocation, community support through measures like boma fencing, and educational initiatives against the harmful practices of poisoning and arbitrary predator killings. To this end, it is important to map population settlements, including bomas that house the livestock, thereby detecting hotspots with a high risk of wildlife attack. Accurately mapping human-predator conflict hotspots lays the groundwork for targeted and effective intervention strategies. This is a vital step toward preserving the intricate balance between human needs and wildlife conservation. Domain experts and organizations working directly on similar problems, such as Kenya Wildlife Trust, need automated and data-driven approaches that augment their capabilities to address the problem and ensure sustainability.

Methods Used

Our study used a twofold machine learning process based on high-resolution WorldView-2 satellite imagery. The first step involved training models to detect settlement buildings and bomas in the region. We leveraged a variety of deep learning architectures—such as U-Net, DeepLabv3+, and FCN—with different backbone models, including the ResNet, ResNeXt, and ViT families. We also explored the effectiveness of class weighting, data augmentation techniques, and pre-training to enhance model performance. Our methodology's second step focused on classifying identified bomas as either populated or not at the time of the image. This involved using a ViT encoder on cropped patches around bomas, aimed at providing an "activeness" signal that can be used to inform potential human–animal conflict zones based on livestock presence.

Our primary dataset comprised two high-resolution satellite images from DigitalGlobe WorldView-2, spanning approximately 3,500 km^2 across the Maasai Mara (see Figure 9.1). Captured on the morning of August 6, 2022, these images consist of RGB-NIR bands with a spatial resolution of 50 cm from the panchromatic band. Image processing included normalizing each RGB-NIR image using per-band minimum and maximum values, pan-sharpening the lower-resolution bands using the panchromatic band, and creating a composite image (e.g., mosaicking).

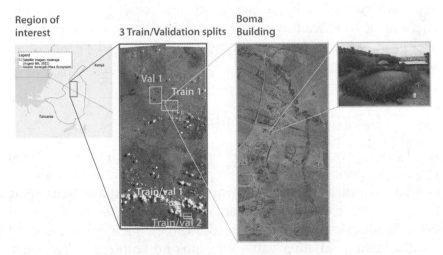

Figure 9.1 The region of interest (left), train/validation splits, and label examples (boma, building).

For the segmentation task, we used QGIS software to create 4,000 weak labels for bomas and buildings. The resulting polygons were then rasterized to match the input image dimensions. The labeling process was iterative and began with a high concentration boma region for initial training, followed by using the model to guide the further addition of hard positive and negative labels. This method included creating a discrepancy map for targeted annotation and expanding the training set to maximize spatial generalizability, thereby addressing out-of-distribution errors like misclassification of clouds or farms.

Our labeling strategy emphasized focusing on "hard-positive" (bomas and buildings) and "hard-negative" (background) examples in sparse imagery. While labeling every boma or building in these regions was impractical, our approach leveraged increasingly accurate model predictions to guide the labeling process, focusing on the most informative areas. Additionally, we used the boma polygons to extract patches that we tagged as "cattle" or "no-cattle," forming a secondary dataset for the cattle presence classification task.

Finally, our training methodology incorporated both static and dynamic hyperparameters, with the latter optimized using Bayesian search methods. Recognizing the challenges posed by sparse labels and extreme class imbalances, we introduced a regularization entropy term to the existing cross-entropy loss function. This approach helped balance precision and recall in our models, enabling us to efficiently map Maasai Mara settlements and their occupancy while handling complex imbalances and uncertainties in our dataset (see Figure 9.2).

Findings

In the semantic segmentation task, our final model exhibited impressive performance, achieving an average *Jaccard similarity coefficient* (a measure of similarities between sample sets, ranging from 0 to 1, with higher numbers indicating greater similarity) of 0.63. For the classification of boma occupancy, our approach focused on determining whether cattle were present within a given boma.

Using a ViT classifier, we achieved an F_1 score of 0.97, underscoring our model's capability to discern patterns indicative of cattle presence.

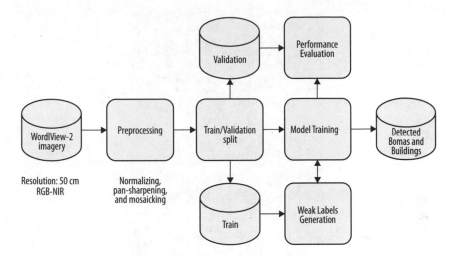

Figure 9.2   Overview of our methodology.

Our experiments on data quantity versus performance revealed that incorporating weighted entropy loss into the loss function significantly enhanced the validation F_1 score, particularly in scenarios with fewer negative labels (0–10 percent). This finding emphasizes the importance of adopting regularization techniques, especially in geospatial domains characterized by sparse data. Finally, by using texture- and color-based augmentation techniques, we were able to use the trained model in other (spatially adjacent) satellite images from 2020 in the conservancies of interest: Mara North Conservancy, Pardamat, and Oloolaimutia—to export weak predictions (see Figure 9.3).

We converted raster predictions into geometries by using techniques ranging from geometry simplification, outlier removal, and shape-based filtering. The final dataset consists of 5,100 empty bomas, around 20,000 buildings, and 160 bomas with cattle. We intend to make it publicly available for download to use alongside the underlying models that generated it.

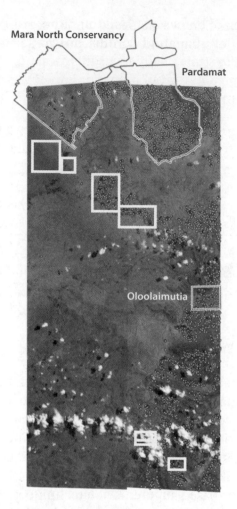

Figure 9.3 The original two images (left/right), train/validation splits (gray), the conservancies, and the predicted boma locations.

Discussion

To support conservancies in their pursuit of predator conservation and in mitigating human–wildlife conflict, our models produced a comprehensive dataset comprising over 5,100 empty bomas, 160 occupied bomas, and approximately 20,000 buildings. Through the detailed mapping of bomas and buildings, these organizations gain crucial insights into potential conflict hotspots. This information empowers them to strategically focus their resources, whether it be in constructing predator-proof bomas or implementing educational and economic support initiatives for local communities. By facilitating better-informed decision-making, this data becomes a pivotal tool in nurturing an environment where humans and wildlife can coexist harmoniously. Moreover, by embracing the open data movement, we aim to catalyze further research and foster collaborations in the field of conservation and geospatial machine learning.

However, our methodology is not without its limitations. One significant limitation is the issue of data scarcity, a common hurdle in African Savannas and similar environments. Additionally, our model's current scope is limited in terms of spatial and temporal generalizability, primarily due to the diverse visual landscape of the region and the specific time frame of data collection. Adapting our model to different geographic or temporal contexts would necessitate further refinement and adjustment.

There are numerous opportunities for expanding and enhancing our work. Addressing data scarcity with innovative data gathering or more advanced data augmentation methods could significantly boost the model's performance. Furthermore, extending our model's application to a wider range of spatial and temporal settings, perhaps through techniques like transfer learning or domain adaptation, presents an exciting research direction. Incorporating additional variables such as climate data, land cover types, and wildlife movement patterns could also enrich our dataset, offering a more nuanced understanding of human–wildlife conflict zones.

In summary, while recognizing its current limitations, our study marks a promising advancement in applying AI to conservation in regions where data is scarce. It underscores the potential of technology to bridge the data gap and, more importantly, highlights the real-world impact AI can have in harmonizing human settlements with wildlife habitats. This balance is critical to preserving biodiversity and enhancing the well-being of both humans and wildlife in these delicate ecosystems.

What We Learned

Throughout the course of this project, several key learnings have emerged, each providing valuable insights into both the technical and practical aspects of applying data-driven approaches to assist conservation efforts.

First, working in the Maasai Mara region highlighted the prevalent issue of data scarcity in African Savannas and similar environments. It underscored the need for innovative solutions to gather and augment data effectively. Additionally, the project shed light on the limitations posed by the spatial and temporal diversity of the region, emphasizing the importance of developing adaptable and generalizable models that can function across various landscapes and time periods.

Second, our experience reinforced the importance of using advanced techniques like weighted entropy loss regularization and strategic data augmentation. These methods significantly improved model performance, particularly in contexts with sparse data and class imbalances. This learning is instrumental for future projects in similar domains, where data challenges are a common occurrence.

Third, our project highlighted the value of collaboration with domain experts in the use of open data when seeking to advance conservation efforts. Such collaboration complements the capabilities of each partner. By making our dataset publicly available, we not only facilitated further research in the field but also encouraged collaborative approaches to problem-solving in conservation. This approach aligns with the growing trend of open data and shared resources in the scientific community.

Finally, our work in the Maasai Mara serves as a case study for the broader applications of AI in conservation globally. The techniques and methodologies developed here can be adapted and applied to other regions facing similar challenges. This project has shown that with careful consideration of the unique environmental and social contexts, AI can be a powerful tool in the global effort to preserve biodiversity and foster sustainable coexistence between humans and wildlife.

Chapter 10

Mapping Industrial Poultry Operations at Scale

—Caleb Robinson and Daniel Ho

Executive Summary

Annually, concentrated animal feeding operations (CAFOs) are estimated to generate more than 13 times the amount of human waste. Inadequate handling of that waste can contaminate nearby lands and waterways with pathogens, pharmaceuticals, heavy metals, and hormones; that contamination causes nitrogen and phosphorous runoffs, which can severely affect water quality and can result in toxic algal blooms. CAFOs are also associated with higher levels of air pollution. All of the downstream effects of CAFOs adversely impact public health and contribute to climate change.

Historically, CAFOs have been difficult to regulate, largely because of challenges identifying where CAFOs are located. To help the Environmental Protection Agency (EPA) and state EPAs, we developed convolutional neural network models that used one meter/pixel aerial imagery data from the National Agricultural Imagery Program (NAIP) to detect poultry CAFOs across the continental United States and to generate the first national open-source dataset of poultry CAFOs.

Why Is This Important?

While many factors contribute to climate change, current agricultural practices do so disproportionately. The entire meat-processing activity—from the planting, harvesting, and transport of feed for animals to the housing, raising, processing, and transportation of the meat—consumes energy and contributes massive amounts of waste. The waste includes fertilizer and antibiotic and pharmaceutical runoff, carbon and methane emissions, and waste produced by the animals themselves.

Some of the impact of that waste can be mitigated through implementation of safe waste-management processes and regulation thereof; however, to be effective at surveying and regulating CAFOs' adherence to those practices, regulators need to be able to identify CAFOs.

By applying artificial intelligence–informed modeling to existing datasets that have been labeled, training models to learn the characteristics of what constitutes a poultry farm, and applying the model to a larger geographic space, we were able to generate a national map of poultry farm locations. By using historical data, new farms can be identified. And because the size of poultry farms can be estimated as well, these maps can help regulators identify farms, prioritize which ones to visit, and develop efficient and effective monitoring systems.

Methods Used

We used a fully automated, open-source process that did not rely on the *Census of Agriculture*—a report that purports to provide a

complete count of U.S. farms and ranches and the people who operate them. While previous studies have used the Census of Agriculture, that use is limited for two reasons:

- First, the census is conducted every five years; therefore, there
  are lags in the availability of the data.
- Second, data is self-reported; if a farmer does not report, information on farmers and their activities will not be included in
  the Census.

To address these limitations, we used a two-step modeling
process. First, we used publicly available, high-resolution (one
meter/pixel), four-band (red, green, blue, and near-infrared)
aerial imagery of the Delmarva Peninsula (that includes parts of
Delaware, Maryland, and Virginia) that already had poultry barns
labeled—the Soroka and Duren dataset of CAFO facility polygons
(see Figure 10.1).

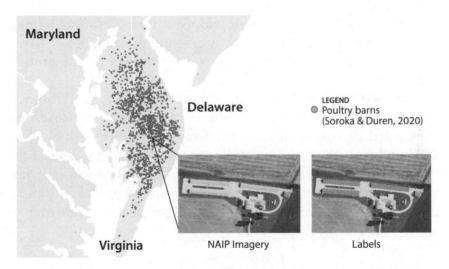

Figure 10.1   The labeled Delmarva Peninsula dataset.

This supervised learning process generated a model that could
be more widely applied to other parts of the United States. Importantly, to eliminate potential confounders—like orientation to

prevailing wind patterns in the Delmarva Peninsula—we trained the model with rotation augmentation by randomly "flipping" objects horizontally or vertically, so that the model was more generalizable. Further, we temporally augmented the model to account for differences in imagery over time. This process allowed us to use historical data to identify new CAFOs as well as make estimates of the construction dates of CAFOs.

Second, we developed a rule-based filtering methodology to remove false-positive predictions made by our model. We then validated our model by comparing its predictions to a hand-labeled dataset of poultry CAFOs from ten counties in California that was not used in model development. Importantly, because the landscape, surroundings, and adjacent facilities in the Delmarva Peninsula and California were different, the application of the Delmarva-generated model to California was a challenging test that enhanced the model's generalizability to the rest of the United States.

Through this process, we developed a method for combining image segmentation with data augmentation and object-based filtering to scale CAFO detection using a small set of ground truth labels.

We used aerial data on streets to conduct object-based filtering for two reasons. First, CAFOs require access to major roads for livestock distribution. Second, roadways themselves can be visually similar to CAFO barns and represent a valuable dataset for filtering out false positives. For instance, Figure 10.2 shows examples of false positives (roads and barren ground on the left) and a true negative (airport hangars, on the right) that we were able to use to train the model for more precision and accuracy.

Findings

Using the model, we developed a national open-source poultry CAFO dataset with facility locations and size estimates based on building footprints (see Figure 10.3).

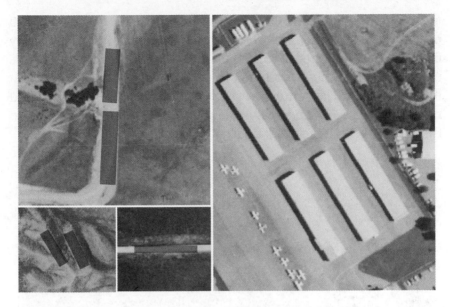

Figure 10.2 Examples of false positives (pictures on the left) and a true negative (picture on the right) that were identified in training the model.

Figure 10.3 A map of poultry CAFOs for the continental United States (Robinson C et al., 2021 / IEEE / CC BY 4.0).

We were able to calculate the predicted number of poultry farms per ten kilometers squared for easy discernment of where poultry farms are concentrated. Zooming in to finer-resolution maps allows users to identify the predicted specific location and size of individual poultry CAFOs, particularly that the Census of Agriculture had not captured (see Figure 10.4). In some counties, this amounts to thousands of undercounted poultry barns.

Figure 10.4   Modeled predictions of poultry CAFOs in counties in Delaware and South Carolina, wherein the Census of Agriculture reported zero poultry operations (Caleb Robinson (Chapter Contributor)).

We evaluated model performance using precision, recall, and the F_2 score. We chose the F_2 metric to more heavily weight recall in model evaluation, as it is possible to reduce the number of false positives in postprocessing but not the number of false negatives. We found that rotational augmentation was critically important because distributions of orientation of predicted poultry barns varied considerably across states. In out-of-sample validation with the California dataset, we found that our model had a recall of 87 percent and a precision of 83 percent. Our results compared favorably to other state-of-the-art open-source models.

Discussion

We used a multi-step process to train a model with labeled data from the Delmarva Peninsula, augmented that data so that the model would be more generalizable to different U.S. geographies, incorporated information on streets to minimize false positives, tested that model using a labeled dataset from California that had not been used to develop the original model, and generated an open-source map that estimates location, size, and age of poultry CAFOs across the continental United States. Our study has substantial implications for environmental research and governance:

- Epidemiological researchers can use information generated from our model to examine the impact of livestock disease spread.
- Environmental groups can use this information to identify and monitor specific facilities.
- Government agencies can use this information to strategically prioritize inspections and understand permitting failures.

Further, our model can substantially reduce the time that those users spend manually scanning for poultry CAFOs by providing a set of likely CAFOs with high recall. In addition, our results highlight the limitations of the Census of Agriculture due to coverage gaps, high nonresponse rates, and internally contradictory data. Finally, our results illustrate advantages to a hybrid approach that leverages the segmentation of regular objects (like barns) and expert-based heuristics, which can be used to implement methods that accommodate different environmental backgrounds that might impair object identification.

Our study has several limitations. First, it was imperfect, and results varied by geography. Second, while we validated our model using data from ten counties in California, we could not validate it using other data sources. Third, our analysis was limited to poultry CAFOs and was based on identification of barns used in poultry farming; modeling cattle or hog CAFOs would require identifying outdoor feedlots or manure storage systems, specific to those industries, respectively. Fourth, other object-level features could be used to improve the model; however, those features may not be comprehensively available across the continental United States. Finally, we were constrained by ground truth data; if imagery or CAFO construction standards change, our models will need to be reconstructed.

What We Learned

We learned that it is possible to leverage limited high-fidelity data when ground truth data is expensive to acquire in new domains. Further, the inclusion of expert heuristics—to anticipate geographic differences in areas where the model was not trained that might limit the model's generalizability—makes the model more widely applicable. We specifically learned not to let models use orientation from Delmarva to drive identification across states as orientation of poultry farms is based on wind (for ventilation), because wind patterns—and therefore barn orientations—differ across states (something we were able to use the model to verify).

We also learned that application of machine learning methods can markedly improve the ability of government regulators and other interested parties to estimate the location of CAFOs. While our model is not perfect, it gives those parties a better chance of identifying CAFOs than they would otherwise have. Therefore, the leveraging of available data to generate informed estimates of locations, sizes, and ages of CAFOs can help them be much more efficient in their study or monitoring of CAFOs.

The full article on which this summary is based is:

Robinson C, Chugg B, Anderson B, Lavista JM, Ho DE. "Mapping industrial poultry operations at scale with deep learning and aerial imagery." *IEEE Journal of Selected Topics in Applied Earth Observations and Remote Sensing* 2021; 15: 7458-7471. doi: 10.1109/JSTARS.2022.3191544.

Chapter 11
Identifying Solar Energy Locations in India

—Anthony Ortiz and Joseph Kiesecker

Executive Summary

To avoid the most catastrophic impacts of climate change, countries will have to reduce greenhouse gas emissions by 50 percent by 2030 and achieve net zero emissions by 2050. With 73 percent of global emissions tied to energy use, a rapid transition to renewable energy is urgently needed. Solar energy is positioned to be a major contributing source of the energy transition and India is a burgeoning hub for solar energy. However, the land used for solar energy, farms has other uses, such as biodiversity conservation, agriculture, or urban development. We first sought to use artificial intelligence to identify solar farms to estimate when those projects were built. Then, we overlaid that information onto land-use maps so that policymakers could understand the land-use impact of previously developed solar projects. Using the locations of current solar farms, we predicted areas suitable for development to help developers and government make informed decisions about the siting of future projects.

To do this work, we developed a semantic segmentation model that used lower-resolution (10 meters) satellite imagery that is freely available worldwide. We integrated pixel-wise labels and hard negative mining techniques to identify 1,363 solar farms in India, including 1,035 that had never before been mapped. Our model had a mean accuracy of identification of solar farms of 92 percent. We found that about 7 percent of solar developments occurred in habitats crucial for both biodiversity and carbon storage and nearly two-thirds occurred in agricultural areas, suggesting that those lands might not have been the most ideal for farm development.

While renewable energy is critical to climate change mitigation, it is crucial to balance this need with other land-use considerations. Solar farms are often large-scale projects that can disrupt local ecosystems or agricultural activities. Therefore, special data on solar installations is vital for proactively identifying potential conflicts between renewable energy and other land uses. The model we developed can help track solar energy deployment; if applied widely, it could be used to hold countries accountable for their climate commitments, tracking their progress on their nationally determined contribution to the Paris climate commitment. In addition, it can help ensure renewable energy development doesn't happen at the expense of other land-use values important to people and nature.

Why Is This Important?

India has ambitious goals for climate change mitigation and has set a target of having an installed capacity of 500 gigawatts of renewable energy output by 2030. With solar energy expected to contribute 60 percent of this capacity, India seeks to emerge as a global leader in combatting climate change. The lower production costs of renewable energy—especially solar energy—make it a financially competitive alternative to conventional energy sources like coal and other fossil fuels.

But solar energy farms consume substantial amounts of land, and the large scale of their solar energy production expansion presents challenges related to land use and the potential socio-ecological impacts that policymakers must consider. These include concerns about destruction of natural habitats, loss of agricultural production, and even increases in greenhouse gas emissions if the farms are sited improperly. Moreover, the conversion of lands critical for agriculture or local communities can lead to socio-ecological conflicts, thereby slowing adoption rates. These concerns are exacerbated in the absence of geospatial data that could guide strategic planning.

In this complex milieu, our work addresses the lack of information on solar farms and alternative land uses by creating the first country-wide database of solar photovoltaic farms in India. Here, we introduce a novel method for creating datasets using semantic segmentation models, which are particularly valuable when labeled data is sparse. Further, we quantify the land cover change occasioned by solar energy expansion—a critical metric for sustainable development. With enhanced geospatial data, policymakers can site projects in low-conflict areas, thereby aligning ecological integrity with energy security. Further, our work serves as a model for other countries looking to balance rapid renewable energy expansion with sustainable land use.

Methods Used

We used a multi-step process for creating datasets of remotely sensed objects using limited labeled data and that incorporated human expertise, satellite imagery, and machine learning. We combined traditional data sources, semi-supervised learning techniques, and post-processing steps to efficiently generate a dataset for detecting utility-scale solar arrays in India.

For the initial development of the model, we used Microsoft's Planetary Computer to query all available Sentinel-2 cloud-free imagery between 2015 and 2020; twelve of the thirteen available spectral bands were used. We processed this data using Temporal Cluster Matching (TCM)—an algorithm designed for aligning time-series changes in satellite imagery. TCM allows you to date the inception of each solar farm, with the median *Kullback-Leibler divergence* (a measure of how one probability distribution differs from another) serving as a threshold to pinpoint the exact scene indicating the farm's initial development.

For analyzing land cover changes, we integrated the identified year of initial development with the Copernicus Global Land Service and National Remote Sensing Centre Land Use Land Cover datasets. This helped assess the types of land that are most affected by the installation of solar farms, over time. Sentinel-2 imagery was then used to corroborate those findings. To optimize the model, we used an iterative bootstrapping approach by adding difficult negative samples to the training set.

We trained the model using an unsupervised convolutional neural network (CNN) and fine-tuned the CNN using a semi-supervised fine-tuning process that incorporated human–machine interaction using a web application. We used pixel-wise intersection over the union and farm-wise recall to validate the model's effectiveness. We used the fine-tuned model to generate pixel-wise semantic labels for all available point labels and combined them with Sentinel-2 imagery to produce a segmentation dataset of 234 image patches that were divided into training (80 percent), validation (10 percent), and test (10 percent) sets (see Figure 11.1).

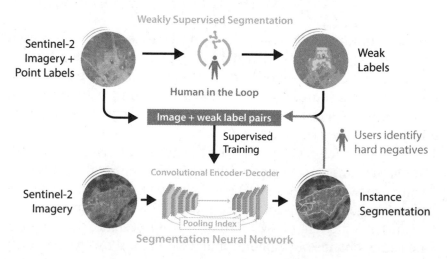

Figure 11.1　Methods used (Anthony Ortiz et al. 2022 / Springer Nature / CC BY 4.0).

We conducted manual data validation using multiple base map layers on QGIS and Google Earth applications. We also used historical high-resolution imagery and public reports for cross-validation.

Findings

The resulting dataset, stored in vector form, included 1,363 validated solar farms, clustered from 4,421 manually validated predictions. The dataset was comprehensive, contained unique identifiers, and provided the area, geographic coordinates, and location by Indian state (see Figure 11.2).

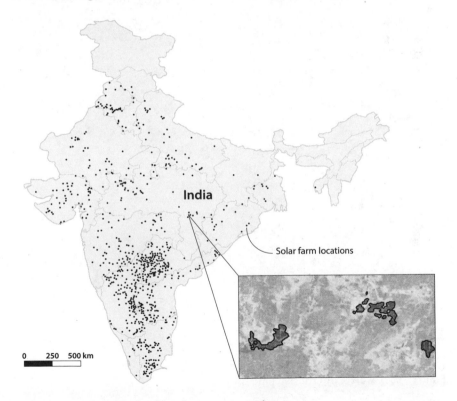

Figure 11.2   Map of solar farm locations in India.

We validated the model using Pearson correlation analysis between installed solar capacity in the state of Karnataka and the solar farm area predicted by the model, finding a correlation coefficient of 0.957. Manual validation showed that 92.5 percent of model predictions accurately represent solar installations. Our land cover and land use change analyses showed that 74 percent of solar installations in India occur on land types—like agricultural and natural habitat lands—that might raise environmental or food security concerns (see Figure 11.3).

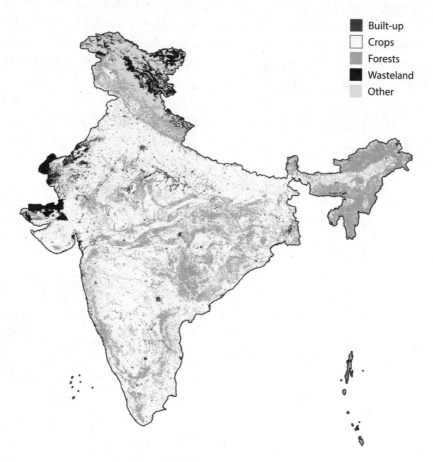

Figure 11.3 Map of alternative land uses.

Discussion

India's expansive renewable energy goals are laudable for their ambition and scope but come with intricate challenges involving land use and ecological conservation. We were able to use novel data acquisition and processing techniques to develop a comprehensive solar farm database that can help policymakers ensure that India's renewable energy roadmap is as sustainable and conflict-free as possible.

Traditionally, automatic identification of photovoltaic arrays has relied on high-resolution satellite imagery, which is often expensive and limited in availability. In contrast, our study demonstrates the viability of using lower-resolution imagery for solar farm detection, offering a scalable and cost-effective approach. Earlier studies have either been limited in scale or completeness and relied on existing databases; our model leveraged widely available data and novel techniques to improve on scale and completeness.

In the context of global climate commitments, such as the Paris Climate Agreement, the techniques we developed could inform the development of a transparent mechanism for tracking solar deployment. This could facilitate accountability in meeting national and international climate targets.

Solar energy is poised to be a pivotal tool for climate change mitigation in India and other countries. Addressing climate change demands accelerated deployment of renewable resources like solar energy. The artificial intelligence semantic segmentation model that we developed could be globally applied to help guide lands suitable for solar projects and reduce land-use conflicts, thus helping public agencies and policymakers better plan and monitor solar development.

What We Learned

We learned that using low-resolution satellite data, collected and compared over time, to feed a multi-step process of machine-learning–driven model development, model enhancement, and model validation can be a powerful tool in the efficient mapping and assessment of solar energy projects. The methods we describe offer a scalable, accurate, and cost-effective way to identify solar panel farms and determine alternative uses of the lands so that policymakers can more efficiently and effectively plan renewable energy investments, understand land-use trade-offs, and determine optimal land use given conflicting interests. Further, datasets like the one we developed could be used on the international stage to transparently serve as an accountability mechanism for national and international commitments to global climate agreements, thereby encouraging those commitments to be honored.

The full article on which this summary is based is:

Ortiz A, Negandhi D, Mysorekar SR, Nagaraju SK, Kiesecker J, Robinson C, Bhatia P, Khurana A, Wang J, Oviedo F, Lavista JM. "An artificial intelligence dataset for solar energy locations in India," *Scientific Data*, 2022; 9: 497. doi: 10.1038/s41597-022-01499-9.

Chapter 12
Mapping Glacial Lakes

—*Anthony Ortiz, Kris Sankaran, Finu Shrestha, Tenzing Chogyal Sherpa, and Mir Matin*

Executive Summary

Understanding the speed and impact of climate change is critical for mitigation efforts. Particular parts of the world are more susceptible to climate change than others and can act as a barometer of the pace of climate change. Glacial lakes are one of those environments and can represent humanitarian threats: when excessive melting weakens the ice shores of those lakes, floods can occur and cause downstream harm. Here, to better understand and measure climate change, we compared several approaches to mapping glacial lakes in the Hindu Kush Himalayas with the anticipated impact that automated mapping could support risk assessments of Glacial Lake Outburst Floods that pose a risk to communities and infrastructure in valleys below glacial lakes.

Incorporating labels from a 2015 survey using Landsat 7 ETM+ SLC-off imagery to guide segmentation on newer higher-resolution satellite images like Sentinel-2 and Bing Maps imagery, we compared our models to previously used ones. We found that a historically guided version of U-Net and a properly initialized form of morphological snakes most effectively segmented the lakes, each providing between an 8–10 percent intersection over union improvement over existing U-Net segmentation approaches. An error analysis highlighted the strengths and limitations of each method. To make our analyses useful, we designed visualizations to support discovery of lakes of potential concern and developed an interactive exploratory interface to facilitate that discovery. We released all the code that we developed that supported our study in public repositories.

Why Is This Important?

Global climate change has accelerated the retreat of glaciers and formed potentially hazardous glacial lakes. These water bodies are constrained by unstable dams made of rock and sediment (*moraine dams*), and their collapse can lead to catastrophic Glacial Lake Outburst Floods, which have been responsible for thousands of deaths and widespread infrastructural damage. Accurate mapping of these glacial lakes over time is critical to assessing the risk of Glacial Lake Outburst Floods occurring and devising effective mitigation measures.

Organizations like the International Centre for Integrated Mountain Development have relied on manual methods or semi-automated techniques to delineate glacial lakes, using either optical or *Synthetic Aperture Radar imagery* (a method of creating images from radio waves). These processes are not only labor intensive but also do not capture the dynamic changes of high-risk glacial lakes very well. In the Hindu Kush Himalayan region, the International Centre for Integrated Mountain Development documented 3,624 glacial lakes, 47 of which were classified as high-risk, using Landsat imagery and the Normalized Difference Water Index. However, because updated analyses of their location and status are infrequent, these lake inventories compromise timely risk assessment and response. Two reasons for the infrequency of the updates are that existing methods are labor intensive and Landsat satellites have a relatively low 30-meter resolution.

Here, we sought to address these limitations by developing innovative methodologies for mapping glacial lakes by incorporating historically guided semantic segmentation models and advanced satellite imagery. While we appreciate previous attempts to automate this process, including the use of hierarchical image segmentation combined with digital elevation maps and the use of U-Net models for glacial lake delineation in recent research, those approaches are sensitive to image conditions and have not fully leveraged historical data to improve accuracy.

Our work underscores the need for advanced, automated methods that can adapt to the rapidly changing dynamics of glacial lake formation and risk. By integrating historical data into cutting-edge semantic segmentation models and using higher-resolution satellite imagery, we demonstrate that our approach outperforms existing methods of glacial lake mapping.

Methods Used

We grappled with the complexities of multitemporal image segmentation given different constraints, including the non-uniformity of label availability over time and the variability of sensor resolutions, to try to develop an automated, useful segmentation strategy that could be used to assess the risk of Glacial Lake Outburst Floods.

We explored several different machine learning approaches. First, we explored U-Net and historically guided U-Net modeling approaches (two types of convolutional neural networks). While the adaptation of U-Net to incorporate historical data as an additional channel is a novel approach to the problem, there is the possibility of overfitting. Although using an ablation mechanism to prevent such model overfitting to past data helps, doing so requires an increased memory footprint that could limit the use of these models, particularly when computational resources are constrained.

Second, we considered a *morphological snake* approach. The adoption of variational methods through morphological snakes uses a family of related methods that allow images to guide the evaluation of curves and surfaces, like those seen in glacial lakes. Given that this approach does not require a training phase, it has advantages for certain real-time applications. However, the computational cost of using a morphological snake approach on large datasets is prohibitive.

Third, we considered *deep level-set evolution,* which is the most advanced, but also the most computationally expensive, approach. This approach incorporates deep, data-specific features that offer more precise segmentation. While using historical guidance could reduce computational load when using this method, its complexity may not necessarily offer a commensurate gain in accuracy.

We used two sources of satellite imagery: Sentinel-2 and Bing Maps. Two examples of Sentinel-2 imagery of growing glacial lakes over two time periods are shown in Figure 12.1.

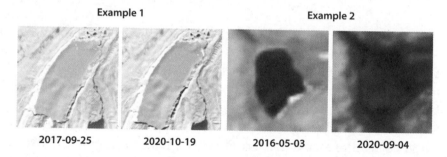

Figure 12.1 Examples of two growing glacial lakes at two time points. The higher resolution on the left is possible because the lake on the left is larger.

We conducted several experiments to determine which approach might be the best and evaluated our models using four metrics: intersection over union, precision, recall, and Fréchet Distance (all defined in Chapter 3, "Commonly Used Processes and Terms"). In our determination of the overall best approach, we considered five additional factors:

- *Scalability*. As a practical matter, we thought it would be beneficial to assess the computational efficiency of these methods as they are scaled for broader impact. Given that the lakes are not isolated phenomena but part of a larger ecosystem, a computationally expensive model might not be feasible for large-scale studies.

- *Temporal coherence.* Because the models rely on multi-temporal data, methods that capture the temporal changes effectively would be more beneficial.
- *Interdisciplinary applications.* Given the importance of monitoring glacial lake boundaries for ecological and human safety reasons, we considered the potential for these segmentation methods to be applied in interdisciplinary contexts (such as climate science or public policy).
- *Uncertainty estimation.* Given the non-uniformity of available labels, we sought to incorporate measures of uncertainty in our predictions.
- *Hardware limitations.* Given that hardware needs to be used for training and inference generation, often in low-resource settings, we considered its potential costs when using different approaches.

Findings

We found that, while no single model had superior performance across all performance metrics, models using the Sentinel-2 dataset generally had better overall performance, and the morphological snake model generally performed better than the other models when using labeled recent imagery (see Table 12.1).

Results were similar when using historical labels from 2015 (see Table 12.2).

Our error evaluation generated a granular analysis of the models' performance using the intersection-over-union performance metric across multiple performance quantiles. The most challenging lakes, usually falling in the lower intersection-over-union quantiles, are responsible for the performance disparities across models. For instance, the U-Net model's precision worsens considerably for challenging tasks despite having comparable performance on easier tasks. However, the historically guided models do not suffer as much in more complex scenarios, possibly due to their utilization of prior information.

Table 12.1 Comparison of the Performance of Models Using Labeled Recent Imagery from the Bing and Sentinel-2 Imagery Datasets

Model	Bing							Sentinel-2		
	IoU (%)	Precision (%)	Recall (%)	Fréchet (px)	Fréchet (m)	IoU (%)	Precision (%)	Recall (%)	Fréchet (px)	Fréchet (m)
U-Net	42.7	48.4	72.3	629.31	327.25	62.5	68.0	84.4	408.27	4083
U-Net Historical	49.8	63.6	72.5	228.57	118.86	67.4	78.4	84.9	239.27	2393
Deep Extreme Level Set Evolution	47.7	58.1	73.5	439.70	228.64	51.4	63.4	65.9	428.78	4288
Deep Extreme Level Set Evolution Historical	37.6	70.7	48.7	211.32	109.89	49.9	89.5	54.9	130.37	1304
Snake	52.8	59.6	79.8	159.70	83.04	70.9	86.4	80.4	111.09	1111

Source: Ortiz A et al., 2022 / IEEE / CC BY 4.0

Table 12.2 Comparison of the Performance of Models Using Imagery Labeled in 2015 and Obtained from the Bing and Sentinel-2 Imagery Datasets

Model	Bing					Sentinel-2				
	IoU (%)	Precision (%)	Recall (%)	Fréchet (px)	Fréchet (m)	IoU (%)	Precision (%)	Recall (%)	Fréchet	Fréchet (m)
U-Net	36.5	42.3	69.0	622.04	323.46	53.0	61.5	76.6	448.81	4488
U-Net Historical	74.7	82.2	90.7	160.75	83.59	80.2	87.6	91.6	279.90	2799
Deep Extreme Level Set Evolution	70.1	76.6	89.4	449.82	233.91	40.4	55.4	51.4	451.75	4518
Deep Extreme Level Set Evolution Historical	53.2	91.0	56.5	115.75	60.19	56.7	98.9	57.3	83.0	830
Snake	58.9	67.1	85.8	120.38	62.60	69.3	89.1	77.6	65.65	657

We show the models' predictions against ground truth for selected lakes in Figure 12.2.

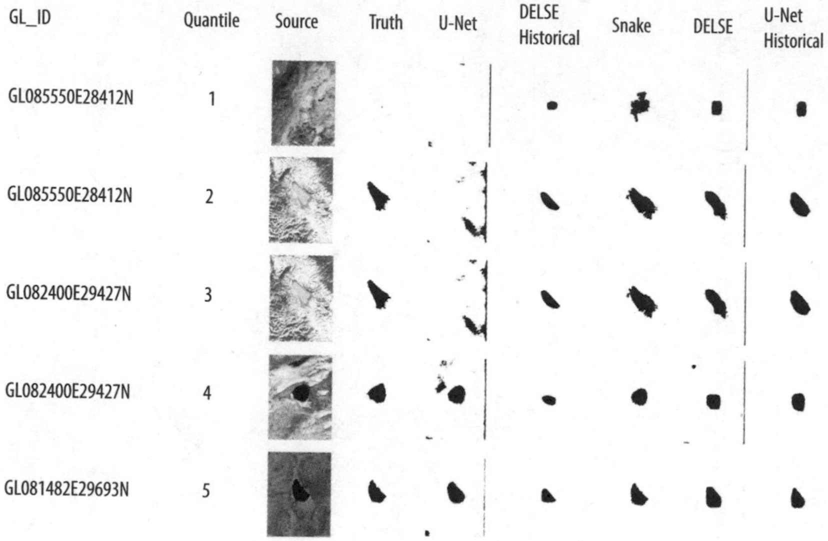

GL_ID	Quantile	Source	Truth	U-Net	DELSE Historical	Snake	DELSE	U-Net Historical
GL085550E28412N	1							
GL085550E28412N	2							
GL082400E29427N	3							
GL082400E29427N	4							
GL081482E29693N	5							

Figure 12.2 Demonstration of the different models' predictions against ground truth for selected lakes.

These comparisons expose the sources of quantitative differences in the models' performance. For example, the morphological snake model often results in rougher boundaries, while both DELSE (a level set model that can learn update rules based on deep, data-specific features) and U-Net are prone to false positives.

Finally, we used linear regression models to assess the relationship between sample collection dates and predicted lake areas. We found a decrease in glacial lake sizes for most lakes in the sample, with a few exceptions (see Figure 12.3).

Discussion

For the purposes of monitoring changes in the size of glacial lakes and their potential to cause catastrophic flooding should they breach, we conducted an in-depth analysis of multiple machine learning models' efficacy in interpreting glacial lake satellite imagery. We highlighted challenges due to variable resolutions of source imagery and the pitfalls of relying solely on historically guided models.

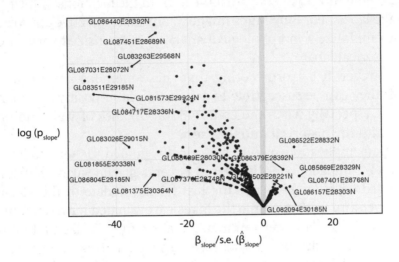

Figure 12.3 A volcano plot of estimated glacial lake area changes. Lakes at the bottom of the "V" do not have detectable trends in glacial lake area. Those to the upper left have significantly decreasing areas; those to the upper right have significantly increasing areas (Ortiz A et al., 2022 / IEEE / CC BY 4.0).

We found that, despite Sentinel-2 satellite imagery having a lower resolution, models based on Sentinel-2 satellite imagery generally outperformed those based on Bing Maps satellite imagery. This finding is likely because of the homogeneity that lower resolution provides, making it easier for the models to predict lake structures. On the other hand, higher resolution introduces intricate variations, such as color and texture differences across the lake, which the models find difficult to learn.

We explored techniques that integrated historical labels into the segmentation of glacial lakes using more recent imagery. Our work serves as a blueprint for Earth observation projects that require label transfer between different imaging modalities. To accomplish this, we employed both advanced level-set evolution techniques and simpler preprocessing strategies.

In the case of Sentinel-2 imagery, we found that augmenting U-Net with an additional channel comprising partially obscured historical labels yielded satisfactory results. This approach minimized the false positives often associated with shadow or snow, as these elements are generally distanced from the locations of historical lake labels. For Bing Maps imagery, our most effective approach was to initialize a morphological snake at a downsized version of the historical label.

However, it is worth noting that these methods are not foolproof: they can be susceptible to generating false-positive segmentations, especially when the contemporary bodies of water do not align with the historical initialization.

Upon application of our historically guided U-Net model to Sentinel-2 imagery, we discovered several glacial lakes that had expanded considerably since the last formal update of the glacial lake inventory in 2015. While the lakes we evaluated have remained relatively stable, a larger number are shrinking. To facilitate others' analysis of lake area trends, we designed a visual query interface. We anticipate that these techniques will enable more frequent updating and analysis of glacial lake regions in the Hindu Kush Himalaya, thus contributing valuable data for Glacial Lake Outburst Flood risk assessments.

Despite these promising results, our study had several limitations:

- First, not all lakes of interest were captured in historical surveys. Future efforts should focus on tightly integrating the identification of new lakes with boundary updates for those already known: this will likely involve an interface capable of both providing and automatically refining weak, partial labels.
- Another limitation was that most models, except for the morphological snake, struggled to handle high-resolution imagery. This is problematic when a single lake features multiple subtly distinguishable textures. We also found that the highly parameterized DELSE model did not outperform a straightforward U-Net modification, possibly due to the limited size of our datasets.

In conclusion, our work offers a methodological framework for using historical labels in the segmentation of more recent glacial lake imagery. While we were successful in reducing false positives and identifying trends in lake sizes, challenges remain, particularly in handling high-resolution imagery and in segmenting newly formed or unrecorded lakes. These issues present fruitful avenues for future research. All the code related to our modeling, interactive visualization, and trend analysis is publicly available, inviting further exploration and application of our methods.

What We Learned

We found that providing data or analyses without also providing an interactive application that engages users in the use of those data and analyses is unlikely to have impact. Therefore, we developed an interface that enables users to examine temporal changes in glacial lake surface areas, primarily by leveraging predictions from the historically guided U-Net model. We focused on making the application user-friendly, allowing users to select lakes, time ranges, and even specific trends to investigate.

Critically, we extended existing segmentation algorithms, using morphological snakes, U-Net, and DELSE algorithms, to incorporate historical glacial lake data, thus guiding segmentation on more precise, higher-resolution imagery from Sentinel-2 and Bing Maps. Further, we compared our findings with those that do not utilize historical data and found that incorporation of historical data improves model accuracy.

Finally, to promote the widespread use and extension of these models, we made our advanced segmentation algorithms available to the broader scientific community by releasing a code repository, thus promoting a more effective and timely approach to Glacial Lake Outburst Floods risk assessment.

The full article on which this summary is based is:

Ortiz A, Tian W, Sherpa TC, Shrestha F, Matin M, Dodhia R, Lavista JM, Sankaran K. "Mapping glacial lakes using historically guided segmentation models." *IEEE Journal of Selected Topics in Applied Earth Observations and Remote Sensing,* 2022: 15(99): 1-15. doi: 10.1109/JSTARS.2022.3215722

Chapter 13

Forecasting and Explaining Degradation of Solar Panels with AI

—Felipe Oviedo and Tonio Buonassisi

Executive Summary

Solar energy is an increasingly important way to address climate change. Solar energy panels use photovoltaics to transform light energy from the sun into stored energy. Degradation of photovoltaics is when their performance suffers over time and under rigorous environmental conditions: degradation means that the panel is not operating at maximal efficiency or effectiveness, and it presents a technical and market hurdle to novel photovoltaic development.

Understanding degradation requires complex measurements on multiple samples over time; therefore, we developed *DeepDeg*, a machine learning model that combines deep learning, explainable machine learning, and physical modeling that can forecast and explain degradation. Using a large and diverse dataset of organic solar cell stability tests and validating the model with a large held-out dataset, we found that, using only a few initial hours of degradation, DeepDeg can accurately and quickly predict degradation dynamics, characterize the degradation, and explain the physiochemical factors driving degradation.

Why Is This Important?

Solar energy is an important arrow in the quiver of fighting climate change. Solar energy incorporates photovoltaics into panels that capture energy from the sun and transform it into energy that can be stored and used by humans. However, *degradation*—meaning a reduction in the efficiency of capture and transformation of light energy over time—remains a significant obstacle to the long-term effectiveness of novel energy devices like photovoltaics and batteries. To be competitive, these devices need to maintain their performance for extended time periods under rigorous environmental conditions.

Commercial photovoltaic modules have low degradation rates of between 0.5 percent to 2 percent, annually. However, emerging photovoltaic technologies have higher degradation rates. The photoactive materials in these newer devices are environmentally sensitive, and their interactions with other solar panel components can introduce further degradation pathways. Traditional methods to study and mitigate degradation—like controlled experiments—take time and generate insights that may be difficult to generalize. Understanding and measuring the degradation of batteries and fuel cells face similar hurdles.

Machine learning offers a transformative solution to these challenges by accelerating the measurement and calculation of degradation, over time. In photovoltaics, machine learning has been used to predict degradation metrics such as power conversion efficiency, primarily in crystalline silicon cells. However, these machine learning approaches demand a thorough understanding of degradation pathways, characterization of those pathways, and vast experimental datasets.

Various machine learning methods—ranging from analytic models to deep learning techniques—have been applied to predict degradation of batteries. A key challenge is balancing the model's performance against its human interpretability: straightforward models, although easier to comprehend, might lack the accuracy achieved by complex deep learning algorithms.

To address shortcomings in the evaluation of photovoltaic degradation, we developed a novel machine learning framework called DeepDeg. Uniquely, DeepDeg separates the tasks of forecasting and explaining the degradation. It employs a deep learning model to make accurate degradation predictions for novel photovoltaics using only the initial hours of a device's current-voltage attributes. Simultaneously, a machine learning explainability component quantifies the influence of various physical factors on degradation metrics.

Methods Used

To better understand and predict photovoltaic degradation over time, we developed DeepDeg, an innovative machine learning model that not only forecasts the degradation of solar cells but also provides in-depth explanations based on physical or chemical driving factors for that degradation.

We designed DeepDeg's architecture to have two components: the *forecasting model* and the *explanation model* (see Figure 13.1).

The forecasting model leveraged initial hours of current-voltage degradation data and other degradation trends to predict future current-voltage characteristics of a given solar cell. Improving on conventional models, we incorporated linear auto-regressive and non-linear convolutional neural network (CNN) mechanisms into DeepDeg's design so it could deliver a complete degradation curve that captures multivariate current-voltage characteristics over time.

To address a critical gap in the current state of knowledge, we incorporated an explanation component into the model by correlating forecasted degradation dynamics with their underlying physical or chemical factors. Using an auxiliary analytical framework based on the one-diode equivalent circuit model, the explanation model attributes time-dependent degradation trends to specific physical parameters, such as changes in shunt resistance. In doing so, the model offers actionable insights for design improvements and further research.

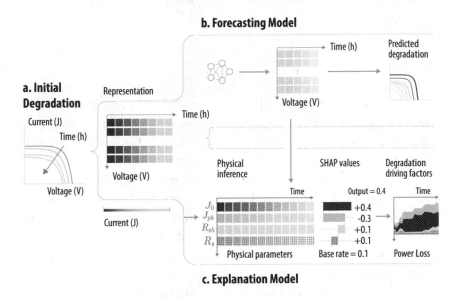

Figure 13.1 Overview of DeepDeg: a) The initial hours of degradation of a photovoltaic device are represented as a multivariate time series of current density-voltage characteristics. b) A forecasting model consisting of a neural network, trained on degradation data from other solar cells, is used to predict future degradation dynamics in a single shot. c) Time-regularized physical inference is used to fit the degradation dynamics to the dynamics of various physical parameters in time according to a device model (Oviedo F et al., 2023 / Cambridge University Press).

We evaluated DeepDeg's robustness using a database of 789 organic photovoltaic solar cells that were composed of various architectures and materials that included over 230,000 hours of degradation data. We tested the model using a challenging and realistic validation scenario of a held-out test set of 31 solar cells that had not been used in model development and that were subjected to different annealing conditions for the charge transport layer—80°C and 200°C. The lower temperature accelerates interface degradation due to excessive recombination and charge accumulation, while the higher temperature curtails this degradation pathway. To integrate reduced time consumption into the model, we used only 15 percent of the total measurement time available in the legacy dataset on which it was trained to make predictions.

Findings

When subjected to grouped five-fold cross-validation, DeepDeg was accurate. Even when trained only on an initial fraction of current-voltage degradation data, DeepDeg outperformed benchmark models in predicting future current-voltage dynamics, as indicated by root mean squared error metrics (see Figure 13.2).

Beyond the improvement in forecasting ability, our explanation model could identify and predict the driving factors of degradation in each test sample. Using top-ranking metrics, DeepDeg exhibited remarkable accuracy in predicting the main degradation driving factors and their contributions to power loss, even when relying on only five percent of the initial data for its predictions.

Furthermore, we compared the estimated change in maximum power point ground truth to DeepDeg's predictions for both annealing conditions (see Figure 13.3).

For devices annealed at 80°C, the model correctly identified that the dominant power loss was driven by the initial power use and time. In contrast, the 200°C condition demonstrated substantially lower power loss, primarily accounted for by the photo-generated current of the solar cell and parallel resistance parameters. While the model underestimated the magnitude of change in maximum power point at 200°C, the relative attribution of driving factors remained consistent, attesting to the model's resilience to forecasting errors. This discrepancy in prediction was likely due to minimal degradation observed during initial measurement hours, thus obfuscating potential degradation dynamics.

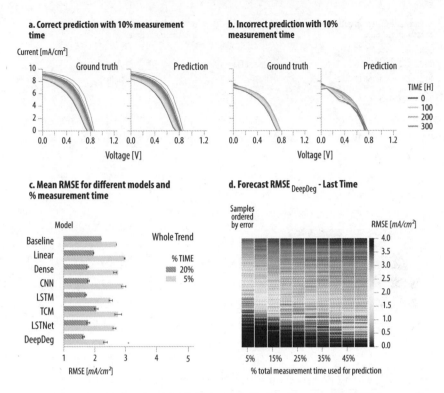

Figure 13.2 Forecasting cross-validation: a) High-accuracy degradation prediction, b) low-accuracy prediction, c) mean root mean squared error across cross-validation test folds for various models (DeepDeg consistently had the lowest error for predicting the whole degradation trend and the last degraded time), d) mean root mean squared error across cross-validation test folds for DeepDeg and the baseline (no prediction) model as a function of the percentage of measurement time used for prediction (Oviedo F et al., 2023 / Cambridge University Press).

A deeper inspection of the inferred equivalent circuit model parameters found distinct characteristics for each annealing condition: the 80°C condition showed higher rates of bulk or interface recombination compared to the 200°C condition. Our predictions aligned closely with the ground truth degradation in both conditions, thereby demonstrating the model's robustness.

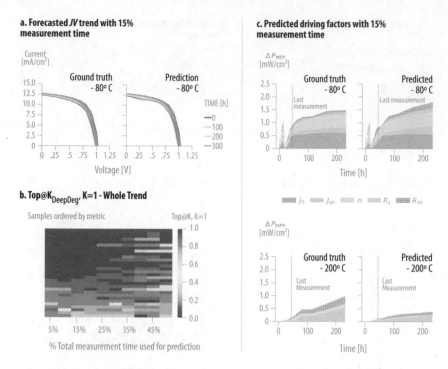

a. Forecasted *JV* trend with 15% measurement time

b. Top@K$_{DeepDeg}$, K=1 - Whole Trend

c. Predicted driving factors with 15% measurement time

Figure 13.3 Held-out test set: a) molecular structure along with the device architecture, b) comparison between the ground truth and DeepDeg forecast for the two annealing conditions, c) inferred enterprise content–management parameters and fitting root mean square errors for the ground truth degradation trends of two annealing conditions, d) comparison of changes in performance explanations for two annealing conditions e) root mean square errors for DeepDeg forecast for all samples in the dataset, and f) metrics of performance and time used for prediction across all samples in the dataset (Oviedo F et al., 2023 / Cambridge University Press).

Interestingly, we found a light-soaking step around 25 hours in both conditions, evident as a sudden recovery in power loss. When it came to final current-voltage characteristics, most were accurately predicted, albeit with greater variance compared to cross-validation test sets. In our evaluation of the model's performance using metrics across the entire time series, we found correct predictions for most tests.

Discussion

We developed DeepDeg, a two-part model of the photovoltaic degradation analysis process that incorporates forecasting and explainability and represents a significant advancement in the field of photovoltaic energy devices and potentially other energy systems. The two-part model integrates flexible physical or chemical models for explicative purposes while harnessing scalable machine learning methods for predictions. We trained DeepDeg on the most extensive dataset of photovoltaic degradation to date, setting a new benchmark in the field.

The performance metrics of DeepDeg are particularly compelling. The model has strong predictive accuracy for long-term degradation as well as the capability to generalize across diverse solar cell materials and architectures. These attributes make DeepDeg a viable tool for expediting experimental screening of novel energy devices, thereby facilitating closed-loop learning and optimization of complete device architectures.

However, the model has several limitations:

- First, DeepDeg may not be useful in predicting novel degradation dynamics for photovoltaics that have characteristics outside of the distribution on which the model was trained. This limitation could be addressed as larger datasets become available for training and as high-throughput experiments enable faster model calibration.
- Second, the quality of degradation explanation is dependent on the accuracy of the devices used. Improved physicochemical models or interpretable statistical models could address this limitation.
- Finally, the model's predictions are limited to accelerated degradation tests under controlled environments: our model may underestimate the impact of more variable and challenging environmental conditions like high humidity and heat.

Nonetheless, the DeepDeg model is a promising way to evaluate other energy devices such as batteries and fuel cells. Particularly where multivariate characteristics provide adequate descriptors of degradation and when physical or chemical models can be used to identify degradation issues, DeepDeg could prove invaluable.

What We Learned

Overall, we learned that DeepDeg introduces a transformative approach to tackling the complex issues of energy device degradation: it not only represents a methodological shift but also holds the promise of broader applicability. Given its capabilities for both prediction and explanation, DeepDeg stands to significantly accelerate the development cycle of novel energy devices and architectures.

We learned that machine learning models can be effective in proactive consideration of the limitations of photovoltaic degradation analysis, which limits the deployment of novel photovoltaic devices. Understanding and addressing the intricacies of the limitations of widespread deployment of any devices or processes designed to mitigate climate change is critical to their success. To make investments in large-scale deployment of such devices, it is necessary to understand when and why they may experience suboptimal behavior. Integrating the forecasting and explainability aspects into our model allowed it to do just that.

Importantly, such models must be tested for accuracy and efficiency. We found that DeepDeg can accurately forecast degradation trends and identify key driving factors with as little as 5–15 percent of the total degradation time, thereby accelerating degradation characterization approximately 5 to 20-fold.

We found that developing a flexible architecture and testing model robustness make for the creation of an essential tool for both researchers and industry professionals aiming to extend the longevity and efficiency of solar cells.

The full article on which this summary is based is:

Oviedo F, Hayden DS, Heumueller T, Wortmann J, Perea JD, Naik R, Xue H, Lavista JM, Fisher J, Brabec CJ, Buonassisi T. "Deep-Deg: forecasting and explaining degradation in novel photovoltaics." *ChemRxiv. Cambridge: Cambridge Open Engage* 2023. doi: 10.26434/chemrxiv-2023-j2pvp

Part III

Humanitarian Action

In the wake of climate change, the frequency and severity of natural disasters like hurricanes and floods have increased. But these types of disasters—and others like earthquakes and avalanches and wars—have existed since the dawn of humanity.

Humans have gotten better at responding to the emergencies that disasters create. But emergency response is often challenged by difficulties obtaining accurate data on, for instance, the extent of damage to a particular locale and the food needs that communities who are impacted by disasters have. Those challenges can both delay emergency response and misdirect scarce resources.

In this part of the book, we provide several examples of how a variety of datasets—from satellite data to household survey

133

data—can be used to rapidly and accurately identify humanitarian needs. Generally, the methods used rely on longitudinal data—to assess the extent of damage that we see today, we need to know whether that damage was present yesterday. Further, the models described herein attempt to provide nuanced data on damage. Many existing models use a binary classification scheme to determine, for instance, building damage as damaged or not damaged. A more nuanced approach attempts to determine the degree of damage that a building sustained, and, further, to estimate the number of people potentially impacted by that damage. This level of information can help emergency response efforts focus on areas where there is the greatest need. Finally, models can be used to anticipate vulnerability to disaster—and those estimates might be predicated on the particular construction of house dwellings and their vulnerability to a particular type of disaster, or to a household's past response to food insecurity.

In the following pages, then, you learn how artificial intelligence can be used to identify risks for severe damage following disasters, to coordinate and improve emergency response, and to give the vulnerable a voice.

Humanitarian action is not solely defined by disaster, however. Humanitarian action also seeks to address populations that have experienced adversity and ensure that they have a voice. In this part, we also provide two examples of how artificial intelligence and advanced data analytics can promote inclusivity, first by helping people with visual impairment identify different currencies and their denominations, and second by identifying areas in which broadband connectivity, which is becoming an essential part of human interconnectedness and activity—is limited. In both of these examples, there are challenges to data use: governments impose regulatory and legal restrictions on the use of high-resolution data on currencies, and, to preserve privacy, steps must be taken to prevent the identification of people in areas wherein broadband connectivity is limited. We provide examples of how artificial intelligence can be used to overcome both of these challenges.

Chapter 14
Post-Disaster Building Damage Assessment

—Shahrzad Gholami

Executive Summary

Climate change is accelerating the frequency and severity of natural disasters. Each year, natural disasters affect over 350 million people and cause trillions of dollars in damage. In the wake of those disasters, providing timely and appropriate emergency responses and humanitarian interventions like shelter, medical aid, and food can be challenging. Artificial intelligence frameworks that leverage available satellite imagery can support existing efforts to provide such interventions. Here, we develop a convolutional neural network model that uses high-resolution satellite imagery from before and after disasters to localize buildings and score their damage into four levels, ranging from not damaged to destroyed.

Due to the emergency nature of disaster response efforts, the value of automating damage assessment lies primarily in its speed, rather than its accuracy. When we compared our results to those generated during an international competition, our solution works three times faster than the fastest winning solution and over 50 times faster than the slowest first place solution. Our model achieved a pixel-wise F1 score of 0.74 for the building localization and a pixel-wise harmonic F1 score of 0.60 for damage classification—both indicators that our model was accurate. Further, our model used a simpler architecture compared to other efforts in the competition. To facilitate the use of our model, we developed a web-based visualizer that can display before and after imagery along with the model's building damage predictions on a custom map. Our work enables humanitarian organizations to deploy the model and visualizer application for emergency response efforts in the field.

Why Is This Important?

Natural disasters pose a severe global challenge. In 2021, natural disasters were a primary cause of hunger for 29 million people. Prompt and effective emergency humanitarian response to these disasters is essential but increasingly difficult due to the escalating scale and volume of disasters, driven by climate change.

In the rapidly evolving field of change detection in satellite imagery, various techniques have been used to enhance emergency humanitarian response and infrastructure monitoring. Convolutional neural networks have emerged as an important technique for processing satellite imagery. Several approaches have been used. One approach has been to use pre-trained convolutional neural network features that are concatenated for both pre- and post-event images. Pixel-wise Euclidean distance can be calculated to form change maps, and thresholding methods can be applied for classification tasks—for instance, to identify which buildings have been impacted and the extent to which they were.

Another approach used Hurricane Harvey data to train convolutional neural networks that were highly accurate in classifying images as damaged or undamaged; however, that approach did not take into account the nuances of building edges and adopted a binary scale (classifying a building as damaged or not) instead of a gradient scale (which would allow policymakers to assess the extent of each building's damage). A third approach used Siamese convolutional neural networks to extract image features pixel by pixel and used weighted contrastive loss to counter the imbalance between changed and unchanged pixels. Siamese convolutional neural networks work in tandem (one usually being a baseline, known network) on two different input sources to compute comparable outputs between baseline and modeled outputs. While this method was better than the others, further improvements have been made to this approach, culminating in a high-resolution, attention-based, two-stream network that unified building localization and classification tasks into an end-to-end model that can help emergency disaster responders identify where the damage is and evaluate the extent of that damage.

Graph-based models can capture similarities between neighboring buildings and can be generalized for application to various types of disasters. However, graph-based models have not consistently outperformed Siamese convolutional neural network models in terms of accuracy.

Here, we propose a Siamese approach inspired by previous work that uses U-Net architecture for building segmentation and assessing building damage levels. We use U-Net's encoders with shared parameters for both pre- and post-disaster imagery in an end-to-end fashion. Further, to ensure that the model could be pragmatically deployed, we tested it under operational emergency conditions. Finally, aligning with other domain-specific visualizers (like those used for wildfire monitoring and fire inspection prioritization), we developed a web visualizer that allows users to see visualizations and predictions of disaster severity where before and after satellite images are available.

Methods Used

In 2019, the "xView2" challenge was launched to gauge computer vision capabilities in damage assessment. The challenge relied on the publicly available xBD dataset, which contains high-resolution imagery of 19 different types of disasters, including floods, earthquakes, and fires, across over 45,000 square kilometers. The dataset consists of 22,068 image tiles, each sized at 1024x1024 pixels, along with 850,736 building polygons that are categorized by damage level—no damage, minor damage, major damage, and destroyed.

The challenge results had some practical limitations. First, because it did not impose any constraints on the computational resources available for model training, winning solutions were resource intensive. Second, because the challenge allowed for potentially biased hand-labeling, results were not optimized for real-time disaster management and emergency response.

To address these limitations, the Microsoft AI for Good Lab partnered with the Netherlands Red Cross to create a machine learning model that used the same high-resolution satellite imagery as that used in the challenge to assess damage levels in affected areas rapidly.

In that effort, we used a novel approach for assessing building damage after natural disasters.

Our model adopted a deep learning approach that used a single pipeline for both building segmentation (the identification of discrete buildings) and damage classification tasks. We used a U-Net model, which is known for its efficacy in image segmentation, as the model's basic architecture (see Figure 14.1).

Unlike other models that incorporate attention layers that enhance some parts of the input data while diminishing other parts, we developed a relatively straightforward architecture, thereby reducing complexity. Our model included an encoder and a decoder, each consisting of multiple convolution blocks, which are used to extract features from the input image. For assessing damage, we used a pair of pre- and post-disaster images, feeding them into the U-Net model using shared weights. The encoded layers from these images were then used to ascertain changes, which were subsequently classified for damage by a separate decoder.

In the experimental phase, we segmented the xBD dataset into train, validation, and test splits at a ratio of 80:10:10. We further divided each tile into 20 patches of 256x256 pixels to manage computational resources. During training, we recognized the inter-connectedness between the building segmentation and damage classification tasks; therefore, we opted for a sequential training approach. Initially, we focused on building segmentation—the identification of discrete buildings—using specific weights to counter the imbalance between building and background pixels (like those depicting the ground or a park or a street). After achieving reasonable performance in building segmentation, we proceeded to the damage classification task, adjusting the *loss* function—the amount of error representing the difference between the model's prediction and the ground truth—to counter the imbalance among different damage categories.

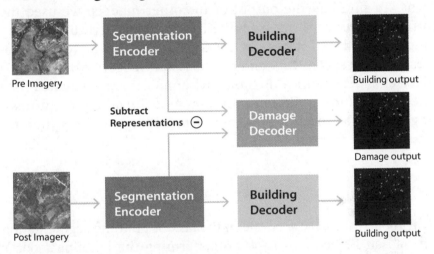

Figure 14.1 In this Siamese U-Net model architecture, pre- and post-disaster imagery are fed into an encoder–decoder style segmentation model (U-Net) with shared weights. The features generated by the segmentation encoder from both inputs are subtracted and passed to an additional damage classification decoder that generates per-pixel damage level predictions. The weights of the damage classification decoder can be fine-tuned for specific disaster types, while relying on building segmentation output from the building decoder (Gholami S et al., 2022 / IEEE).

The model used a multi-class classifier to rate the level of build-ing damage on a scale of 1 to 4, with 1 representing no damage and

4 indicating complete destruction. To examine the accuracy and efficiency of our model, we compared its performance against previous solutions that won the xView2 challenge.

In emergency response, when the goal is to make decisions and provide relief as quickly as possible, the speed of predictive models, gauged by the number of pixels they can process per second, is of paramount importance. Sluggish models not only elevate computing costs but also risk delaying critical decisions. Therefore, we evaluated the inference speed of top-performing models in the xView2 challenge against our model: we used a standardized setup of a Microsoft Azure NC6 virtual machine armed with a NVIDIA Tesla K80 GPU to make those comparisons. To simulate the output of the other models, we used the official inference script from the DIUx-xView GitHub repository and modified it, if necessary, for GPU acceleration. We then processed three sets of pre- and post-disaster imagery from the xBD dataset under identical Python environments and evaluated time metrics, including file input/output, model loading, preprocessing, and post-processing overheads, providing an upper limit for processing a 1024x1024 input.

Findings

Our model was very accurate in the task of building segmentation (it had an F1 score of 0.74, outperforming the baseline model's score from the competition of 0.64). To test the model's robustness to a variety of potential disaster scenarios, we trained it on data that excluded specific disaster events, like the Joplin tornado or Nepal flooding. We found that our model's performance varied depending on the geographical distribution of the training data, and the model's accuracy was lower when tested on disasters occurring in regions not well-represented in the training set, like the Nepal flooding disaster (see Figure 14.2).

We also tested the model's performance when trained solely on specific types of disasters like those related to wind or floods.

Doing so improved the model's performance when applied to entirely new disaster events of the same type. Overall, our model excelled in both building segmentation and damage classification tasks, thereby providing a valuable tool for humanitarian assistance and disaster recovery efforts.

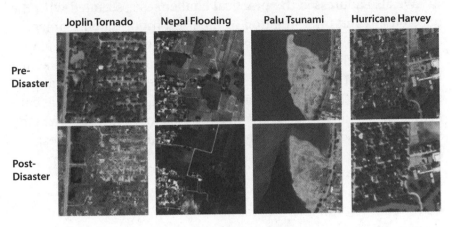

Figure 14.2 Pre- and post-disaster imagery samples of different disasters from DigitalGlobe.

Further, we found that our model was three times faster than the fastest model in the xView2 challenge and over 50 times faster than the one that won first place. In optimized settings, when data processing was improved (by using parallel data-loaders, moving pre- and post-processing to the GPU, maximizing the amount of imagery processed at once, and using the most recent software packages), our model's performance further improved. With those enhancements, our model processed 612.29 square kilometers per hour, a substantial increase over the 89.35 square kilometers under the previous setup. This allowed us to analyze the Hurricane Ida imagery in just two days, costing $14.70, thereby reducing baseline cost estimates by 20 percent.

We found that many of the xView2 challenge's top models used techniques like ensemble learning and test-time augmentation, which sacrificed speed for performance. Optimized for pragmatic implementation, our model produced a more cost-effective and quicker solution. For instance, analyzing the Hurricane Ida dataset would take the xView2 challenge's top-performing model 301.4 days and $6,500 using a NVIDIA Tesla K80 GPU, while our model could accomplish the same in 4.7 days at a cost of $100.

We also addressed the practical challenges associated with the distribution and interpretation of high-resolution satellite imagery and predictions by developing a web-based visualizer that allows users to switch between pre- and post-disaster imagery, adjust the visibility of damage predictions, and integrate additional geographic layers (like streets or riverbanks) for additional spatial context. Our visualizer, built using open-source tools, further offers the advantage of not requiring any specialized GIS software or experience (see Figures 14.3 and 14.4).

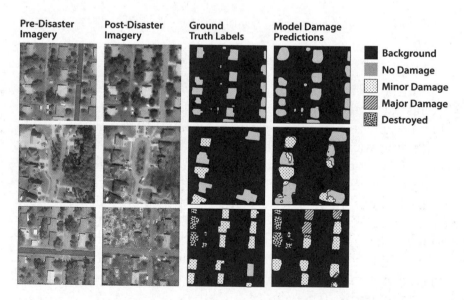

Figure 14.3 Imagery samples with polygons showing building edges and greyscales showing damage level (Gholami S et al., 2022 / IEEE).

Figure 14.4 Full screenshots of pre- and post-disaster images of the 2021 Haiti earthquake as seen through the damage visualizer.

Discussion

To accelerate and improve the use of satellite imagery in emergency response and humanitarian action, we developed a single, integrated, efficient model for identifying both the location and degree of building damage following a disaster. Compared to other work, our model was designed with operational considerations in mind, used a simplified architecture that reduced computational complexity, and focused on speed. We rigorously tested our model's performance and explored its applicability in various disaster scenarios. When benchmarked against the winning solutions of the xView2 challenge, our model was substantially faster and cheaper.

The web-based visualizer that we developed and that displays the "before and after" imagery along with the model's predictions on a custom map improves the model's practical utility by providing an accessible platform for decision-makers, obviating the need for specialized GIS software. This visualizer could not only accelerate disaster response but also facilitate more nuanced interpretations by experts in the field, in near real-time.

In summary, by leveraging machine learning and high-resolution satellite imagery, the collaborative project between Microsoft's AI for Good Lab and the Netherlands Red Cross generated a fast and efficient tool for disaster assessment. This tool not only promises to revolutionize humanitarian responses, but also aims to optimize resource allocation during critical emergency situations.

What We Learned

In light of the rising frequency and severity of natural disasters, there is an urgent need for enhanced strategic responses from humanitarian organizations. A public/private collaboration between Microsoft's AI for Good Lab and the Netherlands Red Cross, successfully developed an implementable convolutional neural network model that harnesses satellite imagery for improved disaster relief efforts.

Collaboration entails learning from stakeholders. Our stakeholder consultations emphasized two key points:

- First, speed trumps accuracy in automated post-disaster damage assessment because ground-level inspections are irreplaceable for determining structural integrity. In other words, spending an inordinate amount of time on precision of the amount of damage that could be seen from satellite imagery does not matter much, as people will need to assess the structural damage of the buildings, in person, at a later date.
- Second, long-term recovery programs require context, not just damage data, necessitating the fusion of our model's outputs with other relevant data, such as data on roads, water supplies, and green space.

We developed our model with those two features in mind. Given that our model may not be universally applicable across diverse geographical regions, more work should be done: incorporating active learning and human–machine collaborations may further improve the model. Nonetheless, our stakeholders have implemented our model within a scalable, distributed computing system that allows for parallel processing and guarantees a fixed computation time, regardless of the number of input images. Furthermore, our model's outputs are disseminated through three channels: our web visualizer, the "Humanitarian Data Exchange" platform, and maps for first responders.

This project represents an interdisciplinary fusion of satellite imagery and AI technologies, aimed at improving the way humanitarian organizations operate in the aftermath of natural disasters.

The co-developed convolutional neural network model represents a transformative approach to post-disaster management by increasing the speed and precision of computing resources, thereby offering a substantial contribution to humanitarian efforts during times of crisis.

The full article on which this summary is based is:

Gholami S, Robinson C, Ortiz A, Yang S, Margutti J, Birge C, Dodhia R, Lavista JM. "On the deployment of post-disaster building damage assessment tools using satellite imagery: a deep learning approach." *IEEE International Conference on Data Mining Workshops* 2022: 1029-1036. doi: 10.1109/ICDMW58026.2022.00134

Chapter 15
Dwelling Type Classification

—Md Nasir and Anshu Sharma

Executive Summary

Neighborhood vulnerability and risk assessment is essential for effective disaster preparedness. Due to their dependency on time-consuming and cost-intensive field surveying, existing systems of neighborhood vulnerability and risk assessment do not provide a scalable way to assess the precise extent of natural-hazard risk at a hyper-local level. Here, we used machine learning to automate the process of identifying dwellings and their type, allowing us to build a potentially more effective and expansive disaster vulnerability assessment system.

First, we used satellite images of low-income settlements and vulnerable areas in India to identify seven different dwelling types. Specifically, we formulated the dwelling type classification as a semantic segmentation task (identifying and classifying discrete dwellings and their types) and trained a U-Net–based neural network model with the data we collected. Then, we used a risk score assessment model that incorporated the determined dwelling type along with a flood inundation model of the regions. We used 2020 data obtained prior to natural hazards that occurred in India thereafter. We collected post-disaster ground-truth data from those regions to validate the efficacy of our model. We found that our model performed well. This work can drive preemptive action by providing household-level risk indicators that can inform decision-making by disaster response organizations, policymakers, and communities at risk.

Why Is This Important?

Over the past two decades, natural disasters have affected more than 4 billion people globally and have caused significant economic losses. Particularly vulnerable is India, which was the seventh most impacted country by weather-related disasters in 2021. Natural disasters often result in extensive damage to housing, disproportionately affecting the economically underprivileged. Here, we developed a technological solution aimed at refining disaster forecasts and enhancing disaster preparedness—not only for India, but also for the world.

To conduct this work, we used a machine learning–based system specifically designed to assess the risk of natural hazards at a granular level. The model we used performed multi-class semantic segmentation tasks (identifying discrete buildings and their types), aiming to enhance the reliability of disaster forecasts. In addition, we used a statistical model for risk scoring, informed by SEEDS, which is an India-based not-for-profit disaster preparedness and response organization.

Dwelling type classification forms the backbone of our risk assessment model. Different roof types—whether plastic, metal, or reinforced concrete—serve as indicators of the building's overall structural integrity. This classification allows for a nuanced understanding of how vulnerable a structure would be to various natural hazards like floods, cyclones, and earthquakes. Contributing factors, such as proximity to water bodies and other geographic elements, were also considered in the risk scoring.

Importantly, while we developed this model using India as an example, its potential application is global. While different countries and regions may have different roof types, models could be generated for specific locales—using local information sources for labeling—to create granular and disaster-specific risk estimation models around the world.

Methods Used

We focused on classifying dwelling types using satellite imagery, a novel approach in machine learning applications to urban landscapes, particularly in India. Prior work in extracting building footprints from satellite images largely relied on convolutional neural networks and focused on generic building identification rather than specific dwelling types. Other research on dwelling classification predominantly used 3D LiDAR data, which offers high granularity but is limited in availability and scope.

One of the main challenges that we faced was the variation in size and shape of buildings within dense Indian urban environments. This required the use of high-resolution satellite images, which are up-to-date and reflect recent developments and construction. To meet these requirements, we obtained satellite imagery of 50 cm resolution from Maxar Technologies that covered Mumbai and Puri regions and were compliant with local regulations. However, these high-resolution images were limited due to their inclusion of only standard RGB (red, green, and blue) bands; additional bands like infrared could have been useful for the dwelling type classification task.

After a comprehensive survey, we identified 14,000 houses that had been manually labeled into 12 categories of roof types. For efficiency, we narrowed the 12 categories down to 7 categories that correlated with risk factors.

We prepared the dataset with imagery from eight areas of interest, four each from Mumbai and Puri. We found that the dataset had a highly skewed distribution of classes, being populated largely by one type of dwelling, which added complexity to the machine learning task. While we attempted to use data-augmentation techniques like horizontal flipping and 90-degree rotations, those techniques yielded no significant performance improvement, likely because the dataset was already diverse in terms of dwelling orientation and size.

We used a neural network–based approach to multi-class semantic segmentation, and we trained the model in a way that could not only identify pixels that represent dwellings but also recognize the type of dwelling (as one of the seven categories) and differentiate them from the background.

For our segmentation model, we used the TernausNet architecture, an extension of U-Net models that uses a VGG11 network as the encoder, pre-trained on ImageNet, to assist with segmentation in smaller datasets. Despite experimenting with different loss functions, multi-class cross-entropy loss yielded the best results.

Therefore, we trained the model using a multi-class cross-entropy loss function with a one-hot encoded label vector for each category. We measured performance using weighted accuracy based on class frequency and weighted pixel-level intersection over union. TernausNet outperformed baseline models, including a traditional U-Net and fully connected convolutional neural network (FCNN) in these metrics. All experiments were performed using the Solaris toolkit with PyTorch as a deep learning framework on Azure DSVM with NVIDIA Tesla K80 GPUs.

Post-processing involved converting segmented dwelling footprints into polygons using the Douglas-Peucker algorithm. This was done not only for shape smoothing, but also to create a low-resource representation of the dwellings for risk assessment.

An overview of the model development process is shown in Figure 15.1.

Findings

We found that the weighted accuracy of the model's predictive performance based on the class frequency of the pixels ranged from 82 to 87 percent, and the weighted intersection over union (or Jaccard index) ranged from 0.75 to 0.81, depending on the model evaluated. Examples of model predictions for dwelling types are provided in Figure 15.2.

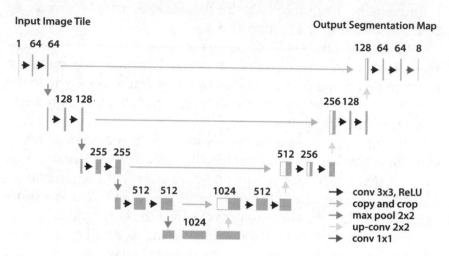

Figure 15.1   An overview of the model development process (Nasir M et al., 2022 / arxiv).

We then used this information to generate risk scores—ranging from 1 to 5—that were assigned to individual dwelling types and their concentrations in communities. This kind of assessment allows for precise, timely warnings that supplement meteorological forecasts. Such granular information is critical for enabling communities to formulate customized response plans, whether they be immediate evacuation or long-term building reinforcement. With a clear understanding of their specific risks, families can also take proactive measures to safeguard their homes and lives.

An overview of the risk score modeling pipeline is shown in Figure 15.3.

Importantly, the model's effectiveness was validated in real-world applications. Initially trained on data from Mumbai and Puri, the system was later deployed in Tamil Nadu and Kerala, regions impacted by the tropical cyclones Nivar and Burevi in late 2020. SEEDS used the model to issue warnings and advisories, thus bridging the gap between broad meteorological forecasts and actionable, localized guidance.

Categories

■ 0 not house
■ 1 RCC
■ 2 CGI_1S
■ 3 CGI_2S
□ 4 CGI_4S
■ 5 TITLE_2S
□ 6 TITLE_4S
□ 7 TARP

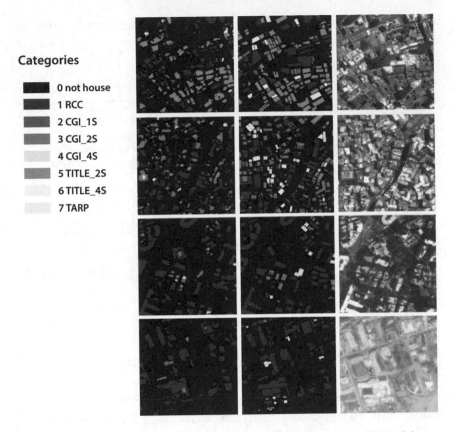

Figure 15.2 Examples of our model's results: predicted label from the model output (left), ground truth (middle), and input imagery (right). Different gray scales in the first columns indicate different dwelling types, with black representing a dwelling-less background.

Discussion

For two states in India, we used publicly available data and machine learning to estimate dwelling types from the composition of their roofs and then used that information to estimate the risks to individual dwellings and communities of suffering damage from natural disasters. The model focused on urban risk, as cities are the focus of growing population densities and have more complex risks. Our results significantly improved upon the granularity of flood early warning systems, enabling more precise and actionable information for vulnerable communities.

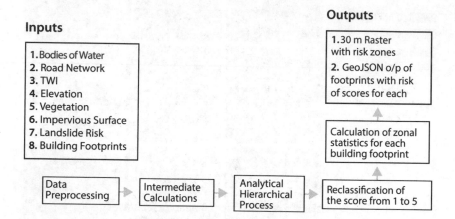

Figure 15.3 An overview of the risk score modeling pipeline (Nasir M et al., 2022 / arxiv).

The model was found to be valid, was effectively used prospectively for risk mitigation, and is currently being revised to extend its application to multiple hazards besides floods, including heatwaves and earthquakes. Further work will improve accuracy by using more advanced modeling and *drone mapping*—which provides higher resolution that satellite imagery—during the annotation phase.

Our study has several limitations. First, while the dwelling identification modeling approach is identical for risk-modeling across changing hazards, the risk scoring approach changes drastically. For example, a plastic sheet or tarpaulin roof house may be very weak and vulnerable to floods but will have lower risk of collapse and casualties in an earthquake scenario. Similarly, a thatch roof (and mud wall) house might have a higher vulnerability to floods but less vulnerability during an earthquake.

Nonetheless, we intend to estimate the degree to which houses of a particular construction material might be damaged by a particular natural disaster. By incorporating attributes unique to each community, such as building materials and topography, future work will create a more accurate, predictive, community-specific model, thus allowing communities to be better prepared in advance and develop custom response plans.

What We Learned

We learned that we could apply a novel approach to determining risk profiles for dwellings and communities by focusing on the fundamental basis for their risk to different natural disasters: their construction. We then leveraged that information and knowledge about the potential impact of different natural disasters on particular dwelling types (and their concentrations in communities) and, where possible, as a function of proximity to those hazards (like rivers for flooding). Applying this modeling to existing data, we were able to markedly enhance the predictive capacities of our non-profit partner.

Importantly, we also learned the value of working with such a partner. Founded in 1994, SEEDS is well established and respected in India. The company has partnered with families affected by disasters and climate emergencies in numerous ways: by restoring and upgrading infrastructure, improving access to clean water and sanitation among marginalized communities, and designing nature-based solutions that help communities adapt to climate change in ecologically sensitive areas. Importantly, SEEDS can engage with policymakers to make models available to local, state, and national government agencies with the intent of making the lives of millions safer.

Our work addressed a pressing need for accurate, reliable disaster warnings in vulnerable communities, particularly in high-risk regions like India. By using machine learning models trained on specific attributes of dwellings, our research brought granularity to risk assessment and forecasting. This advancement holds the promise of mitigating disaster impact, offering economically disadvantaged communities a fighting chance against the devastating effects of natural calamities worldwide.

The full article on which this summary is based is:

Nasir M, Sederholm T, Sharma A, Mallu SR, Ghatage SR, Dodhia R, Lavista JM. "Dwelling type classification for disaster risk assessment using satellite imagery." arXiv: 2211.11636. doi: 10.48550/arXiv.2211.11636. (Presented in AI+HADR workshop, Neurips 2022.)

Trevor Noah's interviews and his review of this project can be found at the following links:

- YouTube video: Microsoft's Chief Questions Officer Trevor Noah on How AI Can Help Protect from Extreme Weather (www .youtube.com/watch?v=RP8g62Mes9I)
- AI for Good site's interview with Trevor Noah: Microsoft Research: The Prompt (www.microsoft.com/en-us/research/group/ai-for-good-research-lab/the-prompt)

Chapter 16

Damage Assessment Following the 2023 Earthquake in Turkey

—Caleb Robinson, Simone Fobi, and Anthony Ortiz

Executive Summary

After the earthquake in Turkey on February 6, 2023, our team used artificial intelligence methods and high-resolution satellite imagery to assess the extent of damage to buildings in the affected region. Specifically, we partnered with Turkey's Ministry of Interior Disaster and Emergency Management Presidency to deliver building-level damage estimates for four cities in southeast Turkey using satellite imagery collected during the first three days of the disaster. We estimated that 3,849 buildings were damaged or destroyed across the four cities. We found the city of Kahramanmaraş most heavily affected, with 7.44 percent of buildings in the city sustaining some level of damage visible from satellite imagery.

Why Is This Important?

Climate change, the spread of the human population, and humanity's increasingly effective ability to respond to disasters suggest that monitoring for and rapidly assessing disasters will become progressively important in the future. The availability of data from satellites that can map the entire Earth daily, and at a very granular level, tremendously helps disaster assessment and emergency response: those images can provide "before" data that can be compared to current data to assess changes in building structures, which indicate damage.

The incredible volume of this data precludes its ability to be rapidly assessed by humans. Humans might not only become fatigued, and thereby miss subtle changes that indicate damage, but also require training and specialized expertise to consistently identify different characteristics of satellite imagery. Artificial intelligence–informed models can be trained to identify and characterize structures, compare identified structures to themselves over time to document changes, assess the degree to which structural changes have occurred, and provide a time window during which such changes happened.

This technological application of artificial intelligence to satellite data has multiple uses, including monitoring the changes in agricultural endeavors (from assessment of coverage, makeup, and harvest status of crops to evaluation of the size and growth of industrial poultry farms), monitoring changes in the size of natural phenomenon that reflect global climate change (like assessing glacial lakes and coastal contours), assessing war damage (importantly, being able to document damage to protected buildings like health clinics and schools and providing dates on which the damage occurred, thereby providing support for war crimes prosecution), and conducting virtually immediate assessments of structural damage due to natural disasters, particularly in areas where it might be dangerous for humans to go (like in areas with recent or current flooding, hurricane damage, fire damage, or earthquakes).

As an example of the use of satellite data for rapid damage assessment and emergency response, we show results following the earthquakes and aftershocks that occurred in southern and central Turkey and northern and western Syria on February 6, 2023, which killed almost 50,000 people.

Methods Used

We used satellite imagery from two commercial providers (Planet Labs and Maxar Technologies) that have images at spatial resolutions of 50 cm and 30 cm, respectively. We modeled the problem of identifying damaged buildings from satellite imagery as a semantic segmentation problem—identifying discrete buildings and then assessing their level of damage by comparing to pre-disaster imagery. We focused our work on four cities in southeast Turkey, which are population centers located to the west of the earthquake's epicenter: Kahramanmaraş (population 610,000), Türkoğlu (population 82,843), Nurdağı (population 31,202), and İslahiye (population 52,622) (see Figure 16.1).

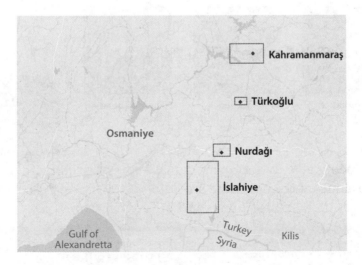

Figure 16.1   Cities on which we focused our analysis (Robinson C et al., 2023 / Microsoft Corporation).

We used convolutional neural networks to estimate whether each pixel in an input satellite image was part of a damaged building, part of an undamaged building, or part of the background (i.e., anything not belonging to the first two classes). We pre-trained a convolutional neural network on the xBD dataset, which provides fine-grained building damage polygons across different types of disasters. We then fine-tuned a convolutional neural network for each of the cities with labels collected using our open-source "satellite-imagery-labeling-tool." This tool allows users to quickly annotate satellite imagery with examples of the three classes and integrate their annotations into a machine learning model training workflow.

After fine-tuning a model for each city, we ran the model using satellite imagery available during the time of interest (before and soon after February 6, 2023) and summarized the model's output using building footprints from Microsoft's or OpenStreetMap's building footprint datasets. For each building footprint in each city, we computed the percentage of the building's footprint that was predicted to be "part of a damaged building" by the convolutional neural network model (see Figure 16.2).

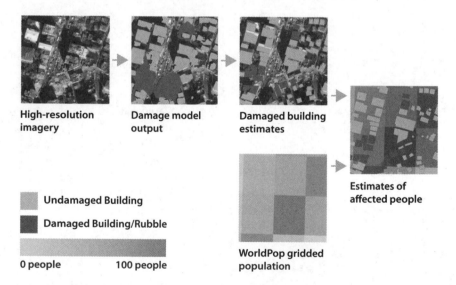

High-resolution imagery

Damage model output

Damaged building estimates

Estimates of affected people

□ Undamaged Building

■ Damaged Building/Rubble

0 people   100 people

WorldPop gridded population

Figure 16.2 Building damage assessment and affected population estimate workflow.

Downstream analyses can apply thresholds of percentage damaged values to quickly contrast the location and number of destroyed buildings to those with minor damage. A weakness of this methodology is that rubble that has been identified as "damage" but that falls outside of a building's footprint cannot be attributed to any nearby building, potentially causing underestimation of the number of damaged buildings. Another weakness is that the building footprints in the Microsoft Building footprint dataset are derived from Bing Basemaps, which include imagery that is potentially outdated for the different cities examined, potentially missing recently constructed buildings.

Finally, we attempted to compute the number of people who were directly affected in the damaged buildings using WorldPop's (www.worldpop.org) unconstrained 2020 gridded population estimates. This data source consists of a grid of 100x100-meter cells that covers the entirety of Turkey, where each cell contains an estimate of the number of people living in that area. We counted the population of a grid cell as "affected" if there was a damaged building in the cell, and we summed the affected population at a city level.

Findings

Across the four cities we examined, we found a total of 3,849 damaged buildings—ranging from partially damaged to destroyed—that impacted 160,411 people (see Table 16.1).

Table 16.1   Results of the Four Study Areas

Region (Image date)	Number of buildings	Number of damaged buildings	% buildings damaged	Estimated people impacted
Kahramanmaraş (2/9)	40,375	3,005	7.44%	148,388
Türkoğlu (2/9)	3,816	185	4.85%	6,202
Nurdağı (2/9)	4,537	331	7.30%	2,163
İslahiye (2/7)	13,215	328	2.48%	3,658

Source: Robinson C et al., 2023 / Microsoft Corporation

Kahramanmaraş was the most heavily affected of the four cities, both proportionally (the fraction of buildings affected) and in magnitude (the total number of buildings damaged). Kahramanmaraş is a major population center in the region that is centrally located between the two major earthquakes (45 kilometers from the first magnitude 7.8 earthquake and 55 kilometers from following magnitude 7.5 earthquake). The damage to buildings in Kahramanmaraş potentially impacted 148,388 people, or 24.3 percent of Kahramanmaraş population. The most significantly damaged area of the city was around the Kültür Park in the city center, shown in Figure 16.3.

Figure 16.3   Extensive damage around the Culture Park area of Kahramanmaraş. (greytones indicate damaged buildings).

Damage in Türkoğlu was distributed throughout the city, with fewer large clusters of damage. In Türkoğlu, 4.85 percent of the buildings were damaged, affecting an estimated 6,202 people. Figure 16.4 shows an example of two destroyed buildings along one of the major streets through the city.

Of the cities we studied, Nurdağı was the closest to the epicenter of the first earthquake. We found significant damage throughout the city, with 7.3 percent of buildings damaged to some extent; however, due to Nurdağı relatively small population, fewer people were affected. Figure 16.5 shows damage to the city center area and a large group of tents that were set up in the response efforts.

Figure 16.4   Several destroyed apartment buildings in Türkoğlu. Greytones indicate damaged buildings.

Figure 16.5   Demonstration of damage in Nurdağı. Greytones indicate damaged buildings.

In İslahiye, 13,215 buildings (2.48 percent of all buildings in the city) were damaged. While İslahiye had the smallest proportion of damaged buildings, they were clustered in densely populated areas, impacting more people. For example, Figure 16.6 shows a group of nine apartment buildings that were all destroyed.

Figure 16.6   A set of nine destroyed five-story apartment buildings in downtown İslahiye. Greytones indicate damaged buildings.

Discussion

In the immediate aftermath of the earthquake that occurred in Turkey on February 6, 2023, we used satellite imagery and artificial intelligence to rapidly assess building damage across three dimensions (undamaged, partially damaged, and destroyed) and enumerate the people likely impacted by that damage.

Critical to this undertaking was that a library of annotated satellite datasets was available for analysis and comparison. To be sure, those datasets are imperfect—as mentioned, they may not include recently constructed buildings and they may not be able to attribute rubble to a particular building. But the concert of current satellite imagery, historical information, and computer power allowed for very rapid and accurate assessments that were used to direct humanitarian relief efforts.

What We Learned

We learned that public–private partnerships can be leveraged to apply new methodologies to old and new datasets to effectively and quickly provide information that is critical to humanitarian relief efforts. Further, the methods and processes we described can have broader applications: they have been applied to wildfire analyses in Canada and Hawaii, flood damage assessment in Africa and India, and hurricane damage in the Caribbean.

With the proliferation of multispectral and hyperspectral satellites that can monitor broad swaths of the electromagnetic spectrum at a high spatial resolution, remotely sensed imagery will become increasingly valuable in the assessment of human activity, monitoring of air and water quality, and damage assessment. As artificial intelligence methods improve, algorithms might be able to predict the impact of decisions, such as those related to urban planning, on emissions, human activity, and climate change. Then, we can calculate the anticipated impact on people or the environment and modify decisions to lessen adverse impacts and maximize the effectiveness of emergency response.

The full article on which this summary is based is:

Robinson C, Gupta R, Nsutezo SF, Pound E, Ortiz A, Rosa M, White K, Dodhia R, Zolli A, Birge C, Lavista JM. "Turkey Building Damage Assessment." which is available at: www.microsoft .com/en-us/research/uploads/prod/2023/02/Turkey-Earthquake-Report-2_MS.pdf

Chapter 17
Food Security Analysis

—Shahrzad Gholami, Erwin Knippenberg, and James Campbell

Executive Summary

Exacerbated by climate change–driven shocks like droughts and floods, *food insecurity*—the lack of consistent access to enough food for every person in a household to live an active, healthy life—is a global problem. For humanitarian programs to ensure timely delivery of assistance, forecasting food insecurity levels and identifying vulnerable households is crucial. Here, we used a machine learning approach trained on high-frequency household survey data to identify predictors of food insecurity at the community level and forecast household-level risks for food insecurity in near real-time.

To develop predictive models, we used data collected monthly through the Measuring Indicators for Resilience Analysis data collection protocol implemented by Catholic Relief Services in southern Malawi. We considered the predictive model as a binary classification of food insecurity that we dichotomized based on two different thresholds, which resulted in two different positive class to negative class ratios (with one class being food insecure and the other class being not food insecure).

When predicting community-level vulnerability, we found that a random forest model outperformed other approaches and that location and self-reported welfare are the best predictors of food insecurity; the model was accurate in predicting food insecurity when predictor features included a historical food insecurity score and 20 additional variables selected by artificial intelligence explainability frameworks. Our findings suggest that the combination of high-frequency, individually collected local data and machine learning algorithms can be used to predict food insecurity at community and household levels and, thereby, improve the efficiency and effectiveness of humanitarian food relief programs.

Why Is This Important?

Affecting nearly 690 million people or 8.9 percent of the global population, food insecurity is an important global humanitarian issue. Food insecurity is defined by the U.S. Department of Agriculture as the lack of consistent access to enough food for every person in a household to live an active, healthy life. According to the UN's Food and Agriculture Organization's 2020 report, populations most vulnerable to food insecurity tend to depend on subsistence agriculture and are disproportionately affected by environmental shocks like droughts and floods. When those shocks happen, households often use impaired coping mechanisms like asset depletion or reduced food intake that are detrimental to their human and financial capital. Further, the long-term impact of these unsustainable and detrimental coping mechanisms can lead to childhood malnutrition, which has lasting educational attainment, earning potential, and health effects.

To be effective and efficient, humanitarian initiatives designed to deter the use of such coping mechanisms need to have access to timely information on food insecurity so that their interventions allocate scarce resources to those for whom the interventions will have the greatest impact. Such initiatives hinge on data collected through remote sensing or embedded sentinel sites. Attempts to predict food insecurity primarily focus on food availability and use satellite data to forecast crop production. However, those predictions often neglect to incorporate factors that are important to the distribution and consumption of food, like its allocation and affordability. Moreover, existing systems like the Integrated Food Security Phase Classification system and Famine Early Warning Systems Network offer mixed predictive accuracy due to their reliance on geospatial and qualitative data.

To address current practice limitations, we used a machine learning framework to predict food insecurity. The framework was trained on data collected through high-frequency household-level sentinel data collection sites, orchestrated by Catholic Relief Services in southern Malawi, that adhered to the Measuring Indicators for Resilience Analysis data collection protocol. That data is immediately available for analysis, providing near real-time information on households' food security status.

In essence, using Malawi as an example, we sought to determine the accuracy of machine learning models in predicting food insecurity at community and individual household levels. Our work sought to underscore the pivotal role of high-frequency sentinel data collection sites and the value of machine learning in forecasting food insecurity in policy and programmatic efforts to allocate scarce resources and address global food insecurity.

Methods Used

We sought to forecast household vulnerability to food insecurity using an advanced machine learning framework that could leverage both cross-sectional and time-series data. Trained on the Measuring Indicators for Resilience Analysis dataset, our approach sought to facilitate nuanced, real-world predictions of food security risks at the household level. To identify the most accurate model, we compared several machine learning approaches, including neural networks, random forests, multilayer perceptron, and convolutional neural networks. To guide this approach, we explored a previously proposed neural network architecture. This foundational work served as a benchmark that allowed us to evaluate the relative effectiveness of random forest models.

We prepared our training dataset as shown in Figure 17.1.

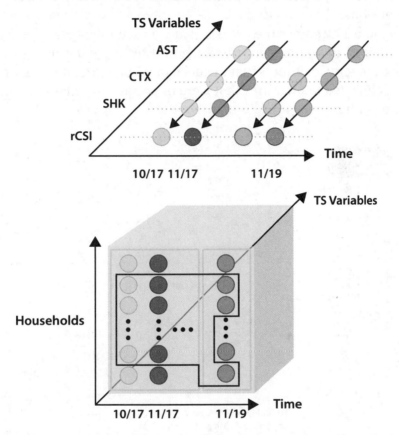

Figure 17.1 Preparation of the machine learning dataset where independent variables are used as predictors for Coping Strategies Index scores over time. The horizonal axis denotes time, the vertical axis denotes households, and the depth axis denotes independent variables (Gholami S et al., 2022 / Cambridge University Press / CC BY 4.0).

In Figure 17.1, for each variable, each time step is represented by a circle: on top, the horizontal axis signifies time steps, and the depth axis denotes variables, including both predictor features and the outcome indicators. Predictor features include information captured through shock, assistance, and contextual data modules in the Measuring Indicators for Resilience Analysis surveys. The vertical axis indicates data that was collected across multiple households, and the dotted line indicates the randomization data splitting scheme (for creating datasets for training and for validation) that was implemented across time and household dimensions.

Figure 17.2 shows the process that we used to prepare the data. We divided the dataset into training and testing datasets, ran the model, generated outputs that included maps of vulnerability scores, and delineated the features that were important in calculating that vulnerability.

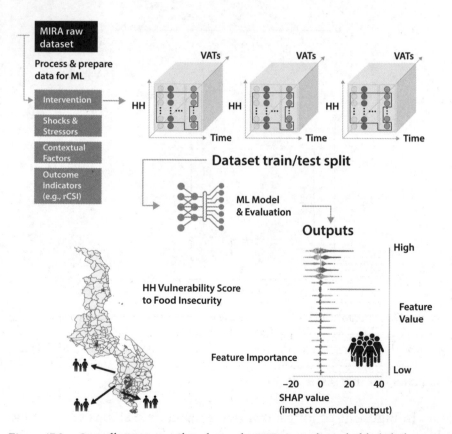

Figure 17.2 Overall process used in the study. HH means households (Gholami S et al., 2022 / Cambridge University Press / CC BY 4.0).

In essence, we obtained data, organized it into a multidimensional dataset that was randomly split into training and testing datasets, used the training dataset to train, evaluate, and optimize the machine learning model, and then tested the optimized model with the randomly selected, held-out testing dataset. Our output included vulnerability scores for food insecurity as well as indicators of which features were most important in the model and the directional relationship between the features and the outcome.

The outcome indicator that we sought to predict is the Reduced Coping Strategies Index score. The Reduced Coping Strategies Index score is a measure of impaired coping due to food insecurity and includes actions that households might take to address food insecurity, such as reducing food intake, changing the types of food eaten, borrowing food from others, taking on new jobs, or sending children out to beg (see Table 17.1).

Table 17.1 Questions and Weights Used to Create Reduced Coping Strategies Index Scores

Reduced Coping Strategies Index Module

In the past seven days, if there have been times when you did not have enough food or money to buy food, how many days has your household had to:
 -Rely on less preferred or less expensive foods? (w=1)
 -Borrow food or rely on help from a friend or relative? (w=2)
 -Engage in piecework or other menial labor? (w=1)
 -Send children out to beg? (w=4)
 -Reduce the number of meals eaten in a day? (w=1)
 -Reduce the size of meals eaten in a day? (w=1)

Abbreviation: rCSI, Reduced Coping Strategies Index
Source: Gholami S et al., 2022 / Cambridge University Press / CC BY 4.0

The Reduced Coping Strategies Index questionnaire can be administered repeatedly to the same households over time. It captures behavioral responses to food insecurity as opposed to a subjective sense of food insecurity. Changes in the Reduced Coping Strategies Index score are felt to necessitate humanitarian action more than a subjective sense of food insecurity.

Our machine learning model used a time-window approach, which is a newer approach than traditional time-series analysis. For splitting the dataset, we used a time-ordered approach. Specifically, we used data from the most recent time period as the test set, while data from all preceding time periods was used for the training set. Using this approach, we preserved the chronological order of the data, which is critical for time-series analysis.

Our final dataset consisted of 37,720 records and 126 predictor variables, processed to fit a monthly format. We analyzed the performance of the model using the measures shown in Table 17.2.

Table 17.2 Measures Used to Evaluate the Performance of the Model, Their Calculations, and Interpretations

Metric	Equation	Interpretation
Precision	$\dfrac{TP}{TP+FP}$	Number of true positives, that is, vulnerable HHs identified, out of positive predictions
Recall	$\dfrac{TP}{TP+FP}$	Number of true positives identified out of total vulnerable HHs
F1	$2\times\dfrac{precision \times recall}{precision + recall}$	Harmonic mean of the precision and recall
Accuracy	$\dfrac{TP\times TN}{TP+FP+TN+FN}$	How well the algorithm has classified positive and negative classes over total cases

Abbreviation: HH, household
Source: Gholami S et al., 2022 / Cambridge University Press / CC BY 4.0

We implemented five-fold cross-validation and random shuffling on the dataset. For each fold, random forest and logistic regression models were trained on 75 percent of the data and evaluated on the remaining 25 percent.

Using this multi-step approach, we sought to not only predict but also understand the nuances that contribute to household vulnerability in the context of food security. The application of multiple machine learning models allowed us to conduct a well-rounded evaluation and enhanced the robustness and reliability of our predictions.

Findings

We found substantial variation in basic household demographic and livelihood information; however, as anticipated, crop farming was the income source for the vast majority of households (see Table 17.3).

Table 17.3   Basic Household Demographics and Livelihood Information

	Mean (SD)	Range
HH size	5.49 (2.47)	[1, 20]
HH head age	44.6 (15.1)	[18, 80]
Years in village	29.86 (18.24)	[1, 80]

Feature	Categories with their percentages
HH head gender Female: 45%; male: 55%	
Primary income	Crop farming: 73.2%; piecework: 19.8%; other: 1.84%; domestic remittances: 1.74%; salaried employment: 1.5%; livestock farming: 0.9%; fish farming: 0.56%; foreign remittances: 0.38%
Secondary income	Crop farming: 32.4%; piecework: 45.7%; other: 5.4%; domestic remittances: 5.4%, salaried employment: 1.94%, livestock farming: 6.3%; fish farming: 1.67%; foreign remittances: 1.25%
Floor dwelling	Smooth mud: 67.4%; sand: 21.3%; smooth cement: 10.85%; wood: 0.38%

Abbreviation: HH, household
Source: Gholami S et al., 2022 / Cambridge University Press / CC BY 4.0

We also found that the distribution of Reduced Coping Strategies Index scores varied, overall, temporally, and across locations (see Figure 17.3).

The variation in scores suggested that we test models in two ways: once with a Reduced Coping Strategies Index score above 16 and once with a Reduced Coping Strategies Index score above 19. Regardless of the Reduced Coping Strategies Index score cutoff used, we found that our random forest model consistently outperformed the logistic regression model across all metrics (see Table 17.4).

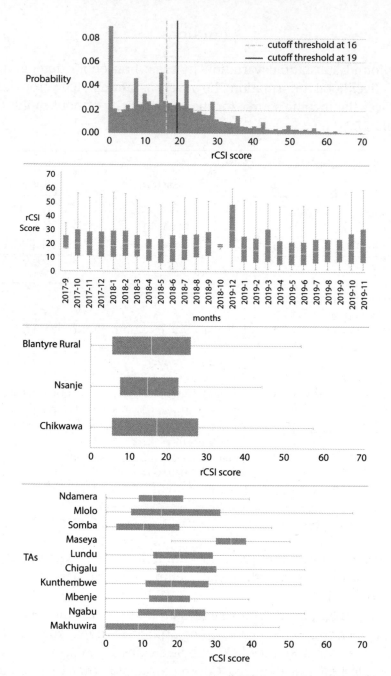

Figure 17.3   Variation in Reduced Coping Strategies Index scores (Gholami S et al., 2022 / Cambridge University Press / CC BY 4.0).

Table 17.4   Performance Scores for the Different Models

Split	Temporal: 7-step Train-1 step test			
Cutoff threshold	19			
Model	MLP	CNN	ResNet	RF
F1	0.74	0.71	0.69	0.73
Precision	0.72	0.67	0.69	0.78
Recall	0.75	0.77	0.69	0.69
Accuracy	0.8	0.77	0.77	0.81
Cutoff threshold	16			
Model	MLP	CNN	ResNet	RF
F1	0.78	0.76	0.76	0.81
Precision	0.77	0.72	0.74	0.82
Recall	0.79	0.8	0.77	0.81
Accuracy	0.8	0.77	0.78	0.83

Abbreviations: CNN, convolutional neural network; MLP, multilayer perceptron; rCSI, reduced Coping Strategy Index; RF, random forest.
Source: Gholami S et al., 2022 / Cambridge University Press / CC BY 4.0

Our Shapley Additive Explanations (SHAP) analysis indicated that food insecurity was a location-specific issue, therefore suggesting that models would need to be retrained for each new site (see Figure 17.4, top).

We found that self-evaluation of future welfare and overall status were influential features in predicting Reduced Coping Strategies Index scores; importantly, when the values for these variables increased, Reduced Coping Strategies Index scores decreased, suggesting less vulnerability. The importance of the different variables in predicting food insecurity varied across the year, suggesting that the scores were somewhat dependent on the crop cycle (see Figure 17.4, bottom).

Using several subsets of predictor features in our machine learning models, we found that configurations that included historical Reduced Coping Strategies Index scores along with SHAP-selected features generated the best results. Twenty-one out of 126 potential indicators accounted for most of the variation in

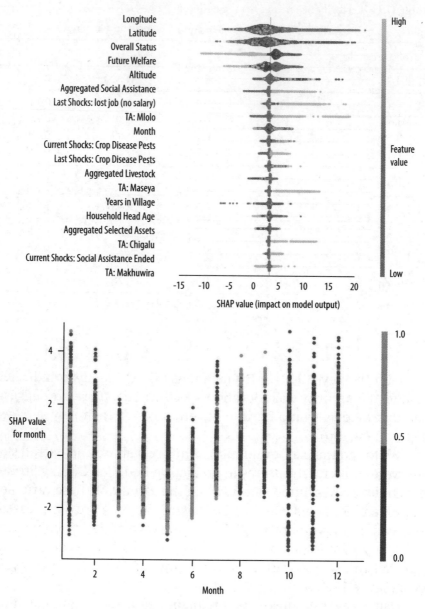

Figure 17.4　Shapley Additive Explanations (SHAP) analysis results, overall (top) and by month (bottom) (Gholami S et al., 2022 / Cambridge University Press / CC BY 4.0).

food insecurity. Those results were robust even with a minimum of 15 months' worth of data, capturing seasonal fluctuations effectively.

We assessed our model's capability to forecast up to four months into the future. Despite the performance drop due to allocating more data for validation, the model maintained a reasonable F1 score between 0.664 and 0.735 and an accuracy between 0.792 and 0.784. Finally, we evaluated Type-I and Type-II errors for the different Reduced Coping Strategies Index cutoff thresholds. With a higher threshold, the false negative rate was around 11 percent, while the lower threshold had a 7 percent false negative rate. The false positive rates varied depending on the threshold but were generally higher. A map of the households for which food security was analyzed and modeled is shown in Figure 17.5.

Discussion

We used machine learning algorithms trained on high-frequency survey data to forecast future levels of Reduced Coping Strategies Index scores that are a valuable measure of food insecurity.

We found that prior levels of food security tend to persist within households over time. Further, we found that location, subjective notions of current and future welfare, seasonal fluctuations, experienced shocks, and social assistance were predictive variables. Unlike previous machine learning efforts that targeted larger administrative areas, our model allows for humanitarian aid organizations to use a more granular approach, enabling targeted assistance down to the community or even household level based on their history of food security. Finally, we found that our model could anticipate food insecurity four months into the future, allowing for more proactive and anticipatory interventions.

Our study highlights the importance of capturing seasonal fluctuations in such data. When a year's worth of monthly data was incorporated into the algorithm, we found a substantial improvement in the model's predictive power.

Figure 17.5   A map of the location of households for which the analyses were performed (Gholami S et al., 2022 / Cambridge University Press / CC BY 4.0).

In conclusion, our work suggests that the integration of machine learning algorithms and high-frequency sentinel data collection is an effective way to predict future food insecurity. Focusing on collection of a minimal key set of variables can optimize efficiency and reduce monitoring costs. Including at least 15 months of seasonal data (which, then, includes multiple crop cycles) substantially improves the model's performance.

What We Learned

While our empirical analysis was rooted in data collected from southern Malawi, the methods that we used have broader applicability. We learned that high-frequency sentinel site data collection is valuable in monitoring food security and, when paired with advanced algorithms, the combination can offer actionable insights for humanitarian aid responders to devise targeted and earlier interventions. Importantly, because about one-sixth of the variables in the model accounted for most of the model's predictive value, it may be possible to reduce the costs of data collection by focusing on a subset of indicators.

We also learned that our machine learning approach significantly outperforms older analytic methods like linear models in predicting food security outcomes. Further, we found value in including data across multiple crop cycles.

Finally, we learned that public–private partnerships like the one we developed to conduct this study can generate novel approaches and valuable insights that can help improve the efficiency and effectiveness of not-for-profit organizatios' spending. The world's problems are increasingly complex and interwoven. Here, climate change is influencing crop production, which then influences food availability and human behaviors. Long-term solutions to these complex problems will require coordinating armies of data scientists and researchers and organizations that carry out interventions— each of whom has somewhat different perspectives—to fight common enemies using sophisticated analytic techniques.

The full article on which this summary is based is:

Gholami S, Knippenberg E, Campbell J, Andriantsimba D, Kamle A, Parthasarathy P, Sankar R, Birge C, Lavista JM. "Food security analysis and forecasting: a machine learning case study in southern Malawi." *Data and Policy* 2022; 4: e33. doi: 10.1017/dap.2022.25.

Chapter 18

BankNote-Net: Open Dataset for Assistive Universal Currency Recognition

—*Felipe Oviedo and Saqib Shaikh*

Executive Summary

Millions of people around the world have low or no vision. Assistive software applications—including optical character recognition, scene identification, person recognition, and currency recognition—have been developed to help such people engage in day-to-day activities. Recognition of different denominations of banknotes can be accomplished using computer vision models; however, the datasets and models available for this task are limited, both in terms of dataset size and the variety of currencies covered. Here, we collected 24,826 images of banknotes in a variety of assistive settings, spanning 17 currencies and 112 denominations. Using supervised contrastive learning, we developed a machine learning model for universal currency recognition.

This model learned regulation-compliant embeddings of banknote images in a variety of contexts: these can be shared publicly (as a highly compressed vector representation) and can be used to train and test specialized downstream models for any currency, including those not covered by our dataset or for which only a few real images per denomination are available. We deployed a variation of this model for public use in the latest version of Microsoft's Seeing AI application, and we share our encoder model and the embeddings as an open dataset in a BankNote-Net repository.

Why Is This Important?

Visual impairment is a growing global issue. An estimated 43 million people worldwide are blind, and over 200 million suffer from moderate to severe vision impairment. A disproportionately high percentage of these individuals are women (55 percent) and reside in low and middle-income countries (89 percent). Projections suggest that by 2050, numbers could increase to 61 million and 235 million for blindness and moderate to severe vision impairment, respectively.

To address the increasing problem of visual impairment, the software community has developed a variety of assistive technologies, such as mobile applications and wearables. These technologies help visually impaired individuals with multiple tasks, such as navigation, public transport utilization, scene comprehension, and person and currency note recognition. Microsoft's Seeing AI application leverages AI technology for vision-to-speech conversion, has an average of 100,000 monthly users across 80 countries, and supports 19 languages.

Machine learning models are often used for currency recognition: algorithms have been tailored for different global currencies like the Indian rupee, the U.S. dollar, and the euro. These models use a range of techniques from classical computer vision methods like Linear Discriminant Analysis and Support Vector Machines to advanced deep learning algorithms. Regardless of the method used, training and testing these models requires large datasets consisting of images of all currency denominations.

Unfortunately, there is a paucity of comprehensive public datasets of currency denominations. This limitation has restricted algorithm development to specific countries and currencies. To address this problem, we created BankNote-Net, a large, open dataset containing 24,826 images of front and back banknote faces spanning 17 currencies and 112 denominations. Importantly, our dataset approximates real-world conditions faced by visually impaired individuals by incorporating a variety of orientations, lighting conditions, backgrounds, and other complicating factors like occlusions and blurriness.

To address this problem, we used supervised contrastive learning to train our models on this dataset. Our model was capable of multi-class classification across the 17 currencies and 224 classes (considering both faces of the 112 denominations) on which the model was trained. Due to legal restrictions on the reproduction of high-resolution currency images in some jurisdictions, the model was engineered to learn highly compressed and compliant image embeddings.

We then conducted a "leave-one-group-out" cross-validation, demonstrating that these learned embeddings could serve as pre-training models for currencies not currently covered by the BankNote-Net dataset. Through the publicly available BankNote-Net repository dataset, we shared these embeddings and the pre-trained encoding model. Overall, using this multifaceted approach, we sought to democratize machine learning solutions for banknote recognition in assistive technologies, thereby improving the lives of visually impaired individuals worldwide.

Methods Used

In the interest of creating reliable machine learning models for banknote recognition in real-world assistive scenarios, we followed a meticulous data collection and model training process. Existing databases—populated by high-quality scans from banknote collectors' websites—were deemed inadequate for the demands of assistive applications. This inadequacy is primarily because the collectors tend to have very good images of banknotes; however, practical application of assistive technology requires imaging data that includes real-world conditions like diverse backgrounds, varying lighting conditions, blurred images, images in which orientation of the banknote is not standard, and occlusion of part of the image. To bridge this gap, we developed a data collection process that captured those features.

Our currency selection process was guided by geographic diversity and focused on areas with high usage of the Microsoft Seeing AI application. We recruited volunteers and Amazon Mechanical Turk workers for each chosen currency: for them, we provided a comprehensive training brochure that outlined image requirements and provided sample images. Each contributor gathered around 100 images for both sides of each currency denomination. A manual validation step checked for inconsistencies and standardized the images to 224x224 pixels.

This process allowed us to collect 24,826 images across 17 currencies. Details of the BankNote-Net dataset, which consists of 112 denominations and 224 classes (for example, a $5 U.S. bill is a class), are shown in Figure 18.1.

We then encoded each image as a 256-dimensional embedding—a low-dimensional, learned representation of discrete variables (in this case, currencies and their denominations)—and made them publicly available.

To learn these embeddings, we trained a neural network image encoder that used supervised contrastive learning loss, which amalgamates contrastive loss with cross-entropy loss, in essence attempting to reduce error in the prediction. The encoder's backbone was MobileNetV2, chosen because it fits the resource constraints of mobile devices. During training, we used data augmentation techniques like random rotation, cropping, and channel shifts. The encoding process that we used is demonstrated in Figure 18.2.

We conducted a "leave-one-group-out" cross-validation scheme to validate the embeddings' predictive power. In this approach, one currency is excluded from the training set and is used for testing. Two data splits—full and few-shot—allowed us to conduct a robust model evaluation.

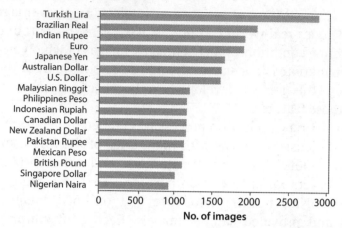

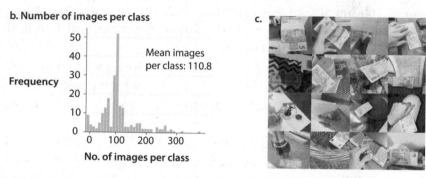

Figure 18.1   Overview of the BankNote-Net dataset, including a) the total number of images per currency, b) the distribution of the number of images per class, and c) examples of currency images (Oviedo F et al., 2022 / arxiv / CC BY 4.0).

Findings

Originally, the Microsoft's Seeing AI application supported recognition of seven currencies that were deployed as independent models for each currency. Using BankNote-Net, we expanded the currencies covered by the Seeing AI application to 17 supported currencies. We performed hyperparameter tuning to maximize model precision for predictions with confidence of 0.99 or above; we chose this approach to minimize false positives during assistive use. This

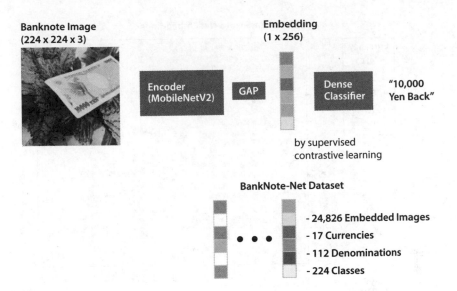

**Banknote Image
(224 x 224 x 3)**

**Embedding
(1 x 256)**

Encoder
(MobileNetV2)

GAP

Dense
Classifier

"10,000
Yen Back"

by supervised
contrastive learning

BankNote-Net Dataset

● ● ●

- 24,826 Embedded Images
- 17 Currencies
- 112 Denominations
- 224 Classes

Figure 18.2 An overview of the approach we used. We used a convolutional neural network (MobileNetV2) as an encoder for assistive banknote images. Using supervised contrastive learning, the models learn a highly compressed and descriptive embedding for each image. We then used these embeddings for downstream tasks, such as banknote recognition.

single universal model has been deployed in the last version of the Seeing AI mobile application. Further, the embeddings, labels, and pre-trained MobileNetV2 encoder model that we developed are available in the BankNote-Net repository.

Because of the legal restrictions regarding the reproduction of high-resolution banknote images in some jurisdictions, we released our dataset in the form of embeddings rather than actual images. Our embeddings naturally cluster individual currencies together, improving predictive performance (see Figure 18.3, top). Further, our encoding representation is several orders of magnitude smaller than alternative compression algorithms, making high-resolution reconstruction infeasible (see Figure 18.3, bottom).

We found that BankNote-Net embeddings consistently out-performed the other methods, particularly in few-shot learning settings. We found that our model generalized well to unseen currencies, even with limited data.

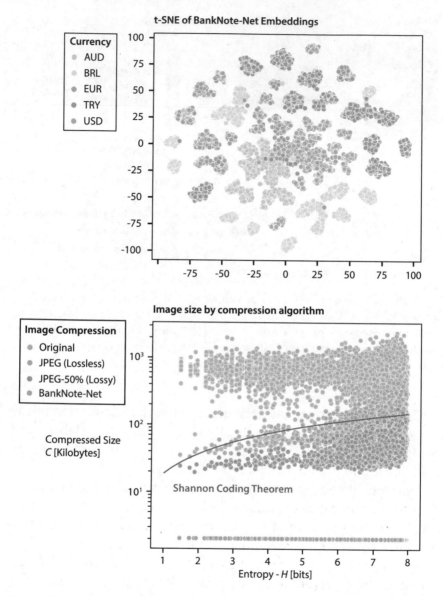

Figure 18.3   Clustering of individual currencies, which improves predictive performance (top) and demonstration of how our encoding representation compares to other compression algorithms (bottom) (Oviedo F et al., 2022 / arxiv / CC BY 4.0).

Discussion

We curated BankNote-Net, an expansive and diverse dataset covering 17 currencies and 224 classes that was explicitly designed for use in visual assistive applications requiring banknote recognition. We used machine learning to produce embeddings that capture a condensed, yet highly informative, representation of each banknote image. Importantly, we found that it is virtually impossible to reverse-engineer these embeddings back into high-resolution images, thereby maintaining data integrity and security. Because these embeddings could be widely used in multiple computer vision tasks, BankNote-Net can serve as a valuable resource for the research community.

Our dataset has several limitations:

- First, the images for each currency type were predominantly captured by one or two individuals; despite their efforts to incorporate a diverse range of settings, backgrounds, and orientations, the resulting dataset has a limited number of images with these features.
- The dataset is further limited because of the specifications of the mobile camera used for capture and the limited variety of settings available to the volunteers who captured the images.

These limitations represent a calculated trade-off: in choosing this data collection strategy, our primary goal was to ensure thorough coverage of all denominations for each currency included.

Despite these limitations, the database and embeddings generated exhibit robust generalization capabilities. This extends even to currencies that are not part of the BankNote-Net dataset. Therefore, the dataset holds promise for a range of future applications, including but not limited to the inclusion of currently unsupported currencies or the addition of new banknote designs not yet featured in the dataset.

What We Learned

Our study generated several insights:

- First, examining an existing assistive technology, we identified opportunities to improve it and developed strategic data collection and analytic pathways to do so.
- Second, we learned that a crowdsourcing approach to data collection can be effective for evaluating and developing assistive technologies. While there are inherent limitations to crowdsourcing—several of which we mentioned here—one advantage is that the process provides real-world, pragmatic currency photographs.
- Third, we discovered that embedding methodologies can be used to naturally cluster denominations, thereby improving model performance, as well as preserving the security of currency details and complying with laws.

Looking forward, practical deployment requires optimization of specific performance metrics that go beyond standard measures like precision and recall. For instance, if a particular "high-confidence precision" metric is of interest, users of the dataset may achieve desired results by fine-tuning the encoder on a representative validation dataset. Future work should include diversifying the range of data collectors to mitigate existing biases and expand the dataset's utility.

The full article on which this summary is based is:

Oviedo F, Vinnakota S, Seleznev E, Malhotra H, Shaikh S, Lavista JM. "BankNote-Net: open dataset for assistive universal currency recognition." arXiv: 2204.03738. doi: 10.48550. arXiv.2204.02738.

The model is deployed in production in Microsoft's Seeing AI mobile app.

Chapter 19

Broadband Connectivity

—Mayana Pereira, Amit Misra, and Allen Kim

Executive Summary

Broadband connectivity is critical to the functioning of today's economy, directly impacting gross domestic product in an era of rapid expansion of the digital economy. Highlighting the importance of broadband connectivity, the COVID-19 guidelines of social distancing and the rapid uptake of telehealth services made Internet connectivity necessary for everyday activities such as work, learning, healthcare, and staying in touch with family and friends. To help policymakers and interested organizations better understand broadband connectivity and markets where connectivity might be lacking, we sought to introduce a publicly available Broadband Coverage dataset that reports broadband coverage percentages for the United States at the ZIP Code level. Critical to this release was using differential privacy methods that guarantee that the privacy of individual households is preserved. Further, we calculated error ranges estimates, so that the expected error that is introduced by using differential privacy methods is also available at the ZIP Code level. Here, we describe our error range calculation method and show that this additional data metric does not induce any privacy loss.

Why Is This Important?

Every day our world becomes a little more digital. But reaping the benefits of this digital world—pursuing new educational opportunities through distance learning, feeding the world through precision agriculture, growing a small business by leveraging the cloud, and accessing better healthcare through telemedicine—is only possible for those with a broadband connection. The importance of such connectivity was highlighted during the COVID-19 pandemic, when people relied on Internet access to work, interact with others, and obtain healthcare.

The Federal Communications Commission's 2021 Fourteenth Broadband Deployment Report found that broadband was not available to at least 14.5 million people in the United States, 11.3 million of whom live in rural areas. The accuracy of estimates of numbers and locations of people without broadband access is important: such data is used by federal, state, and local agencies to decide where to target public funds dedicated to closing the broadband gap. Inaccuracies could mean that millions of Americans already lacking access to broadband will be invisible and that could decrease the likelihood of those in need obtaining additional broadband funding or broadband service. We sought to improve the accuracy of broadband connectivity estimates so that others can use our dataset and methods to develop solutions to improving broadband access or addressing problems with broadband access.

But accuracy in making those estimates—particularly in geographic areas where there are few residents—could threaten their privacy. Here, we explain the data privatization process that we implemented to safely estimate coverage and share our U.S. Broadband Coverage dataset. Leveraging differential privacy methods, we ensured that data remained anonymized while also outlining implementation details and specifications for privacy loss. Further, we describe an empirical methodology for estimating the error range of broadband connectivity for each ZIP Code and demonstrate that doing so does not result in additional privacy losses, which makes the method and the dataset significant assets for research and policy-making purposes.

Methods Used

We used broadband coverage estimates collected from Microsoft Services and divided the dataset into ZIP Code estimates. The coverage estimates were determined by Microsoft Services by identifying the connection of various devices to the Internet at varying Internet speeds; we used this data to compute Broadband Coverage Estimates, which represent the fraction of households in a ZIP Code with an Internet connection speed above 25 Mbps. We applied the Laplace Mechanism—which randomly adds noise to estimates, with a mean of zero—to these counts with an epsilon value of 0.1. Because using the Laplace Mechanism can sometimes result in negative counts, our method restates negative estimates to zero without affecting privacy loss, because differential privacy is immune to post-processing.

The computation of privacy loss is important for preserving privacy and providing privacy guarantees. Privacy loss computation uses both parallel and sequential composition properties of differential privacy mechanisms to calculate a total privacy loss of epsilon equal to 0.2. The total privacy loss accounts for privacy loss from aggregating Internet speed data as well as privacy loss from Microsoft Services device counts.

We then calculated estimates of error ranges of our results because we introduced noise to preserve privacy. We made these estimates using a simulation process that considers ZIP Codes with different population sizes and then computes key statistical measures like the mean absolute error, the 95th percentile error, and the mean signed deviation for each ZIP Code. The process that we used is shown in Figure 19.1.

The mean absolute error provides an average range within which the non-private broadband coverage estimate will most likely fall; the 95th percentile error offers a statistical boundary, indicating that 95 percent of the time, the estimate will reside within this range. The mean signed deviation serves as an estimator for any bias introduced using differential privacy mechanisms.

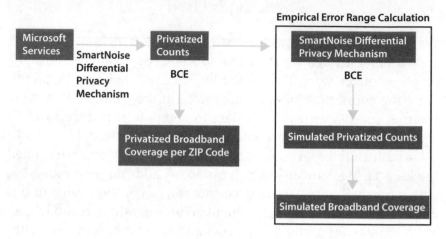

Figure 19.1   Process for estimating the error introduced by differential privacy.

All differential privacy processing was done using the OpenDP SmartNoise library. The SmartNoise library includes a comprehensive set of differential privacy mechanisms, algorithms, and validators that is open-source and is maintained by the OpenDP initiative led by Harvard. Using these methods, we addressed the need for privacy protection while maintaining the dataset's usefulness for policymakers and researchers alike.

Findings

For the purpose of analyzing, understanding, improving, and addressing problems related to broadband access, we released county-level broadband usage percentage data in April 2020. We added ZIP Code–level views of the same information in December 2020 (see Figure 19.2).

Because the ZIP Code–level dataset provides a more granular view of broadband usage percentages by households, we took the aforementioned additional step to ensure data privacy guarantees by utilizing differential privacy, a technique that adds noise to data aggregations, thereby preventing identification of specific individuals in the dataset. We estimated broadband usage by combining privatized data from multiple Microsoft services. As differential privacy adds noise to protect privacy, the noise added to ZIP Codes with a small number of households can impact the usefulness of the data. To ensure transparency into how ZIP Codes with different population magnitudes are affected, we calculated error range data (see Figure 19.3).

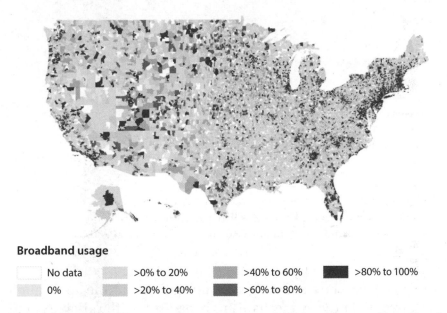

Broadband usage

No data	>0% to 20%	>40% to 60%	>80% to 100%
0%	>20% to 40%	>60% to 80%	

Figure 19.2   Map of the United States by ZIP Code with indicators of broadband usage (Pereira M et al., 2021 / arxiv).

Our analysis found that calculated error estimates vary with population size: the expected error decreases as the population size of a ZIP Code increases. This finding suggests that larger populations require the introduction of less noise to adequately mask individual data, while smaller populations require the introduction of more noise to achieve the same level of privacy.

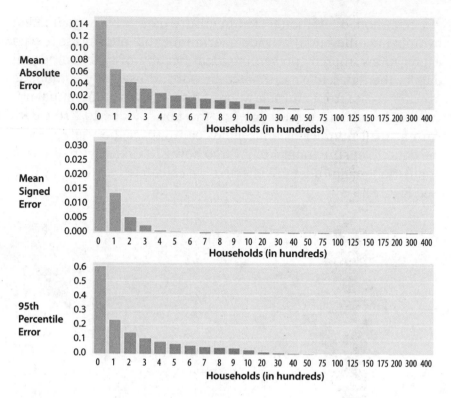

Figure 19.3   Measures of error for several population ranges. Expected mean absolute error, mean signed error, and 95th percentile of the error caused by the privatization mechanism for different population thresholds (Pereira M et al., 2021 / arxiv).

This nuanced understanding has implications for the application of differential privacy mechanisms in datasets with variable population densities.

Discussion

In this chapter, we describe the steps used to ensure that the Broadband Coverage Estimates dataset can provide valuable information while preserving privacy of Microsoft Services data. We were able to estimate broadband coverage across the United States, at the ZIP Code level. Additionally, we developed a simple method for estimating error via a simulation process. Information on estimation errors can help explain the impact of the differential privacy application in different subgroup sizes. The main advantage of the method that we used for error generation is that it does not cause any additional privacy losses.

What We Learned

We developed a privacy-conscious dataset that can serve as a resource regarding broadband access for researchers and policymakers. The dataset can be used to identify areas wherein broadband access is lacking—so that policymakers can focus resources on expanding access in those areas—while ensuring the privacy of individual households.

We also learned that, to solve important social problems, innovative use of extant datasets should be considered. Here, we used a Microsoft dataset that captures download speeds; it is reasonable to assume that higher download speeds indicate better broadband connectivity. And while any dataset is limited—this one, for instance, by not being applicable to households that do not use Microsoft products—and comes with caveats, analysis of even flawed datasets can still provide insights that can be useful to policymakers. Using an existing dataset can be much less expensive than collecting primary data and it takes much less time to analyze.

Finally, we learned that while the error estimates are important for understanding the reliability of the privatized data, they do not account for other types of errors, like sampling errors and biases that are inherent in the broadband coverage estimation, perhaps driven by the aforementioned dataset limitations. The limitations inherent in any dataset highlight the need to use a multi-dimensional approach to assessing the accuracy and reliability of any developed model.

The full article on which this summary is based is:

Pereira M, Kim A, Allen J, White K, Lavista J, Dodhia R. "US Broadband Coverage Data Set: A differentially private dataset release." arXiv:2103.14035v2. doi: 10.48550/arXiv.2103.14035

Chapter 20

Monitoring the Syrian War with Natural Language Processing

—Rahul Dodhia and Michael Scholtens

Executive Summary

The civil war in Syria may no longer be in the public eye, but The Carter Center has been monitoring it since 2013. The Carter Center collects reports of incidents in the war, conducts detailed analyses, and reports these to organizations like the United Nations, the European Union, and interested non-governmental organizations.

The Center manually classifies conflict events into 13 incident types. However, manual classification is a time-consuming process and hard to scale. To address this, we fine-tuned an existing language model on a sample of The Carter Center's Syrian conflict data. The resulting model achieved 96 percent accuracy on held-out test data and 90 percent on out-of-sample data. When reviewed by experts, the model could successfully identify events that should be classified as multiple incident types, such as events categorized as clashes, but which might also be categorized as shelling: the previous methodology had allowed only a single classification.

Overall, our language model reduced the time needed to transform conflict data, giving The Carter Center the ability to produce reports in a timelier manner and scale the number of reports that could be processed. It also made a breadth of conflict datasets accessible by automating cumbersome manual transformations. Our work contributes to incorporating technology into the peace-building field.

Why Is This Important?

Wars cause destruction at large scales, causing devastating loss of life and leaving behind the detritus of socioeconomic catastrophes. While the importance of diplomats, humanitarian organizations, and aid agencies that constantly strive to build peace—or at least mitigate the harms of war on civilian populations—cannot be overstated, the efficacy of these peace-building activities largely hinges on the availability and reliability of data related to the dynamics of conflicts.

Unfortunately, data on conflicts is often flawed, for several reasons. First, political actors may manipulate information to further their own agendas. Second, the lack of a standardized format for data collection means that quick and insightful analysis becomes difficult. Inconsistencies seen in available data can be metaphorically compared to attempting to assemble a jigsaw puzzle using mismatched pieces from various sets.

One organization that attempts to overcome these limitations is The Armed Conflict Location & Event Data (ACLED) Project. Since 2014, ACLED has been collecting data on several conflicts around the world, and, since 2018, it has been The Carter Center's main source of data about the Syrian civil war. The Carter Center analyzes these data for stakeholders such as mediators and humanitarian interventionists, creating and disseminating reports that offer granular insights into the intricate dynamics prevailing in a region undergoing rapid sociopolitical change.

This data and analytics effort presents organizations and individuals engaged at various strategic levels with a more lucid regional context. For example, the Syrian war has destroyed the lives of hundreds of thousands of civilians, and its psychological and economic repercussions will be felt by numerous subsequent generations. But among the worst of the tangible remains of war are unexploded ordnances. With the data collected by ACLED and The Carter Center, humanitarian organizations can devise strategies to identify the locations and types of these weapons.

In conflict zones, the value of such detailed, up-to-date information is amplified, because observational access is often limited due to safety concerns and logistical challenges. Possessing access to contemporary and detailed data ensures that stakeholders can devise more precise and informed interventions. This helps ensure that strategies are tailored to yield maximum efficacy in the context of Syrian dynamics.

With reports of new events arriving each day, The Carter Center grapples with the challenge of processing them in a timely manner to ensure timely analysis and dissemination among its subscribers. This challenge is not only quantitative, but also qualitative: The Carter Center's analysts spend considerable time adapting data to make it fit the specific needs of their downstream analyses. Such adjustments are not only a matter of data compatibility; they also reflect the inherent intricacies of conflicts. When individuals attempt to categorize or narrate these events, they invariably infuse them with their own interpretations and worldviews. This inevitable subjectivity introduces the risk of bias, which can obscure an objective, large-scale understanding of the conflict at hand.

Given these considerations and the sheer volume of information needing analysis, professionals in the field of conflict resolution began wondering how emerging technologies, specifically artificial intelligence, could be harnessed to manage their data. Here, we describe how we used a large language model (LLM) to help process the data to rapidly create contextually rich and interpretable content.

Methods Used

From ACLED, we obtained a dataset consisting of text snippets that described events in the Syrian conflict between 2018 and 2019. This dataset comprised 7,847 text snippets, each narrated in a text length ranging from 10 to 90 words.

The Carter Center has developed a list of incident types by which each snippet can be described (see Table 20.1). It is important to recognize that a single conflict event can encapsulate more than one type of incident, and the list may change as reporting demands shift. To address this challenge, each event-type combination was allocated a separate row; however, the unique identifier for each conflict event remained consistent. As a result, the dataset expanded to encompass 8,942 conflict events, spread across multiple distinct incident types (shown in Table 20.1). Out of these, we selected three specific incident types—shelling, clashes, and strategic developments—as the foundation for fine-tuning the NLP model.

Table 20.1   Typology Used to Classify Events in Syria's Civil War.

General	Event	Incident Type
Violent events	Battles	Armed clash
		Government regains territory
		Non-state actor overtakes territory
	Explosions/remote violence	Chemical weapon
		Air/drone strike
		Suicide bomb
		Shelling/artillery/missile attack
		Remote explosive/landmine/IED
		Grenade
	Violence against civilians	Sexual violence
		Attack
		Abduction/forced disappearance
Demonstrations	Protests	Peaceful protest
		Protest with intervention
		Excessive force against protesters
	Riots	Violent demonstration
		Mob violence

(continues)

Table 20.1 *(continued)*

General	Event	Incident Type
Non-violent actions	Strategic developments	Agreement
		Arrests
		Change to group/activity
		Disrupted weapons use
		Headquarters or base established
		Looting/property destruction
		Non-violent transfer of territory
		Other

Source: Trivedi A et al., 2020 / Springer Nature

To analyze the dataset, we leveraged the concept of "transfer learning," a popular technique used in modern machine learning, particularly when adapting large neural network models to specialized data. The idea involves taking knowledge learned from one task and applying it to a new, related task, thus saving time and computing resources because the new model does not have to be trained from scratch. We used a pre-trained BERT model for our text classification task. BERT is a text classification model open-sourced by Google in 2019; it was one of the early transformer-based models that replaced recurrent neural networks. The base version of BERT used in this project had 110 million parameters, and the model could generate multiple labels per text snippet.

We contrasted the BERT transformer model with other machine learning approaches, each with their own advantages. For example, multinomial logit and Naïve Bayes models are simple and computationally efficient, and an analyst can gain insight into which features are driving its performance. Convolutional neural networks that were originally developed for computer vision tasks have been shown to be successful in language classification tasks. The neural network can learn features that an analyst may not know are important. However, transformer models like BERT, and recently ChatGPT, can capture even more intricate features that are relevant.

Findings

While none of the models failed to accurately classify text into one of the test categories, the BERT transformer model that we used was the best performing of the ones tested (see Table 20.2). When comparing performance accuracy of each model on a set of data that was not used in training, the multinomial logit seemed the most promising; however, it did not perform as well when generalizing to the 2017 dataset from ACLED. The convolutional neural network model also had good performance, but was very expensive in terms of computing power.

Table 20.2   Accuracy of the Four Classification Models

Model	Accuracy
Multinomial Naïve Bayesian	0.81
Multinomial Logit	0.88
Convolutional Neural Network	0.90
BERT Transformer Model	0.97

After some adjustments, the transformer model exhibited an impressive 96 percent accuracy when tested on The Carter Center's validation data, making it the best choice for implementation into The Carter Center's workflow.

To test the model further, we obtained from ACLED an additional set of 31,193 events from 2017. This expanded dataset provided a more comprehensive framework for assessing the trained model's accuracy and adaptability in real-world scenarios. Experts manually reviewed random samples of the results, with a particular interest in events that could be classified into multiple types, such as a clash that also involved heavy shelling. Impressively, the transformer model demonstrated an accuracy of 90 percent on the new data, and remarkable precision in its identification of events while also being able to attribute multiple types to these events. For example, the transformer model could discern clashes, and then—by picking up hints from the textual context—identify that shelling was also involved, making the model's output closer to that of a human expert when examining the texts.

Discussion

Transformer-based models have emerged as powerful semantic tools, allowing scientists to extract nuanced insights from vast and intricate textual datasets. The field of conflict reporting, while rich in information, often presents its own set of challenges, predominantly those of lacking structured formatting, which makes organizing text into tabular format for analysis difficult and restrictive. Further, the absence of structure invariably complicates the analytic process, obfuscating potential insights that could be derived from the data.

While ACLED has significantly contributed to structuring this otherwise disordered data landscape, we were able to use machine learning techniques and a transformative model to improve the analytic process.

One of the advantages of this improved methodology is the automation of the data classification process. Non-profit organizations can redirect resources from manual classification to critical analysis, thereby focusing on the heart of conflict resolution. Furthermore, by incorporating a diverse array of conflict datasets, our methodology can mitigate the perennial challenge of reporting bias. Finally, automation not only expedites the processing of existing data but also stimulates more intentional and comprehensive data collection, thus enriching resulting analyses and reports.

What We Learned

We learned that one of the greatest contributors of transformer models like BERT to this domain is their potential to classify data more accurately than human classifiers. When the transformer classifications deviated from manual categorizations, the difference did not necessarily imply an error on the model's part. Instead, the model's choice often shed light on alternative, yet valid, perspectives on the data, thereby enriching the overall analysis.

We also learned that the potential synergy between technology and peace initiatives offers promising, desirable, and even imperative avenues for enhanced global conflict management. As artificial intelligence technology continues to improve, other data modalities could be included in the conflict management repertoire. Videos and satellite images—both now commonplace—might be used to provide further nuance to conflict analysis. In combination, the NLP process described here and other tools yet to be developed promise not only to shed light on the horrors of war, but also to help humanitarians assist the innocents who are affected and resolve conflicts earlier.

The full article on which this summary is based is:

Trivedi A, Keator K, Scholtens M, Haigood B, Dodhia R, Lavista JM, Sankar R, Verma A. "How to Handle Armed Conflict Data in a Real-World Scenario?" *Philosophy and Technology* 2020; 34 (1): 111-123. doi: 10.1007/s13347-020-00424-5.

Chapter 21

The Proliferation of Misinformation Online

—*Will Fein, Mayana Pereira, Jane Wang, Kevin Greene,*
Lucas Meyer, Rahul Dodhia, and Jacob Shapiro

Executive Summary

Over the course of a very fruitful collaboration with researchers from Princeton's Empirical Studies of Conflict Project, we conducted an analysis that shed light into how users navigate to and from unreliable news sites online and then used our findings to motivate a machine learning model with practical use in identifying other unreliable sites.

In the initial analysis, we identified factors that contribute to the phenomenon of *rabbit holes*—specifically, the browsing patterns of users who, after encountering misinformation, tend to delve even deeper into engaging with untrustworthy content. This analysis highlights the stark differences in the way users reach reliable and unreliable news sites and how engagement with these sites differs as a result of linking structures.

We found that readers on unreliable sites click more *internal* links—links that refer readers to other articles within the site—making these sites "stickier." We also found compelling evidence that reliable and unreliable news sites are largely disconnected from each other; unreliable sites provide few exits to reliable sources of news and reliable sources of news rarely send readers to unreliable sites.

We then used these findings to motivate a machine learning model capable of identifying unreliable sites based on patterns of ingoing and outgoing traffic and proposed a framework to feasibly deploy our model in the real world. The model reached 98 percent precision, meeting or exceeding results from similar experiments. More importantly, real-world experiments demonstrated the practical value of the deployment framework we proposed for using this model to identify new misinformation sites at scale.

Why Is This Important?

The serious negative effects of misinformation have been made evident by numerous academic studies, as well as by public incidents like "Pizzagate." While misinformation is not a new phenomenon, the growth of social media online news platforms has enabled false stories to spread to more people more quickly than they would through traditional media.

The material Internet users see is influenced not only by their own choices, but also by the options presented to them—or indeed recommended to them—by the sites they visit. These sites are financially motivated to keep users on their platform engaging with more material. There are several ways to profit from increased user engagement—including subscriptions and donations—but the principal method of monetization is ad revenue. The implication is that, for unreliable sites that promote misinformation, efforts to keep users in their ecosystems create the potential for "rabbit holes" of unreliable content.

Additionally, there may be incentives for unreliable sites to send users to other unreliable sites via links embedded in their articles. Such incentives could include referral programs or the ideological alignment of these sites. If these patterns exist, they could also contribute to the formation of misinformation rabbit holes, as users encounter multiple unreliable sites reinforcing the same false narratives.

As part of Microsoft, the AI for Good Lab has the remarkable opportunity to conduct research using first-party data that can shed light on how people around the world interact with digital technologies. Accompanying this opportunity is a responsibility to investigate how these technologies are serving the users they are meant to benefit.

In this collaboration, the AI For Good Lab and subject matter experts from Princeton University's Empirical Studies of Conflict Project worked to develop insights on how Internet users use both reliable and unreliable websites and applied those insights to the development of a machine learning model that could be deployed at scale to identify new misinformation sites.

Methods Used

For this work, we used two datasets that provided evaluations of the credibility of news sites and one anonymized first-party dataset on Internet browsing.

We obtained data on the credibility of news sites at the publisher level from two sources:

- NewsGuard, a journalism and technology company that researches and rates the credibility of news websites. Using NewsGuard's rubric, sites that receive a score below 60 out of 100 fail to meet basic standards of credibility and transparency: sites that scored below 60 were treated as unreliable in this work; those that scored 60 or above were considered reliable.

- Miburo (now Microsoft Threat Analysis Center) consists of a team of strategic analysts who specialize in detecting and countering the malign influence of foreign states. Miburo provided expert identification of sites owned by or affiliated with the Russian government, which were considered unreliable.

We obtained anonymized data on the Internet from Edge, Microsoft's web browser. All the data used was collected from users who had opted in, and the data was anonymized and aggregated at the point of collection to remove all personal identifying information. This Internet browsing dataset consisted of three features: a timestamp, the page that the user was leaving, and the page to which the user was navigating.

In the "rabbit holes" analysis, we only examined site navigation through HREF links, removing navigation via the favorites bar, back/forward buttons, and other methods that do not involve clicking embedded links.

For every site rated by NewsGuard, we used this navigation dataset to quantify:

- The number of referrals that kept the user on the same site. Referrals occur when a user clicks an embedded link and navigates to a new page. The self-referrals counted here represent instances in which users click a link and are directed to additional content within the same website. Though all websites share the financial incentive to keep users on their sites, we hypothesized that visitors to unreliable sites would show a greater propensity to click internal referral links and therefore would be more likely to enter so-called "rabbit holes."
- The number of referrals that led to unreliable sites, quantified as the number of instances in which users clicked an embedded link and were directed to an unreliable site, excluding users who navigated to a new page on the same unreliable site.
- The number of referrals that led to reliable sites, quantified as the number of instances in which users clicked an embedded link and were directed to a reliable site, excluding users who navigated to a new page on the same reliable site.

We characterized each site by a set of features based on these metrics. These features included the proportion of incoming traffic from self-referrals, reliable sites, and unreliable sites, and the proportion of outgoing traffic landing on reliable and unreliable sites.

This navigation dataset includes all direct navigations to and from pages on unreliable sites, accurately reflecting how users are interacting with these sites. It does not necessarily include all possible navigations, however, as there may be additional embedded links that were never clicked. Therefore, after analyzing the differences in navigation trends across reliable and unreliable sites, we replicated our results using a dataset that captured which embedded links existed on each site. In this corroborating work, we looked at the proportion of embedded links that led to reliable and unreliable sites.

It became clear that navigation patterns provide valuable information about whether a site is reliable or unreliable, so we next constructed a navigation graph using the Edge data. In the graph, each node is a different site. When the data contains a navigation from site A to site B, a directed edge is drawn from the node that represents site A (Node A) to the node that represents site B (Node B). The final weight of the edge from node A to node B is equal to the number of instances in which a user navigated from site A to site B (see Figure 21.1). Many of the sites in the graph have one of two labels, which are based on the expert site ratings:

- Authoritative, which we used to refer to reliable domains
- Misinformation, which we used to refer to unreliable domains

To build a machine learning model motivated by our initial findings, we created a set of features from this graph. We counted the number of visits from reliable sites and to reliable sites and did the same for visits to and from unreliable sites. We repeated this process for additional categories of websites believed to be relevant based on existing literature. These categories of websites were:

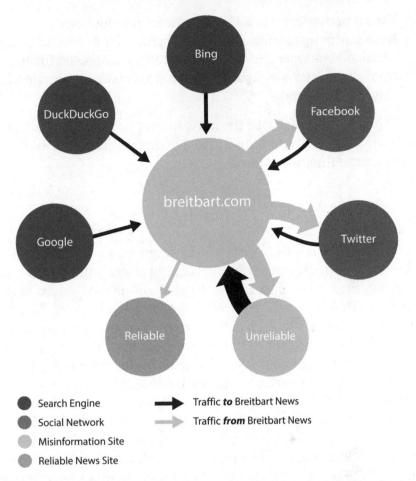

Figure 21.1 A simplified example of a navigation graph node. Breitbart.com sends a lot of traffic to Facebook, Twitter, and other unreliable sites and receives inbound traffic from these sites as well. Breitbart.com sends some traffic to reliable sites but does not receive inbound traffic from those sites. Search Engines send traffic to Breitbart.com but Breitbart.com does not send readers to search engines.

- **Search engines:** Google, Bing, and DuckDuckGo
- **Social media sites:** Facebook, Twitter, TikTok, LinkedIn, Telegram, and WhatsApp
- **News aggregators:** MSN, Bloomberg, news.google, and news.yahoo

- **Email providers:** Gmail, mail.yahoo, and Outlook
- **Russian propaganda sites**: Miburo provided a list of known Russian state-operated and -affiliated news sites. Traffic to and from these sites was used to create features for the multi-class classification model.

These features describe the navigational pattern into and out of each site, allowing us to train a model to detect misinformation sites based on the findings of the first study.

Findings

In our initial analysis, we sought to understand whether unreliable sites are more successful at keeping users within their platform. We calculated for each site the share of all navigations to that site that came from self-referrals. For example, Breitbart, the most visited unreliable site in the study, receives roughly 96 percent of its inbound traffic as self-referrals. Surprisingly, this very high self-referral percentage was below the median value for unreliable sites (98 percent); the median value for reliable sites was 75 percent, which is statistically significantly lower than for unreliable sites.

We also found that unreliable sites are statistically significantly more likely than reliable sites to direct users to unreliable sites—and to obtain users from other unreliable sites—via embedded links. While reliable sites tend to direct users to other reliable sites, unreliable sites rarely direct users to reliable sites.

As a sensitivity analysis, we analyzed data that included self-referrals and data that excluded self-referrals. In both instances, we found that unreliable sites were more likely to refer users to unreliable sites and reliable sites were more likely to refer users to reliable sites. Interestingly, when self-referrals were removed, the volume of referrals among unreliable sites decreased substantially. This suggests that self-referrals are the primary avenue by which users find themselves in misinformation rabbit holes.

Because previous research suggests that the readers who visit unreliable sites are different from those who visit reliable sites, we replicated these results with a dataset representing which links are present, instead of which links are clicked. We chose a random sample of 100 unreliable sites and 100 reliable sites, collected a random sample of 25 articles from each, and extracted all the embedded URLs from the text of each article. These URLs were then checked against News-Guard's ratings to get a reliability rating to generate a dataset identifying the types of links that existed on reliable and unreliable sites.

In the analysis of this dataset, we also found that reliable sites commonly link to other reliable sites, while unreliable sites rarely do. Conversely, unreliable sites frequently link to other unreliable sites, which reliable sites rarely do.

Overall, it was clear that reliable and unreliable sites were largely disconnected. We used this insight to develop a classification model that was able to label sites as either reliable or unreliable with high fidelity while providing enough interpretability to convey what highly predictive features it was using to make its evaluations. We trained a random forest model using features extracted from the navigation graph. These features included referrals to and from unreliable sites, referrals to and from reliable sites, and referrals to and from other classes of sites, like social media platforms and search engines.

After training, our random forest model achieved 98 percent precision and 91 percent recall, meaning that 98 percent of the websites labeled as "misinformation" by the model were indeed misinformation, and the model's labels successfully found 91 percent of the misinformation models that existed in the dataset. This performance matched or exceeded previously published results.

Because we chose a random forest model, we were able to use the Gini importance to determine which features were most important in finding misinformation domains. The two most important features were referrals to known misinformation sites and referrals from known misinformation sites. This finding confirms the intuition developed in the initial analyses: misinformation sites are largely disconnected from reliable news sites and this fact can be used to identify previously unknown misinformation sites.

We then extended our model to a multi-class classification problem. To do so, we used the list of known Russian state-owned or -affiliated propaganda sites provided by Miburo. We used the same navigation graph used to create model features. Instead of labeling "misinformation" or "not misinformation," the model was asked to label "misinformation," "propaganda," or "neither." This model was also highly successful, achieving 99 percent precision and 96 percent recall when identifying propaganda sites.

While several previously developed models have high levels of accuracy in identifying misinformation sites, few have shown practical utility. Since no machine learning models are perfect, systems proposed to detect misinformation sites use models to identify sites suspected of spreading misinformation and then refer these sites to expert human reviewers. The vast majority of sites on the Internet are not misinformation, though, and even models that demonstrate high precision when tested against benchmark datasets have been shown to perform worse when asked to identify new misinformation sites. This means that the human reviewers are asked to review thousands of sites, most of which are not spreaders of misinformation.

We proposed a new deployment procedure that leverages the navigation graph again. We only run the machine learning model on unlabeled sites connected to known misinformation sites—that is, sites that have either received traffic from a known misinformation site or sent traffic to a known misinformation site. To measure the utility of deploying our model in this way, we asked experts to review a random sample of 300 completely new sites labeled as misinformation by the model. The model achieved 78 percent precision in this real-world experiment, over ten times greater than the 5 percent precision reported in previous work. The same real-world experiment was run for the multi-class model, and it achieved 56 percent precision, also sufficient to suggest practical utility.

Discussion

We conducted novel research about the existence of misinformation rabbit holes on unreliable news sites and found that the principal driver of rabbit holes is self-referral, a behavior that occurs more often on unreliable sites when compared to reliable sites. Additionally, we found that while users commonly navigate from reliable site to reliable site—and from unreliable site to unreliable site—very few referrals exist between reliable and unreliable sites.

It is clear from this research that the composition of inbound and outbound traffic for unreliable sites is quite distinct from that of reliable sites. This clear difference in the traffic patterns of unreliable and reliable domains provided the inspiration to train machine learning models to detect previously unknown misinformation sites.

While other models have reached high levels of accuracy in benchmark datasets, we made our model both accurate and useful. By using the initial analysis to motivate the structure of our model, we ensured that our model was learning from genuinely informative features. We also chose a sufficiently interpretable model and provided insights on which traffic features were leading the model to suspect sites of spreading misinformation. Finally, we proposed a full deployment framework that considered the practical complications of using the model to detect new misinformation sites in the real world.

What We Learned

We learned the tremendous value of collaboration between academic research groups and mission-driven teams within companies like Microsoft. Teams like AI for Good can provide unique datasets and expertise on these datasets. Researchers like the Princeton team bring a nuanced understanding of the issues at play and the discourse around the proliferation of misinformation. With a unique combination of data, domain knowledge, and technical expertise, collaborations like this one can contribute novel insights into the proliferation of online misinformation.

In addition, we learned the value of training models with the goal of augmenting human expertise, not replacing it. When working to detect sites that spread misinformation, no model will ever be so precise that it will never have a false positive—a site wrongly suspected of spreading misinformation. It will always be necessary to have a human in the loop validating the model's results. Since human reviewers have limited capacity, we focused on precision, and we didn't stop at training a model with good performance metrics. We went beyond the model and proposed an end-to-end solution that includes human reviewers and considers their capacity.

Finally, we learned that pragmatism is key to successful deployment. It is often easier to train a model and achieve high accuracy levels on held-out data than it is to propose a useful real-world system built on a machine learning model. Without the deployment process that includes filtering the navigation graph, our model would have rated 350 million sites every month, referring an unwieldy 800,000 suspected misinformation websites to human reviewers. Instead, with our proposed framework, the model evaluates 32,000 sites per month and refers fewer than 1,000 to human review.

Appreciating each of these lessons allowed us to build a model grounded in research and feasible to deploy.

The full articles on which this summary is based are:

Greene KT, Pereira M, Pisharody N, Dodhia R, Ferres JL, and Shapiro JN. "Using Website Referrals to Identify Misinformation Rabbit Holes." (available at https://files.osf.io/v1/resources/ x4dh7/providers/osfstorage/6487b927a31091009ad10d0a?action= download&direct&version=1)

Pereira M, Greene K, Pisharody N, Dodhia R, Shapiro JN, and Lavista J. "Navigating the Web of Misinformation: A Framework for Misinformation Domain Detection Using Browser Traffic." arXiv preprint arXiv:2307.13180

Chapter 22
Unlocking the Potential of AI with Open Data

—Anthony Cintron Roman and Kevin Xu

Executive Summary

With over 100 million users, GitHub is the world's largest platform for collaborative software development. Also used extensively for open data collaboration—which means that data are freely and readily available to users—GitHub hosts more than 800 million open data files, totaling 142 terabytes of data. Here, we consider the potential of open data on GitHub and how open data can accelerate AI research. We explore GitHub's open data landscape and patterns of how users share datasets. We found that GitHub is one of the largest hosts of open data in the world and has experienced an accelerated growth of open data assets in the recent past. Leading by example, we released the three datasets that we collected to support this analysis as open datasets. By examining the open data landscape on GitHub, we sought to empower users and organizations to leverage existing open datasets and improve their discoverability—ultimately contributing to the ongoing AI revolution and its opportunities to help address complex societal issues.

Why Is This Important?

Artificial intelligence has the potential to facilitate digital innovation, promote experimentation, improve efficiency, and accelerate progress in addressing societal issues. By providing large quantities of data that are readily available for use in developing AI-powered models, open data is foundational to realizing this potential. Sectors like healthcare, education, and environmental conservation have seen noteworthy advancements due to the availability of open data to generate such models.

Serving as a leading platform for developers to share and collaborate on code, GitHub is central to this open data–driven transformation. With over 100 million users and a 27 percent annual growth rate, in addition to serving as a hub for software development, GitHub is one of the largest open data platforms in the world. GitHub houses more than 11 million data repositories that include more than 800 million open data files.

In 2020, Microsoft initiated the Open Data Campaign to help organizations understand the advantages of open data and expand open data access. To support this effort, we leveraged internal access to the data backend for GitHub's public application programming interfaces to conduct an in-depth analysis of metadata from GitHub's public data repositories. We created a dataset that includes counts of different file types found on GitHub, the username or organization that uploaded them, and the year they were added. Further, we explored the licenses of the repositories they are part of and compiled a list of websites that are active hosts of open data. This compilation should help individual users and organizations that are active on GitHub fully harness the potential of the available datasets and increase the discoverability and utility of these datasets.

The transformative power of AI is widely known, and open data access is critical to unleashing that power. GitHub, with its expansive user base and myriad repositories, plays an indispensable role in this ecosystem. Microsoft's Open Data Campaign and the analysis that we provide here support ongoing efforts to democratize data and accelerate AI-driven advancements.

Methods Used

To conduct our analysis, we curated three open datasets—Data Counts, License Counts, and Open Data Websites—each made available under the CDLA-Permissive-2.0 license on GitHub.

The Data Counts dataset includes a comprehensive tabulation of various types of data files on GitHub. It organizes this information by the user or organization that posted the file and the year it was uploaded. This dataset was created using GitHub's internal data services and was filtered to ensure data accuracy. We included some extensions and excluded others based on criteria such as file names, file paths, and the nature of the users. We used the Data Counts dataset to identify trends in the types of data files posted over time, the users or organizations contributing most to specific types of files, and the rate at which these files were posted. Though we have attempted to mitigate errors, there is an inherent lack of validation of each file's content.

The License Counts dataset expands on the Data Counts dataset by providing information on licensing. This dataset provides information on the license under which files are released, the file format, and the year that files were added to GitHub.

The Open Data Websites dataset was manually curated and includes 205 websites that host open data. We classified these websites according to whether they were hosted by governments, non-profit organizations, or private sector organizations, and we calculated the number of datasets each type of entity hosts.

We collected data from multiple sources, including data.gov and Google data search. We limited our analysis to websites that directly host open data and were accessible through web search, were in English, and existed as of February 11, 2023.

Findings

We found that, as of February 11, 2023, GitHub hosted the greatest number of data assets by far (see Table 22.1).

Table 22.1   Number of Data Assets in Each of the Top Ten Open Data Sites

Website	Data Assets	Sector
github.com	802M files/11.3M repos	Private
figshare.com/search	1.6M	Private
datadiscoverystudio.org/geoportal	1.6M	Non-profit
data.europa.eu/catalogue-statistics	1.3M	Government
data.gov.in	499K	Government
maps.amsterdam.nl/open_geodata	372k	Government
catalog.data.gov/dataset	245K	Government
researchdata.ands.org.au	203K	Government
kaggle.com	197K	Private
zenodo.org	178K	Non-profit

Source: Roman AC et al., 2023 / arxiv / CC BY 4.0

GitHub hosted more than 11.3 million public repositories that contained over 802 million structured and machine-readable data files and that were contributed by more than 4.2 million users. Notably, between 2019 and 2023, there was a surge in data file uploads: 81 percent of all uploads were contributed to GitHub during that time period (see Figure 22.1).

Organizations owned 1.3 million of these repositories and contributed 31 percent of the data files. Over 80 percent of all data files were in JSON and CSV formats (see Table 22.2).

Further, about 85 percent of the data files were classified as general research files, though geospatial, acoustic, and chemistry files collectively represented about 13 percent of all data files examined (see Table 22.3).

We found that data can be uploaded directly to a repository, linked from external storage, or contributed by a combination of the two. GitHub offers a Large File System (Git LFS) to accommodate files that exceed the default size limit of 100MB, extending up to 5GB depending on the type of account that the user has.

Some organizations break large datasets down into multiple repositories to adhere to GitHub's limitations on repository sizes.

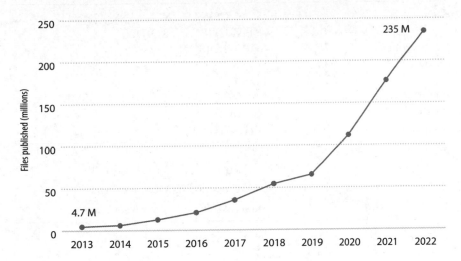

Figure 22.1 Number of data assets by year added to GitHub from 2013 to 2022 (Roman AC et al., 2023 / arxiv / CC BY 4.0).

Table 22.2   Top Ten Data File Formats on GitHub

File Format	Data Assets
JSON	483.7M
CSV	168.2M
GEOJSON	44.2M
WAV	43.7M
PDB	14.7M
TIF	14M
XLSX	7.8M
TSV	5.5M
FASTA	4.2M
PARQUET	3.2M

Source: Roman AC et al., 2023 / arxiv / CC BY 4.0

Licensing protocols offer clarity on how data can be used, shared, or attributed, and GitHub attempts to automatically classify repositories based on known licenses. Of the data files on GitHub, over 9 million had an open data license as recognized by the Open Knowledge Foundation (OKF) (see Table 22.4).

Table 22.3   Number of Data Assets on GitHub by Research Category

Category	Data Assets	Formats
General	689.3M	JSON, CSV, TSV, XLS, XLSX, TIFF, TIF, PARQUET, AVRO, DBF
Geospatial	47.5M	SHP, GEOJSON, SHX
Acoustic	43.7M	WAV
Chemistry	14.7M	PDB
Bioinformatics	4.4M	FASTA, FASTQ, BIOM, SBGN, SBML
Medical Imaging	2.6M	NII, DCM
Genomics	215K	GVF, GVCF, VCF

Source: Roman AC et al., 2023 / arxiv / CC BY 4.0

Table 22.4   Percentage of Data Assets Classified by License Category

License Category	Data Assets	Percentage
"Open Data" License	9.0M	1.1%
Unidentified License	59.9M	7.5%
Other Open Licenses	124.9M	15.6%
No License Detected	609.0M	75.9%

Source: Roman AC et al., 2023 / arxiv / CC BY 4.0

We identified four GitHub accounts that, collectively, have published over 40 million data files (see Table 22.5). The whosonfirst owner contributed more than half of those files, the vast majority being in a GEOJSON format. Two museums and the "Where on Earth" (woeplanet) owner contributed the remainder.

Table 22.5   Four GitHub Account Owners that Have Published Over 40 Million Data Files

Owner	GEOJSON	JSON	TSV	WAV	CSV	SHP	TIFF	Total
whosonfirst-data	24,056,588	7,321	0	0	52	9	0	24,063,970
sfomuseum-data	8,522,469	1,595	0	0	1	0	0	8,524,065
woeplanet-data	5,762,402	1,239,622	444	0	6	0	0	7,002,474
Fitzwilliam-Museum	2	1,430,103	0	304	35	0	2	1,430,446
Total	38,341,461	2,678,641	444	304	94	9	2	41,020,955

Source: Roman AC et al., 2023 / arxiv / CC BY 4.0

GitHub currently offers Collections, Topics, and standard search functions that have been largely designed for code discovery but may also be useful for locating data files. However, we found that only a fraction of repositories and data assets can be found using those search functions.

Discussion

We conducted an analysis of open data available on GitHub in early 2023 and found that GitHub hosts the vast majority of open data assets, contributions to GitHub have accelerated in the recent past, most files are in JSON or CSV formats, most data assets are of a non-specific research focus, most files did not have a detectable license, and the distribution of the volumes of files made by contributors to GitHub is skewed.

Our findings suggest that GitHub is a fertile ground for hosting and sharing datasets that are vital for AI research. Datasets like the Stanford Question Answering Dataset (SQuAD), the OpenAI GPT-2 Dataset, and the Common Objects in Context (COCO) dataset are key examples. SQuAD is an instrumental dataset containing over 100,000 question–answer pairs derived from Wikipedia articles, mainly used for training natural language processing and machine comprehension algorithms. On the other hand, the GPT-2 dataset from OpenAI is a large-scale language model trained on a diverse array of Internet texts. The COCO dataset, containing over 200,000 labeled images across 80 categories, is used for object detection, segmentation, and captioning tasks.

Open data enhances the quality of artificial intelligence models by providing practitioners with a diverse range of materials to train and fine-tune them. GitHub's ability to host these large datasets means that researchers have access to much more extensive and diverse data than was previously the case, thus contributing to the advancement of AI research.

Our evaluation of GitHub had several limitations:

- First, we limited our analysis to data assets with certain file extensions and excluded certain repositories and file paths.

For instance, we excluded organizations like Project Gutenberg, which has uploaded over 43,000 ebooks in TXT format, due to the difficulty of distinguishing between data and non-data files.

- Second, our analysis assumed that the listed repository-level license is an accurate reflection of the individual files it contains.
- Third, our analysis included only data from public, non-forked repositories and omitted certain potentially useful content like compressed versions of files (e.g., CSV.GZ).
- Finally, search engine biases may affect the comprehensiveness of this dataset.

Despite these limitations, our analysis provides a comprehensive overview of open data availability and trends as of March 2023, making them valuable resources for further research and analysis.

What We Learned

In our study of GitHub's open access datasets, we developed several novel methods for evaluating the volume, characteristics, and contribution sources of open data assets. To date, analyses have used filters based on file metadata like extensions, names, paths, and counts per user. Such filtering techniques are flawed, primarily because they do not account for the multifaceted reasons users upload files to GitHub. Future analyses should, therefore, focus on adopting content-based classification approaches that leverage the text within the repository's documentation files for a more accurate assessment. Such approaches will allow for broader and more accurate analysis of repositories, potentially including general-purpose extensions like .TXT files that were excluded from this study.

The vast amount of data on GitHub has the potential to significantly advance artificial intelligence research. The platform itself can be used to foster collaboration and promote the development of more sophisticated artificial intelligence models, as evidenced by community AI initiatives hosted on GitHub like LAION.AI. However, the vast majority of files did not have any detectable license, potentially limiting the use of these files and making it imperative to assign licenses in the future.

In March 2023, Google took a significant step in advancing artificial intelligence research by releasing a groundbreaking dataset on GitHub. This dataset will be an important resource for researchers and practitioners in the field of text-to-image research. Moreover, the dataset's release exemplifies the variety of datasets that are available on GitHub. Other datasets—like SQuAD, OpenAI's GPT-2, and COCO—will allow AI practitioners to refine their models, thereby advancing innovations in the field.

Access to large datasets is crucial for the development and scaling of AI models. By hosting open data on GitHub, greater numbers of researchers can easily access and utilize these datasets. Furthermore, GitHub's collaborative environment promotes an open and transparent AI research community.

Finally, open data on GitHub can contribute to the democratization of AI research, as it allows researchers from various backgrounds and institutions to access and utilize the same datasets. This can promote more diverse perspectives in artificial intelligence research, ultimately leading to more innovative and inclusive AI solutions.

The full article on which this summary is based is:

Roman AC, Xu K, Smith A, Torres J, Robinson C, Lavista JM. "Open data on GitHub: unlocking the potential of AI." arXiv:2306 .06191. doi: 10.48550/arXiv.2306.06191.

Part IV

Health

Health is perhaps the area in which the application of artificial intelligence models, machine learning, and sophisticated analytic techniques can have the greatest impact on humanity. Such application can extend our lives, improve their quality, and enhance productivity. While the other two areas covered in the book have a clear health impact (climate change impacts population health and humanitarian action acts to restore and preserve population health), this section of the book focuses on how artificial intelligence can be used to improve provider productivity (and, thereby, extend the provider workforce and improve access to care). These examples illustrate how AI can analyze large datasets that capture patients' interactions with healthcare systems and the diagnoses that they receive, as well as facilitate access to the latest medical knowledge. The overall goal of such work includes keeping providers up-to-date with recent developments, enabling patients to be informed about their own conditions and treatments, and helping policymakers determine their next best steps for improving public health.

Public health and healthcare delivery have different, sometimes conflicting, goals. Public health seeks to improve the health of the population. While it contributes to this goal, perhaps surprisingly, healthcare delivery accounts for only between 20 and 40 percent of a population's health: the rest is determined by social determinants of health, which are the economic, environmental, and social conditions in which we live. The tension between the two goals is reflected in funding: in the United States, only about 3 percent of total annual health expenditures is spent on public health while the other 97 percent—about $4 trillion a year, or 18 percent of gross domestic product—is spent on healthcare delivery.

The goal of healthcare delivery organizations and providers is to achieve the quadruple aim, defined as follows:

- Improving the patient experience
- Improving the provider experience
- Improving care access, equity, quality, and outcomes
- Reducing per-capita healthcare costs

Artificial intelligence can help improve performance in each of these quadrants. It can be used to improve the patient experience by improving access to information (through, for instance, use of ChatGPT and search engines) and care (by expanding the provider workforce by allowing community health workers to do more, or by making it easier for patients to make appointments or get and understand test results). It can be used to improve provider experiences, by helping them screen patients so they only see the patients who need their care, or by helping them focus on the parts of an x-ray that most need their attention. Artificial intelligence can improve care quality, access, equity, and outcomes by helping both providers and patients do the next right thing, keeping both patients and providers current with the latest information and recommendations, and helping health systems address care inequities and opportunities to improve care outcomes by applying the best patient care pathways indiscriminately.

Finally, artificial intelligence can help drive down the per-capita costs of care in two ways. First, by facilitating or eliminating time-consuming operational components, such as note writing, coding, and scheduling. Automation of these tasks not only reduces labor inputs but also improves the provider experience: providers did not endure years of training to type. Second, by better using their time, providers can monitor many more patients. Most providers spend the majority of their time seeing patients who may not need to be seen: their time can be better used when artificial intelligence algorithms direct appropriate patients to self-care, help providers operate at the top of their licenses by ensuring that they see only patients who need to be seen, and identify patient care needs that most require their attention.

To be sure, artificial intelligence algorithms should be responsibly and ethically developed and applied. But, when done so, they have the potential to revolutionize how healthcare is delivered, improve the health of the population, promote health equity, and reduce healthcare costs.

Chapter 23
Detecting Middle Ear Disease

—Yixi Xu and Al-Rahim Habib

Executive Summary

Hearing loss affects about 1.5 billion people—or about 20 percent of the global population—and it is anticipated to impact over 2.5 billion people by 2050. The economic burden of hearing loss nears $1 trillion in the United States alone. Globally, about 34 million children suffer from hearing loss; preventable hearing loss in children includes chronic middle ear infection that can be detected by otoscopy (looking into the ear with a magnification device). We sought to evaluate the generalizability of artificial intelligence algorithms that use deep learning methods to identify middle ear disease from otoscopic images. To do so, we used 1,842 normal and abnormal otoscopic images that were collected from three independent sources in Van, Turkey; Santiago, Chile; and Ohio in the United States.

We used deep learning methods to develop models, and we evaluated their internal and external performance using area under the curve (AUC) estimates. Further, we conducted a pooled assessment by combining all three cohorts with five-fold cross-validation.

We found that artificial intelligence–informed otoscopy algorithms had high internal performance (mean AUC: 0.95, 95% Confidence Interval (CI): 0.80–1.00) but lower performance when tested on external otoscopic images not used for training (mean AUC: 0.76, 95% CI: 0.61–0.91). Model performance when applied to the combined cohort had better pooled performance (AUC: 0.96, standard error: 0.01). Further efforts are required to explore data augmentation and preprocessing techniques that might improve external performance and develop a robust, generalizable algorithm for real-world clinical applications.

Why Is This Important?

Hearing loss affects an estimated 1.5 billion people worldwide, or nearly 20 percent of the global population. Hearing loss is anticipated to swell to over 2.5 billion people by 2050. When considering healthcare costs, educational expenses, productivity losses, and societal impacts, the economic burden of hearing loss in the United States approached $1 trillion annually.

Globally, about 34 million children suffer from hearing loss; because a significant proportion of preventable hearing loss in children is attributed to infections such as mumps, measles, and middle ear infections, most cases of childhood hearing loss can be prevented.

Otoscopy, a diagnostic procedure used to examine the ear, is a crucial part of ear health assessments and is performed by a range of healthcare providers, from mid-level providers to specialized otolaryngologists. Otoscopy is instrumental in identifying ear infections that could potentially lead to hearing loss if left untreated. However, the efficacy of otoscopy in generating accurate diagnoses significantly depends on the expertise of the practitioner: non-otolaryngologists often struggle to differentiate between various types of ear diseases such as acute otitis media and otitis media with effusion. Accurate diagnosis of these conditions is important for early intervention and could mitigate long-term hearing loss, improve speech and language development, and reduce healthcare costs.

Because of the interpretative variability in otoscopy, deep learning–based image classification algorithms have been developed. Unlike traditional machine learning methods that rely on predefined features, deep learning algorithms use neural networks to learn patterns directly from raw data. These algorithms offer the promise of improving diagnostic performance of non-expert practitioners to levels comparable to otolaryngologists. Otolaryngologists demonstrate superior diagnostic accuracy, particularly in identifying nuanced pathological characteristics like tympanic membrane perforations, but are scarce, highly trained specialists to whom most of the world's population has limited access.

Previous research using deep learning in otoscopy shows promising results. A recent meta-analysis revealed that algorithms achieved 91 percent accuracy in differentiating between normal and abnormal otoscopic images; a pooled analysis demonstrated 98 percent accuracy in multi-classification algorithms used to identify different ear disease types.

However, these studies have limitations. One of the major concerns is the significant heterogeneity between different models, leading to questions about their generalizability in real-world environments. Factors such as data source, capture devices, types of ear diseases, and the deep learning methods used can affect a model's performance. To date, the issue of the generalizability of deep learning algorithms for otoscopy has not been thoroughly explored.

Here, we sought to construct a deep learning–based image classifier capable of differentiating normal from abnormal otoscopic images and to produce an algorithm robust enough to adapt to variations in data quality, capture devices, and subtypes of ear diseases. Further, we wanted to evaluate the algorithm's generalizability using images not utilized in the training phase.

Methods Used

We focused on the application of artificial intelligence, particularly deep learning algorithms, for classifying otoscopic images to diagnose ear conditions. This study was conducted following ethical guidelines such as the Helsinki Declaration, STARD, and CONSORT-AI, and used three separate cohorts of otoscopic images, each with institutional review board approval from their respective institutions.

We trained and evaluated models using three cohorts. Cohort A from Turkey included 848 images captured at Van Özel Akdamar Hospital that were classified by two otolaryngologists and one pediatrician into normal, acute otitis media (AOM), and chronic otitis media (COM). Cohort B from Chile included 540 images from the University of Chile Clinical Hospital, classified by one otolaryngologist into normal or COM. Cohort C from the United States included 454 images from Nationwide Children's Hospital and Ohio State University, which were classified by one otolaryngologist as either normal or otitis media with effusion (OME). Images where the tympanic membrane (TM) could not be visualized were excluded.

We trained deep learning models to classify the images into either normal or abnormal, with abnormal subcategories including AOM, OME, and COM. We used four different neural net architectures: ResNet-50, VGGNet-16, DenseNet-161, and Vision Transformer. All images were resized to 224x224 pixels, and the models were trained for 200 epochs using Stochastic Gradient Descent as the optimizer with a learning rate of 0.003. We used a cross-entropy loss function and Microsoft's Azure Machine Learning Studio for training.

Each cohort was randomly divided into training, validation, and testing sets with proportions of 70 percent, 10 percent, and 20 percent, respectively. The model that performed the best during the validation phase was selected for further testing. To gauge external validity, the finalized models were also tested on the remaining two cohorts. Additionally, each experiment was run three times to compute the mean and standard deviation of key metrics like accuracy, area under the curve, sensitivity, and specificity, thereby providing a robust understanding of model performance (see Figure 23.1).

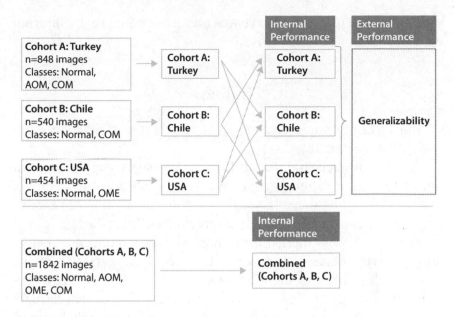

Figure 23.1   The processes used to assess internal and external performance of the different cohorts (Habib A et al., 2023 / Springer Nature / CC BY 4.0).

We assessed pooled performance by merging data from all three cohorts and applying five-fold cross-validation, as follows: we partitioned the pooled data into five separate groups or folds, trained the model using three folds, validated the model on one fold, and tested it in the remaining folds. We did this iteratively until each fold had been utilized as a test fold once, and we averaged metrics to assess pooled performance.

To determine model performance, we calculated the area under the curve, accuracy, sensitivity, and specificity for each cohort. We assessed internal performance by training and testing models on otoscopic images from the same cohort and external validation and generalizability by using models trained on one cohort to validate the other two. We calculated mean differences in area under the curve between internal and external performance comparisons. We used bootstrapping methods to compare receiver operating characteristics curves with a null hypothesis stating that the external validation area under the curve was greater or equal to the internal validation area under the curve.

Findings

Of the 1,842 otoscopic images, 1,117 were categorized as normal and 725 as abnormal.

Internal models trained on Cohort A images yielded an area under the curve ranging from 0.82 to 0.86, with accuracy levels between 80 and 84 percent, sensitivity between 57 and 70 percent, and specificity between 90 and 91 percent (see Table 23.1).

Internal models trained on Cohort B images attained a perfect area under the curve of 1.00, with 100 percent accuracy, sensitivity, and specificity. Internal models trained on Cohort C images also performed admirably, achieving area under the curve scores between 0.98 and 0.99, with accuracy rates of 91 to 95 percent, sensitivity between 91 and 96 percent, and specificity ranging from 89 to 96 percent.

In terms of external validation, models trained on Cohort A and tested on Cohort B had area under the curve scores between 0.80 and 0.87, with accuracy levels ranging from 62 to 77 percent, sensitivity ranging from 76 to 96 percent, and specificity ranging from 47 to 78 percent. When these models were tested on Cohort C, they achieved area under the curve scores of between 0.61 and 0.82, with accuracy levels of 65 to 76 percent, sensitivity ranging from 80 to 92 percent, and specificity ranging from 25 to 69 percent.

Models trained on Cohort B and tested on Cohort A yielded area under the curve scores between 0.60 and 0.67, with accuracy rates of 59 to 65 percent, but low sensitivity ranging from 4 to 54 percent and high specificity between 61 and 99 percent. These models, when tested on Cohort C, had area under the curve scores between 0.87 and 0.91, with accuracy levels of 72 to 80 percent, sensitivities between 62 and 73 percent, and specificities ranging from 88 to 95 percent.

Models trained on Cohort C and tested on Cohort A had area under the curve scores between 0.54 and 0.68, with accuracies ranging from 44 to 70 percent, sensitivities between 14 and 82 percent,

Table 23.1 Summary of Internal and External Performance Between Cohorts to Differentiate Normal Versus Abnormal Otoscopic Images Trained Using ResNet-50, DenseNet-161, VGG16, and Vision Transformer

Experiments			ResNet-50		DenseNet-161		VGGNet-16		Vision Transformer	
Train	**Validate**		**Acc % (SD)**	**AUC**	**Acc % (SD)**	**AUC**	**Acc % (SD)**	**AUC**	**Acc % (SD)**	**AUC**
Cohort A	Cohort A (Internal)		78 (0.02)	0.83 (0.01)	83 (0.01)	0.86 (0.01)	82 (0.01)	0.84 (0.0)	82 (0.0)	0.85 (0.02)
	Cohort B (External)		75 (0.05)	0.88 (0.01)	65 (0.04)	0.84 (0.03)	80 (0.03)	0.89 (0.02)	62 (0.06)	0.86 (0.02)
	Cohort C (External)		75 (0.01)	0.81 (0.02)	67 (0.03)	0.71 (0.05)	73 (0.03)	0.78 (0.05)	65 (0.02)	0.64 (0.06)
Cohort B	Cohort B (Internal)		100 (0.0)	1.0 (0.0)	100 (0.0)	1.0 (0.0)	100 (0.0)	1.0 (0.0)	100 (0.0)	1.0 (0.0)
	Cohort A (External)		59 (0.04)	0.62 (0.02)	56 (0.07)	0.67 (0.05)	64 (0.02)	0.63 (0.01)	67 (0.03)	0.62 (0.05)
	Cohort C (External)		76 (0.02)	0.87 (0.03)	81 (0.01)	0.89 (0.01)	77 (0.01)	0.9 (0.01)	67 (0.03)	0.82 (0.04)
Cohort C	Cohort C (Internal)		92 (0.01)	0.99 (0.0)	92 (0.01)	0.98 (0.0)	94 (0.01)	0.99 (0.0)	96 (0.01)	0.99 (0.0)
	Cohort A (External)		53 (0.12)	0.69 (0.01)	52 (0.04)	0.66 (0.03)	66 (0.01)	0.58 (0.02)	53 (0.11)	0.57 (0.03)
	Cohort B (External)		37 (0.02)	0.86 (0.01)	36 (0.01)	0.92 (0.01)	41 (0.03)	0.92 (0.02)	38 (0.02)	0.9 (0.01)

Abbreviations: Acc, accuracy; AUC, area under the receiver operating characteristics curve; SD, standard deviation.
Source: Habib A et al, 2023 / Springer Nature / CC BY 4.0

and specificities ranging from 26 to 96 percent. When tested on Cohort B, these models had area under the curve scores ranging from 0.85 to 0.94; however, the models had poor accuracy rates of 34 to 45 percent, high sensitivity at 100 percent, and extremely low specificity between 1 and 17 percent.

Area under the curve scores for externally trained models were significantly lower than those for internally trained models. Specifically, the range of the mean difference in area under the curve scores for the DenseNet-161 architecture was between 0.07 and 0.39. Among the cohorts, Cohort A showed the smallest discrepancy between internal and external area under the curve metrics, with a range of mean differences from -0.05 to 0.07.

Models trained on a combined dataset from all cohorts achieved 90 to 91 percent accuracy, had an area under the curve score of 0.96, sensitivities that ranged from 84 to 87 percent, and specificities that were between 93 and 95 percent (see Table 23.2). Of all architectures used for this pooled data, DenseNet-161 had the highest area under the curve scores and the smallest standard deviation in the five-fold cross-validation process.

Table 23.2 Summary of Pooled Performance for Differentiating Normal from Abnormal Otoscopic Images Using the Combined Dataset (Cohorts A, B, and C) as Trained on a Convolutional Neural Network Architecture

Model Architecture	Acc (SD)	AUC (SD)	Sen (SD)	Spec (SD)
ResNet-50	0.91 (0.02)	0.96 (0.01)	0.87 (0.04)	0.93 (0.01)
DenseNet-161	0.91 (0.02)	0.96 (0.01)	0.86 (0.04)	0.94 (0.01)
VGG16	0.90 (0.02)	0.96 (0.01)	0.84 (0.02)	0.94 (0.02)
Vision Transformer	0.92 (0.01)	0.96 (0.01)	0.86 (0.01)	0.95 (0.01)

Abbreviations: Acc, accuracy; AUC, area under the receiver operating characteristics curve; Sen sensitivity, Spec specificity, SD, standard deviation.
Source: Habib A et al., 2023 / Springer Nature / CC BY 4.0

Discussion

We examined the generalizability of artificial intelligence–informed binary classification of otoscopic images using convolutional neural networks. We found a high degree of internal performance for each individual cohort; however, performance decreased when the models were applied to external validation sets.

We also found that performance metrics varied between the cohorts when externally validated. For instance, when exposed to different models, Cohort A had the smallest drop in performance in accuracy, area under the curve scores, and sensitivity. On the other hand, Cohort B had the smallest drop in specificity but the greatest drop in area under the curve and sensitivity. These performance variations indicate that evaluation of the model's external validity needs to be considered in the context of specific outcome measures.

We also found that the DenseNet-161 model had the highest internal performance when the data was pooled, suggesting that aggregating data from multiple sources could potentially mitigate the decrease in performance seen in external validation. However, more complex convolutional neural network architectures may require increased computational resources and could be more susceptible to overfitting.

Interestingly, the convolutional neural networks were able to differentiate between otitis media with effusion and normal tympanic membranes even when the models were not trained on otitis media with effusion images. This finding highlights the convolutional neural networks' architectural design and capacity for feature extraction, although the addition of acute otitis media in one cohort seemed to negatively affect this ability.

What We Learned

While our study establishes a promising foundation for the use of artificial intelligence in otoscopy, it also identified several limitations:

- The first is that the performance of the models was compromised by data collection methods that were not standardized across cohorts.

- Second, our models may be limited by lack of full information, for instance, if ear disease diagnoses that were used to label images were not solely based on otoscopic images but were supplemented with other clinical information.
- Finally, the ground truth labels were not verified by expert consensus, introducing potential inter-rater variability and bias.

Despite these shortcomings, there is considerable potential application of artificial intelligence in otoscopy, particularly in underserved or remote areas. Autonomous artificial intelligence tools could improve both triage and clinical decision-making, especially in settings where healthcare access is limited. However, to achieve this, artificial intelligence algorithms must be accurate, reliable, and generalizable, while also being accessible and sustainable. More work is needed to standardize diagnostic definitions and to expand the databases used for training the algorithms. Future research should investigate data augmentation and preprocessing techniques that might enhance external performance. Overall, while convolutional neural networks show promise in assisting with otoscopic diagnosis, our study highlights that external validation and generalizability are critical challenges that must be addressed.

The full article on which this summary is based is:

Habib A, Xu Y, Bock K, Mohanty S, Sederholm T, Weeks WB, Dodhia R, Lavista JM, Perry C, Sacks R, Singh N. "Evaluating the generalizability of deep learning image classification algorithms to detect middle ear disease using otoscopy." *Scientific Reports* 2023; 13: 5368. doi: 10.1038/s41598-023-31921-0.

Chapter 24
Detecting Leprosy in Vulnerable Populations

—Yixi Xu and Ann Aerts

Executive Summary

Leprosy is a chronic bacterial infection that damages the nerves, eyes, respiratory tracts, and skin. While the global burden has been reduced by about 99 percent, thanks to the widespread free availability of multidrug therapy, about 200,000 new patients are still diagnosed annually. India, Brazil, Indonesia, and Sub-Saharan Africa see the highest incidence of leprosy. While the disease can be cured, its incubation time can lag between a few months and 20 years. Delayed diagnosis and treatment leave many patients with untreated leprosy and that can lead to irreversible nerve damage, often resulting in disfiguring disabilities. As people with leprosy are often stigmatized and excluded from their communities, it is important to accelerate detection of the disease to enable health providers to offer prompt treatment.

Most forms of leprosy have dermatological features that can be used—with clinical symptoms—to diagnose patients, even in the absence of confirmatory pathology testing. However, there are

235

other diseases that may look similar—such as syphilis, psoriasis, lymphoma, and neurofibromatosis.

Here, we used artificial intelligence models that incorporated photographs of patients' skin lesions and clinical features to help health providers—who might live at a distance from patients, particularly those living in underserved or rural settings—diagnose patients and differentiate those with leprosy from other conditions.

Why Is This Important?

Most people in the world do not have ready access to healthcare. Access to healthcare includes the availability of healthcare providers (from physicians to nurses to community health workers) who can diagnose healthcare conditions, to pharmaceuticals that can be used to treat those conditions, to healthcare facilities that can house interactions with healthcare professionals and facilitate healthcare visits, surgeries, and childbirth centers. Further, "access" should imply quality of care, as low-quality care can seriously harm people. Quality of care and lack of access to care disproportionately affect the most vulnerable, poor, and disenfranchised.

Traditionally, developing the infrastructure necessary for creating a robust provider workforce, a strong supply chain network for medical supplies, and safe and functional health facilities take decades. Particularly in low- and middle-income countries, that development must compete with investments in education, roads, and other necessities. However, because of the widespread availability of mobile phones, broadband networks, and inexpensive smartphones, access to high-quality care could be substantially improved by virtual means, such as visual imagery and artificial intelligence–enhanced algorithms that can help providers diagnose and treat patients at a distance.

Particularly for the rarest specialties—like ophthalmologists, dermatologists, neurologists, and otolaryngologists—such algorithms can effectively overcome some of the health worker shortages. Only patients with high likelihood of having a particular disease will need to be seen and treated by the specialists, addressing the barrier of access.

Therefore, leveraging mobile phone and broadband infrastructure to offer a diagnosis acceleration tool using photos and clinical information from the patient can massively expand access, accelerate the diagnosis and treatment process, and ultimately prevent the occurrence of long-term sequelae of treatable diseases.

Methods Used

In this study, we included patients who had "leprosy-like lesions," including macules, plaques, or nodules. Following a protocol, researchers collected three photographs of those lesions and obtained skin biopsies (that were later verified to be leprosy based on tissue morphology or the presence of the bacteria most commonly associated with leprosy). Further, during the intake process, researchers collected patients' socio-demographic data and clinical symptoms and performed a dermato-neurological exam.

We entered photographic, clinical, and patient data into three separate machine learning models, and used the final, combined model to test model validity in an unseen group of patients, as shown in Figure 24.1.

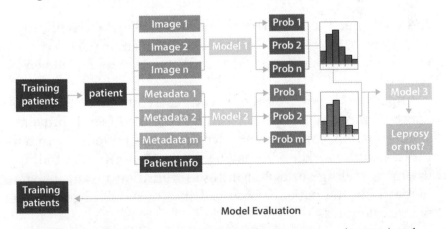

Figure 24.1   Model development and testing. (Barbieri RR, et al., 2022 / With permission of Elsevier)

In essence, we fed photographic and clinical data into separate models, each of which was processed to identify features that were consistent or inconsistent with a diagnosis of leprosy. The processed data generated probability histograms that were integrated into a third model that also included patient socio-demographic data to finally calculate the probability that the patient had leprosy.

We tested a third model on an independent and randomly selected group of 40 patients to determine how good it was at predicting whether a patient had leprosy. While the same data had been collected on these patients, their information had not been used to train the models. Therefore, this testing—which is critical to considering real-world clinical application of an artificial intelligence protocol—was done even though those 40 patients were previously unseen but had a similar set of photographic, clinical, and socio-demographic data. Importantly, the data collection and skin photography processes did not require a skilled medical professional. A community health worker following a simple data collection protocol could collect all of the data used in the predictive model.

Findings

We found that the model performed well, with a classification accuracy of 90 percent and an area under the curve (AUC) of 96.5 percent. The top ten features that predicted leprosy are shown in Figure 24.2.

Importantly, none of these features required collection of data or pictures by a physician or highly skilled health provider. All information could be collected from the patient or a community health worker who had been provided minimal training on what a scaling surface or diffuse infiltration meant, by simply matching the patient's observed skin to standardized photographic examples.

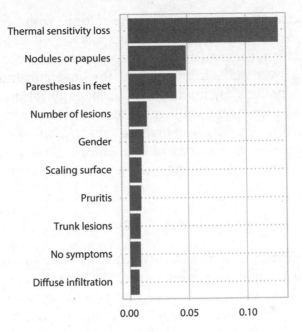

Figure 24.2 The ten most important features in the model (Barbieri RR, et al., 2022 / With permission of Elsevier).

Discussion

We developed an artificial intelligence–based model that could be used by non-clinicians to help determine whether a patient had leprosy. We found that the model was highly accurate and reliable; further, the most important features for determining the likelihood of leprosy could be obtained from a smartphone application without the need for a clinician. Importantly, we found that photographic information alone was not as useful as information that included clinical signs and symptoms directly provided by the patient, such as the color, number, and sensitivity of the lesion or pain.

These types of artificial intelligence–based models—trained on a group of patients for whom the diagnostic outcome is known, tested on a group of patients for whom the diagnostic outcome is not known but can be verified, and then widely deployed in an inexpensive and user-friendly manner—have tremendous potential for widespread application, particularly in settings with limited access to quality care or skilled health professionals.

Importantly, these artificial intelligence–based algorithms have advantages over statistical methods that are currently used in clinical evaluations. By holding out a randomly selected subset of patients, researchers can validate an algorithm before clinical application. Further, artificial intelligence and machine learning tools can incorporate a multiplicity of interactions. Most currently used statistical methods are limited to a few interaction terms.

What We Learned

While the developed model is not a panacea—like all work done on a particular population, results may not be generalizable to populations in different geographic settings or, particularly when photography is used, with different skin tones. For this reason, we conducted the study in Brazil, where people from almost all skin types could be included, and this allowed us to show that highly accurate and reliable models could be developed for widespread application. These models depend on data that can be elicited directly from patients and minimally trained community health workers, without the need for highly trained clinicians.

Such models could be developed for a multitude of clinical applications—from skin lesions to clinical pathways to reading of radiographs and pathology slides. When widely applied, those applications could effectively expand the health professional workforce, improve access to quality care for everyone, and dramatically accelerate adequate diagnosis and treatment.

The full article on which this summary is based is:

Barbieri RR, Xu Y, Setian L, Souza-Santos PT, Trivedi A, Cristofono J, Bhering R, White K, Sales AM, Miller G, Nery JAC, Sharman M, Bumann R, Zhang S, Goldust M, Sarno EN, Mirza F, Cavaliero A, Timmer S, Bonfiglioli E, Smith C, Scollard D, Navarini AA, Aerts A, Lavista JM, Moraes MO. "Reimagining leprosy elimination with AI analysis of a combination of skin lesion images with demographic and clinical data." *Lancet Regional Health Americas* 2022; 9: 100192. doi: 10.1016/j.lana.2022.100192.

Chapter 25
Automated Segmentation of Prostate Cancer Metastases

—Yixi Xu

Executive Summary

Automated and accurate segmentation of lesions in radiological images of metastatic castration-resistant prostate cancer can facilitate personalized radiopharmaceutical therapy and advanced treatment response monitoring. Here, we sought to develop a convolutional neural networks-based framework for fully automated detection and segmentation of metastatic prostate cancer lesions in whole-body Positron Emission Tomography/Computed Tomography (PET/CT) images. We used 525 whole-body PET/CT images of patients with metastatic prostate cancer. Those scans used the [18F] DCFPyL radiotracer that targets the prostate-specific membrane antigen (PSMA). We trained U-Net (1)-based convolutional neural networks to identify lesions on paired axial PET/CT slices.

We used both batch-wise Dice loss and weighted batch-wise Dice loss approaches to minimize error, and we quantified lesion detection accuracy of each approach, with a particular emphasis on lesion size, intensity, and location. We used 418 images for model training, 30 for model validation, and 77 for model testing. Further, we allowed our model to take up to 12 neighboring axial slices to determine how incorporating a three-dimensional context influenced model performance. We then selected the optimal number of neighboring axial slices that maximized the detection rate on the 30 validation images and trained five neural networks with different architectures.

We found that the weighted batch-wise Dice loss approach significantly improved the lesion detection rate, the lesion-wise Dice similarity coefficient, and the lesion-wise sensitivity compared to the baseline. Including the first two neighboring axial slices into the model increased model performance; however, we found a minimal effect from including more distant neighboring slices. When including two neighboring slices and using the weighted Dice loss function to train three models, we were able to detect 80 percent of all testing lesions and 93 percent of lesions that had a maximum standardized uptake value of [^{18}F]DCFPyL greater than 5.0. We, therefore, demonstrated that convolutional neural networks can detect and segment prostate cancer metastases in PET/CT images.

Segmentation performance strongly depended on the intensity, size, and the location of lesions, and might be improved by using specialized loss functions; models performed best when detecting lesions with higher standardized uptake values of [^{18}F]DCFPyL.

Why Is This Important?

Prostate cancer is the second most frequently diagnosed cancer among men. Its aggressive form—metastatic castration-resistant prostate cancer—is responsible for over 350,000 deaths worldwide each year. A recent treatment breakthrough has been using diagnostic imaging to quantify the total tumor burden, predict therapeutic response, and optimize dosing. However, the laborious nature of lesion detection and delineation in images has hindered the widespread adoption of total tumor burden quantification in clinical settings.

Technological advancements in PET/CT—particularly the use of tracers like [^{18}F]DCFPyL that target the prostate-specific membrane antigen—have improved the ability to detect and quantify metastases in metastatic castration-resistant prostate cancer. These tracers illuminate high-contrast and focal lesions, making them easier to demarcate and quantify, making this process increasingly important in treatment decision-making and patient management. A challenge to using this technique is that identifying those lesions is labor-intensive work that requires highly skilled healthcare workers.

To address that problem, we focused on automating segmentation of metastatic prostate cancer lesions in [^{18}F]DCFPyL-enhanced images, specifically for total tumor burden quantification. Prior studies have predominantly addressed intraprostatic tumor segmentation manually, semi-automatically, or fully automatically. For instance, one study demonstrated that manual contouring achieved a median Dice similarity coefficient (a measure comparing human segmentation to automated segmentation that ranges from 0 to 1, with higher numbers indicating greater alignment) of 0.90 in primary prostate tumors. Using a convolutional neural network for the same purpose produced a median Dice similarity coefficient above 0.8 on all three validation cohorts.

However, metastatic lesions outside the prostate present unique challenges, such as the problematic detection of local tumor recurrence adjacent to the urinary bladder. To date, no comprehensive research has been conducted on the automated detection and segmentation of metastatic castration-resistant prostate cancer lesions in whole-body prostate-specific membrane antigen [^{18}F]DCFPyL-enhanced PET/CT images.

Methods Used

We analyzed 525 whole-body [^{18}F]DCFPyL radiotracer-enhanced PET/CT images of patients with metastatic prostate cancer. All subjects consented to be part of an ongoing clinical trial, and the ethics board at the University of British Columbia approved the project. The radiotracer was injected following a four-hour fast and after a 120-minute uptake period. Images were captured using GE Discovery 600 or 690 scanners. The image dimensions for Positron Emission Tomography were 192x192 pixels while those for Computed Tomography were 512x512 pixels.

For preprocessing, CT images were down-sampled to match PET images' voxel size. We normalized radiotracer dose variations by standardizing the uptake values of [^{18}F]DCFPyL. Each PET/CT had up to five lesions manually delineated by a nuclear medicine physician; these lesion contours were converted to binary masks for neural network training.

We randomly divided the 525 images into three subsets: 418 training, 30 validation, and 77 testing images. Each model we developed was trained using the training set, then validated, and then tested. We repeated this process for two additional random splits to ensure robust model performance. We used U-Nets with ResNet-34, VGG-16, and DenseNet-121 backbones, MA-Net, and UNet++ models. Each model architecture had its unique feature: MA-Net incorporated self-attention mechanisms, while UNet++ was designed specifically for medical imaging segmentation tasks.

We used paired PET/CT slices and their axial positions as model inputs. We tested several configurations by varying the number of neighboring slices included in the input. We chose Stochastic Gradient Descent as the training algorithm, with a learning rate of 0.003 and batch size of 32. We used a batch-wise Dice loss function approach, modified to address batch-level imbalances. Additionally, to adjust for lesion volumes, we used a weighted version of the Dice loss function.

We evaluated our models at both the lesion and the image level. We calculated the lesion-wise detection rate by averaging results over all the lesions to determine whether at least part of each lesion had been detected. On the other hand, we designed our image-wise performance evaluation to capture the rate of false positives. We computed the Dice similarity coefficient at the lesion level and at the image level and we calculated model sensitivity.

We compared the performance of different models across various lesion characteristics such as Mean Tumor Volume, mean and maximum standardized [^{18}F]DCFPyL uptake values, and Total Lesion Activity. We also calculated the distance from the lesion to the bladder, with that distance serving as a proxy for distance from the lesion to the prostate. We used pre-checked bladder masks to make these calculations and excluded images with weak bladder mask predictions from the analysis.

Findings

We found that our models were better at detecting medium or large-sized lesions than small ones; lesions with lower standardized [^{18}F]DCFPyL uptake values and Total Lesion Activity were harder to detect. Further, we found that lesions farther from the bladder were more challenging to identify.

Incorporating neighboring slices into the main imaging slice improved our model's performance by capturing three-dimensional information (see Figure 25.1).

We found that adding the first two neighboring slices significantly improved performance; however, from both lesion-wise and image-wise perspectives, adding additional slices did not significantly contribute to model performance.

We found that using weighted Dice loss resulted in higher detection rates and higher lesion-wise Dice similarity coefficients, particularly for smaller lesions (see Figure 25.2).

However, image-wise Dice similarity coefficients did not substantially improve when using a weighted Dice loss approach as opposed to a standard Dice loss approach; further, we found some evidence that the weighted Dice loss approach could generate more false positives.

We also found that our model was better at detecting lesions with larger mean tumor volumes, higher standardized [^{18}F]DCFPyL uptake values, and greater Total Lesion Activity. However,

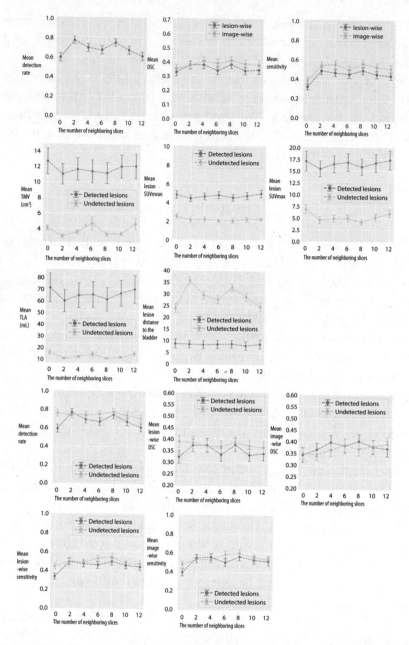

Figure 25.1 The impact of adding additional neighboring slices on detection rate, Dice similarity coefficient values, model sensitivity, total mean volume, mean and maximum standardized [^{18}F]DCFPyL uptake values, total lesion activity, bladder distance, lesion detection rates, lesion-wise Dice similarity coefficient values, image-wise Dice similarity coefficient values, lesion-wise sensitivity, and image-wise sensitivity (Xu Y, et al., 2023 / With permission of Elsevier).

it struggled with lower standardized [^{18}F]DCFPyL uptake value lesions (see Figure 25.3).

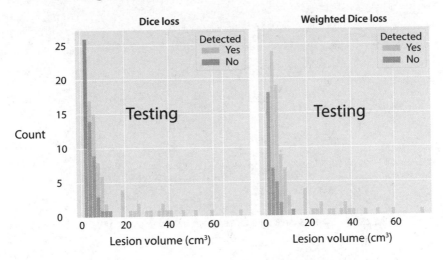

Figure 25.2 Evaluation metrics comparing Dice loss and weighted Dice loss approaches (Xu Y, et al., 2023 / With permission of Elsevier).

Also, we found that the Dice similarity coefficients and lesion detection rates could fluctuate when using a weighted Dice loss approach, a behavior not observed when using a standard Dice loss approach. These fluctuations may be attributed to the *curse of dimensionality*—which is when the addition of more dimensions degrades performance—as more slices are added. After comparing various configurations, the best-performing model included using a weighted Dice loss function and two neighboring slices. Two additional experiments reaffirmed the effectiveness of the model and showed a consistent detection rate of 80 percent and higher detection rates for lesions with maximum standardized [^{18}F]DCFPyL uptake values that were greater than 5.0.

We compared different neural network architectures like U-Net with various backbones—MA-Net and UNet++. Each architecture had strengths and weaknesses. For example, U-Net with DenseNet-121 had the highest detection rate and Dice similarity coefficient values but also yielded the most false positives. Conversely, U-Net with ResNet-34 had lower lesion detection rates, but performed similarly in lesion-wise Dice similarity coefficient values.

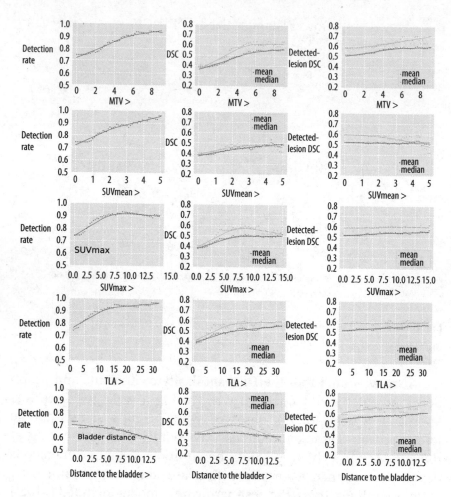

Figure 25.3   Model performance as a function of different measures of the lesion. The first column shows the mean detection rate, the second column shows the mean and median Dice similarity coefficient values, and the third column shows the Dice similarity coefficient detected lesion rates as a function of the mean total volume, standardized [18F]DCFPyL uptake values, maximum standardized [18F]DCFPyL uptake values, total lesion activity, and distance of the lesion to the bladder (Xu Y, et al., 2023 / With permission of Elsevier).

Discussion

We developed and evaluated a neural network model designed to detect metastatic castration-resistant prostate cancer lesions using [^{18}F]DCFPyL-enhanced PET/CT images. Our model was better at detecting larger lesions and those with higher standardized [^{18}F]DCFPyL uptake values, but it struggled with low standardized [^{18}F]DCFPyL uptake value lesions and those situated farther from the bladder. We found that using a weighted Dice loss approach, coupled with a well-chosen neural network architecture and an optimal number of neighboring slices, can significantly improve the model's performance.

Our findings revealed that standard neural network architectures are capable of detecting and segmenting large and high-intensity lesions with moderate success. However, the real challenge lies in accurately segmenting small or low-intensity lesions. We introduced the weighted Dice loss function, designed specifically for lesion segmentation, as a promising approach to improve the detection of these small lesions. We found that the weighted Dice loss function performs better when smaller batch image sizes are used.

Our research also examined the ability of models to detect lesions with low standardized uptake values. We found that the models performed well when standardized [^{18}F]DCFPyL uptake values were above 5.0, but poorly when they were lower. The likely causes for this poor performance include high image noise and patient-to-patient variability in uptake levels. Further, lesions appearing closer to the bladder were more difficult to detect, aligning with guidelines that suggest reducing bladder activity might improve lesion detection.

Our results suggest that lesion detection could benefit from including contextual information from healthy organs. This approach might incorporate a multi-target model capable of segmenting not only metastatic lesions but also the bladder, which may offer a better context for the neural network models. Supporting this approach are findings from prior work that found improved segmentation performance when multiple organs were targeted when evaluating prostate-specific membrane antigen PET images.

We found that lesion volume also plays an important role in detectability. Smaller lesions are harder to detect, but this is also strongly correlated with their low standardized [^{18}F]DCFPyL uptake values. Thus, improving the detection of lesions with low values will likely also improve the detectability of small lesions.

Future work should focus on improving the detection of lesions with lower standardized [^{18}F]DCFPyL uptake values by designing custom loss functions that take into account lesion intensity, using additional data augmentation techniques, and reducing the number of false lesions by developing methods to better separate signal from noise.

One limitation of our study is that we used data from a single medical center. As more datasets become available that span medical centers, researchers should be able to develop deeper insights into the relationships between lesion size, intensity, and detectability of theses cancers.

Despite these limitations, our research provides a foundation for future work in this area. Future efforts should build specially tailored models that could discriminate more effectively between signal and noise, include multi-scale contextual information, and be trained on a more extensive and diverse dataset. The ultimate goal is to improve the automation process for lesion segmentation and quantification, thereby enhancing the diagnosis, treatment, and outcomes for prostate cancer patients.

What We Learned

We addressed the challenge of automating the identification of metastatic lesions in prostate-specific membrane antigen [^{18}F]DCFPyL-enhanced PET/CT images for patients with metastatic prostate cancer. The task of identifying these lesions is labor-intensive, especially for those with moderate to advanced stages of the disease.

Our focus was on determining whether neural networks could be useful in detecting and segmenting these lesions.

We found that the models we developed are useful, but imperfect. Several lesion characteristics affected model performance. But our work demonstrated that metastatic prostate cancer lesions can be detected and segmented using deep convolutional neural networks and that this provides first performance estimates of commonly used network architectures.

Radiology is an expensive component of healthcare delivery. Humans can make errors in identifying radiological lesions, and those errors can delay diagnosis and appropriate treatment. Human errors may be facilitated by human fatigue and lack of signal—radiologists have busy days, and they spend much of those days scanning images that are normal.

While artificial intelligence will never replace radiologists, it may improve their efficiency and effectiveness. In this example, by identifying likely lesions, artificial intelligence could help radiologists focus their attention on those areas of the PET or CT scan that are likely to have metastatic lesions, as identified by the model. By focusing on high-risk areas, radiologists might be able to review more scans, be more accurate in their diagnostic efforts, and accelerate treatment.

The full article on which this summary is based is:

Xu Y, Klyuzhin I, Harsini S, Ortiz A, Zhang S, Bénard F, Dodhia R, Uribe CF, Rahmin A, Lavista JM. "Automatic segmentation of prostate cancer metastases in PSMA PET/CT images using deep neural networks with weighted batch-wise Dice loss." *Computers in Biology and Medicine* 2023; 158: 106882. doi: 10.1016/j.compbiomed.2023.106882.

Chapter 26
Screening Premature Infants for Retinopathy of Prematurity in Low-Resource Settings

—*Anthony Ortiz, Juan M. Lavista Ferres, Guillermo Monteoliva,
and Maria Ana Martinez-Castellanos*

Executive Summary

Retinopathy of prematurity (ROP) is a vision-threatening disorder affecting premature infants. Because of medical advancements, more prematurely born children survive, causing the incidence of ROP to rise. ROP is treatable: pediatric ophthalmologists can use lasers to stop abnormal vascular development that can otherwise lead to retinal detachment, visual impairment, and blindness. Usually, pediatric ophthalmologists are needed to screen for ROP as well as treat it; however, these specialists are exceedingly rare, particularly in low-resource settings.

Here, we describe the development of a three-step process that can be used by lightly trained personnel—who are not pediatric ophthalmologists—to screen premature infants for ROP. Using a smartphone's camera, the trained personnel can capture a video of the infant's retina and upload the video to our application that immediately determines whether the video contains adequate frames of retinal images (so that the videographer can obtain another video, while the patient is there and prepped for videography, if there are no good images). The application then uses the best obtained retinal images to determine the probability that the image indicates ROP and provides that information to a pediatric ophthalmologist for further diagnostic workup, if warranted. Because ROP can develop over time, using unique patient identifiers, measures of ROP probability can be collected throughout infancy, while the child is susceptible. Since the purpose of our work was to screen patients for further evaluation by scarce specialists, results are always validated by a pediatric ophthalmologist. Because it is worse—from a patient care perspective—to miss an ROP case than it is to raise a concern about ROP when there is low probability of ROP, we optimized our ROP model for sensitivity, which measures the proportion of ROP patients who were correctly determined to have ROP. We found that our model outperformed pediatric ophthalmologists on that measure. Therefore, we were able to create a process that could use video input from trained—but not highly skilled—healthcare workers to screen patients for ROP in an efficient and effective way, thereby essentially extending the pediatric ophthalmologist workforce. Our work demonstrates how artificial intelligence–informed models can be trained to assist the diagnosis and treatment process, expand screening in low-resource settings, and better use scarce resources like pediatric ophthalmologists.

Why Is This Important?

Retinopathy of prematurity (ROP) is a vision-threatening disorder affecting premature infants. It results from abnormal retinal vascular development. In later stages, fibrovascular proliferation leads to retinal detachment, visual impairment, and blindness. ROP has become the leading cause of preventable childhood blindness throughout the world.

There is a significant increase in ROP cases across the globe, particularly in the Global South. This is a result of improvements in maternal and infant health. ROP primarily affects premature infants weighing 2 ¾ pounds (1,250 grams) or less who were born before 31 weeks of gestation (a full-term pregnancy has a gestation of 38–42 weeks); historically, these babies had low rates of survival. However, because of improvements in medicine and healthcare, many more babies are surviving prematurity. There are treatments available for ROP and, if detected and treated early, blindness is preventable.

To enable timely intervention, a screening and monitoring system has been implemented for infants at risk of developing ROP in most developed countries. In the United States, the initial screening occurs within the first four weeks after birth with regular weekly examinations needed until it becomes evident either that the eyes will not develop a condition requiring treatment or treatment is required. Treatment should be administered within 48 hours of recognition of ROP, as ROP can progress rapidly.

That treatment—laser application to the areas of concern in the retina—must be performed by a pediatric ophthalmologist, which is a rare type of specialist that treats eye disorders. As of March 2022, in the United States, four states and 90 percent of counties had no pediatric ophthalmologists. The situation is considerably worse in developing countries—particularly in Latin America where the incidence of ROP is rising quickly. There, pediatric ophthalmologists are even more scarce, and access to expensive indirect ophthalmoscope devices, required to obtain retinal images for screening, is extremely limited.

Here, we sought to develop an artificial intelligence–assisted solution to help screen prematurely born infants for ROP. We did so using video imagery of the patients' eyes captured with widely accessible cellphone cameras using low-cost magnifiers. Figure 26.1 shows how the videos are collected.

We applied a machine learning process to each frame of the video that detects and crops the retinal image and then selects the

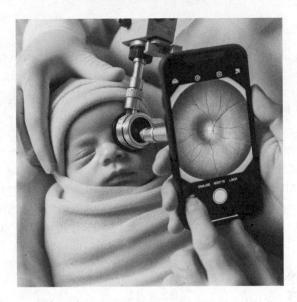

Figure 26.1 Procedure followed to capture a video of the retina using a low-cost magnifier and a cellphone (Hanh Pham, Orbis International / www.cehjournal .org/article/retinopathy-of-prematurity-it-is-time-to-take-action / last accessed 19 December, 2023).

best images. The best images are then analyzed using an image classification model to predict a probability of presence of ROP in the frame. The original video, along with the best retinal images and the model's probability output, is shared with a pediatric ophthalmologist for further evaluation.

Our work represents the first video-based ROP screening solution available in low-resource settings. Our solution allows for ROP screening in areas where there is no access to a pediatric ophthalmologist, since anyone trained to do so can collect the videos, thereby substantially increasing access to ROP screening.

Methods Used

We developed a multi-step analytic workflow that extends from evaluation of collected raw cellphone videos through cropped images to generation of ROP screening results. The solution includes three main components: a retinal image frame selector, an ROP classifier, and a mobile application for interaction with doctors (see Figure 26.2).

Retinal Image Selector

In this phase, our machine learning algorithm examines all frames of the smartphone–collected video and identifies the highest-quality ones, which are then used for ROP probability analysis. First, all video frames are extracted from the raw mobile videos at a specific sampling rate; the individual color video frames are converted to gray scale. Since the magnifiers used for video collection are circular, we used the Circle Hough Transform process to conduct a search of all circles within a frame in a learned radius range. The transformed image is then used to determine the parameters of a circle when several points that fall on the perimeter are known. A circle with a radius and center can be described with parametric equations and can determine the length of the circle's radius, allowing identification of the circle's center.

We then identify good retinal images based on what we know are correct circular dimensions. If we find no circles with the expected dimensions, the frame is disregarded. If multiple circles are detected, those with parameters that are closest to that expected are selected. Using the identified center of the circle, the circle's parameters, and its radius, the machine learning tool crops the retinal image from the original color video frame and resizes it to a fixed 256x256-pixel-sized image.

Some of the circles detected using this process will not be retinal images. To ensure that only retinal images are collected, using a dataset collected for this particular task, we trained an image classifier that used a ResNet network architecture to determine whether the image was a retinal image. The output of this phase is a set of fundus images like the one shown on the right side of Figure 26.2.

ROP Classifier and Model Calibration

The retinal images from the previous step are then sent to an ROP image classifier. To arrive at our final process, we constructed multiple classification models, optimizing them for recall, meaning that we

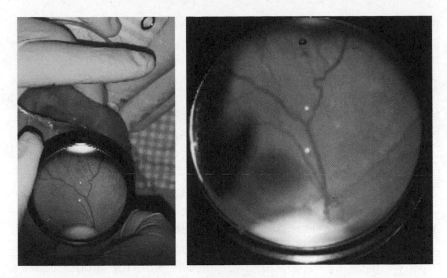

Figure 26.2 A retinal image as seen in the smartphone-based video collection process (left) and a retinal image that was cropped using our analytic pipeline (right).

sought to minimize the frequency of false negatives (images that the model would indicate that the child did not have ROP when, in truth, the image suggested that the child did have ROP). We trained image classifiers using Adam optimization with binary weighted cross-entropy loss until there was convergence, using a learning rate of 0.0001. During training, we used multiple data augmentation techniques, including image rotation, horizontal and vertical flips, and image jittering. Since the predicted probabilities of the image classifier did not reflect the true probability of ROP, we used Temperature Scaling to calibrate output so that it generated the correct probabilities.

Mobile ROP Application Development

To help pediatric ophthalmologists in low-resource settings screen for ROP, we developed a mobile ROP screening application. The application lets those trained to collect the videos from the baby's eyes with their smartphones, upload the video using the application, process the video using the retinal image selector, and then classify the best frames with a probability that they demonstrate ROP. Each selected retinal image and the predicted probability of ROP are sent to a pediatric ophthalmologist. They can then use the application to examine the retinal image in detail and make a final determination for further intervention, if needed. Because each patient has a unique patient identifier, multiple analyses can be conducted over time for monitoring purposes.

To evaluate the accuracy of our process, we conducted experiments using a dataset of videos collected by doctors in Colombia, Mexico, and Argentina. The dataset included 56 videos from 28 patients with ROP and 28 healthy patients. For model validation, we used 12 videos of those videos, and for model testing, we used 459 videos collected by partner doctors. All videos were anonymized. From these videos, two independent frame datasets were created: a frame selection dataset and an ROP classification dataset for analysis.

- **Frame selection dataset.** We iteratively created a frame selection dataset using 370 frames from the train videos and 100 frames from the validation set. We trained our frame selection classifier and used its prediction results from both train and validation videos to add training samples in a hard negative mining fashion. We then evaluated the final frame selection model using the entire set of test videos.
- **ROP classification dataset.** With the help of a team of pediatric ophthalmologists from Colombia, Mexico, and Argentina, we created an ROP classification dataset consisting of 2,227 retinal images that were obtained from the video dataset using the frame selection model. These images were labeled by the ophthalmologists as having or not having ROP. For analytic purposes, the dataset was split as follows: 1,664 train (657 healthy, 1,007 ROP), 272 validation (112 healthy, 160 ROP), 291 test (122 healthy, 169 ROP).

Findings

First, we evaluated the effectiveness of the frame selection pipeline. The goal of the frame selection pipeline was to obtain a useful set of retinal images from each video. To the pipeline's ability to do so, we applied the frame selection framework to all 456 videos from the previously described test set. A prediction was considered correct if there were clear fundus images obtained from the pipeline. When sampling from every five frames, the pipeline could obtain high-quality retinal images from 82.5 percent of the test videos; when sampling from every other frame, high-quality retinal images were obtained from 87.1 percent of the test videos. We also determined the precision of the model's performance—the proportion of all selected frames that were considered high-quality retinal images. Across all test videos, we found a precision of 97.4 percent. In practice, videos were uploaded immediately after collection; we created a feedback loop that alerts the videographer when no valid retinal images were identified so the videographer can collect a new video while the patient is still there and prepared for video collection.

We evaluated the ROP classifier across multiple scenarios. First, we tested model performance at the frame level using the ROP classification dataset and found a test accuracy of 97.8 percent, meaning that 97.8 percent of the time, our model predicted ROP in frames that had been determined by ophthalmologists to have ROP.

Second, we tested how the model performed compared to pediatric ophthalmologists at the patient level. For 50 randomly chosen patients, we ran our frame selection pipeline on their raw videos and selected the three retinal images with the highest-quality ranking from each. These frames were then randomized and shown to two pediatric ophthalmologists who are ROP experts. We compared their performance with the ROP classifier model, at both the patient and frame levels. For the patient-level analysis, if any of the three selected frames was positive for ROP, the patient was considered to have ROP. Specificity measures the proportion of non-ROP patients who were correctly determined not to have ROP, while sensitivity measures the proportion of ROP patients who were correctly determined to have ROP. Since the purpose of our work was to screen patients for further evaluation by scarce specialists, results are always validated by a pediatric ophthalmologist. It is worse—from a patient care perspective—to miss an ROP case than it is to raise a concern about ROP when there is none, so we optimized our ROP model for sensitivity. While our model was not as accurate or as specific as the human experts, it outperformed them in terms of sensitivity by a large margin (see Table 26.1).

Table 26.1 Comparison of the Performance of Our Models with Pediatric Ophthalmologists

	Patient Level			Frame Level		
	Accuracy	Specificity	Sensitivity	Accuracy	Specificity	Sensitivity
Doctor 1	71.1%	72.4%	73.3%	76.6%	78.6%	64.3%
Doctor 2	73.3%	75.9%	66.7%	75.8%	78.6%	64.3%
Doctor 3	72.9%	75.9%	68.8%	77.1%	74.2%	65.9%
Consensus	76.7%	75.9%	73.3%	78.0%	81.9%	71.4%
AI Model	66.7%	55.2%	93.3%	64.9%	64.3%	76.7%

Our mobile application could be used to upload videos at the point of care, determine whether the videos contained adequate retinal imaging for analysis, successfully display the best retinal images and an estimate that the image demonstrates ROP, all while integrating a learning feedback loop (asking the pediatric ophthalmologist for feedback and diagnosis) that will be used to further improve the model as the application is used (see Figure 26.3).

Discussion

In the face of increasing prevalence of ROP—a treatable condition that requires screening—we developed an analytic pipeline that allows for trained personnel (but not highly trained scarce medical specialists like pediatric ophthalmologists) to collect videos of

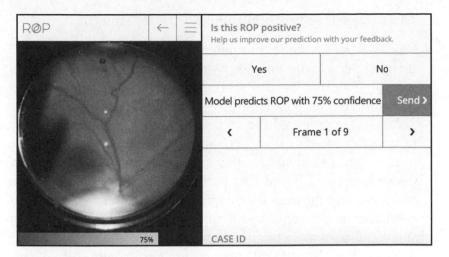

Figure 26.3   An example of our ROP mobile application output after it was used to process the video shown in Figure 26.2. The application shows the best retinal images (allowing the ophthalmologist to scan through several) and the model's probability that the image shows ROP; further, it provides a feedback loop that asks the ophthalmologist whether they think the image demonstrates ROP. That feedback will be used to enhance model performance, going forward. As each patient has a unique identifier, ophthalmologists can monitor patients for changes in ROP probability over time.

preterm infants' retinas and upload those videos to an application. The personnel then receive immediate feedback on the quality of the video (and whether it contains adequate frames of a patient's retina). Assuming there are, the process identifies the best retinal images for further processing, calculates a probability that the selected retinal images indicate that the patient has ROP, and sends the video, the best retinal images, and the calculated probability of ROP to a pediatric ophthalmologist for further evaluation and treatment.

We found that our process was usable and, while optimized to do so, was less likely to misclassify patients who had ROP than pediatric ophthalmologists (although it was less accurate than those ophthalmologists in making an ROP diagnosis).

Our study has several limitations:

- First, we used a limited number of videos and labeled retinal images to create our analytic pipeline, and these were collected in Latin America. Further work is required to assure generalizability to broader populations.
- Second, we compared the accuracy, sensitivity, and specificity of our model to only three pediatric ophthalmologists. While we randomized the images, conducted analyses at the patient and image level, and found that performance of the two ophthalmologists was quite similar, comparisons to a larger number of specialists is warranted. Our integrated feedback mechanism should help improve performance, but the model should still be objectively evaluated and compared to performance of a larger number of specialists.

Despite these limitations, we developed a highly usable process that can dramatically increase screening of ROP in low-resource settings. As screening is one of the major limitations of getting ROP treatment, by offloading the process to less scarce and less-trained personnel, our process can liberate pediatric ophthalmologists to focus more on diagnosis and treatment—something only they can do—and less on conducting screening.

What We Learned

We learned that understanding the medical process—and particularly the rate limiting steps that lead to restrictions in care access—is critical to the development of any models that will be useful in achieving the quadruple aim of healthcare: improving the patient experience; improving the provider experience; improving care access, equity, quality, and outcomes; and reducing healthcare costs.

Here, for example, we identified that screening for ROP consumes pediatric ophthalmologists' time. Like all humans, these specialists need to divide their work life tasks into different activities—in this case, for simplicity, screening and treatment. Understanding this dynamic, appreciating that pediatric ophthalmologists are a labor restriction in treating ROP (they are the only specialists who can treat ROP), and considering ways to offload the screening process to less scarce and less highly trained individuals motivated this project.

That, however, requires a profound understanding of how the screening, evaluation, diagnosis, and treatment process work. Only by partnering with the skilled professionals who do this work can new processes—ones that can be integrated into the current workflow—be developed to maximize their efficiency and effectiveness.

Too often, technologists armed with analytic tools skip this vital part in developing solutions. They create pathways or pipelines that are not easily integrated into the current workflow, that do not improve provider efficiency, and that are not designed to achieve the goals of the quadruple aim. Those solutions are doomed from the start: the only effective solution will be one that is used. And the only way to design a usable solution is to work with the end users of that solution to co-create it.

The work described here extends that described in the following book chapter:

De Kartzow AV, Acevedo PJ, Saidman G, Schbib V, Zuluaga C, Moteoliva G, Carrascal M, Salvatelli A, Patiño S, Marmol J, Lavista J, Castellanos MA. "Smartphone telemedicine networks for retinopathy of prematurity (ROP) in Latin America." In *Digital Eye Care and Teleophthamology: A practical guide to applications*. Eds: Yogesan K, Goldschmidt L, Cuadros J, Ricur G. Springer, 2023. ISBN: 2021240510.

Chapter 27
Long-Term Effects of COVID-19

—Meghana Kshirsagar and Sumit Mukherjee

Executive Summary

While there is ample information on the risk factors of having complications or dying from SARS-CoV-2 (COVID), there is less information on the long-term effects of COVID and the risks of developing them. To address this knowledge gap, we analyzed a large U.S. medical billing claims dataset to identify common long-term diagnoses and symptoms following COVID infection as well as their associations with various social and medical risk factors. From Change Healthcare—a large insurance claims processor—we obtained a dataset that included healthcare claims (including diagnostic information encoded as International Classification of Diseases, 10th revision—ICD-10—codes) as well as various social determinants of health, such as race, income, education level, and veteran status of the individuals. To identify long-term effects associated with COVID infection, we used a self-controlled cohort design observational study to identify ICD-10 codes whose proportion was significantly increased in the outcome period compared to the control period. Further, we used logistic regression to identify statistically significant relationships between social determinants of health and long-term effects following COVID infection.

Among the over 1.37 million COVID patients analyzed, we found 36 out of 1,724 three-digit ICD-10 codes to be statistically significantly increased in the post-COVID period ($p < 0.05$). We also found one combination of ICD-10 codes, corresponding to "other anemias" and "hypertension," that was statistically significantly increased in the post-COVID period ($p < 0.05$). After adjusting for comorbidities and prior conditions, we found that:

- Age and gender were significantly associated with the multiple long-term effects.
- Race was associated only with "other sepsis."
- Income level was associated only with "Alopecia areata."
- Education level was associated only with "Maternal infectious and parasitic diseases" (all $p < 0.05$).

In this large self-controlled cohort study of over one million patients, we found that age and gender were commonly associated with long-term effects following COVID infection, while social determinants of health generally were not.

Why Is This Important?

The social determinants of health—defined by the Institute of Medicine as the conditions in which individuals are born, grow, work, live, and age—influence the health of individuals and populations substantially more than does healthcare. In the United States, while age and comorbidities were associated with higher COVID mortality rates, being a member of a vulnerable population—such as a minority living in a poverty-stricken environment—substantially increased the risk of poor outcomes following COVID infection.

Understanding how the social determinants of health relate to health outcomes is challenging: data reflecting social determinants are multi-factorial, generally time-lagged, and commonly exist at geographic, as opposed to individual, levels. However, by exploring relationships that are not pre-anticipated by humans, artificial intelligence methods—including machine learning—can explore relationships between social determinants and health conditions and outcomes more effectively than traditional regression techniques.

As an example of its potential, we used machine learning and a unique dataset to examine the relationship between long-term sequelae of COVID, other health conditions, and social determinants of health. We chose to explore COVID because, between its appearance in late 2019 and March 2022, it had infected over 200 million people globally and resulted in more than 4.5 million deaths. We knew that COVID infection could cause severe primary illnesses like pneumonia and acute respiratory distress syndrome and trigger immune-mediated pathologies, including lymphopenia during the acute phase of illness. But beyond these short-term health effects, accumulating evidence suggests that COVID might be associated with long-term complications for some individuals; however, there is a dearth of information on what those long-term complications might be.

While most attempts to study long-term complications of COVID have small sample sizes, focus on specific conditions, or both, even large-scale studies and meta-studies had failed to adequately address the potential influence of social and economic factors.

To address this knowledge gap, we used claims data on a large cohort of patients who had been diagnosed with COVID to explore long-term sequelae. For the purposes of this research, long-term sequelae, commonly known as "long COVID," were defined as symptoms persisting for over two months after initial COVID diagnosis.

Therefore, by using a large dataset and machine learning algorithms, we were able to identify conditions that are significantly more likely to occur after COVID diagnosis, to pinpoint the relative timing at which conditions appeared, and to explore associations between long COVID and social determinants of health.

Methods Used

We analyzed a dataset provided by Change Healthcare that included medical billing claims that were obtained between April 1, 2018, and January 31, 2021. The dataset included over 50 million medical claims that were submitted regarding care provided to 2 million patients. These records contained pertinent details of medical encounters, such as diagnoses made and procedures performed that were encoded using the International Classification of Diseases, 10th revision (ICD-10). Around 95 percent of these claims were from commercial insurers, with the remaining 5 percent being submitted by Medicare Advantage or other plans.

The dataset included patient-level social determinants of health, including race, gender, age, income level, education level, and veteran status. Age and gender were derived from the claims themselves, while the other social determinants data were estimates based on community-level data and were available for approximately 44 percent of the patient population.

We limited our analysis to patients who had a COVID infection that was diagnosed between March 1, 2020, and September 30, 2020, as determined through specific ICD-10 codes. From an original study population of 2.7 million, 1.37 million patients remained after eliminating incomplete records. Supplementary social determinants of health data were available for 602,025 of these patients, referred to as the "SDOH cohort," while the rest constitute the "non-SDOH cohort."

We used a self-controlled cohort design, wherein post-COVID diagnosis ICD-10 codes were compared with pre-diagnosis ICD-10 codes, where the pre-COVID and post-COVID periods were both three-month-long windows. We defined the index date as the date a COVID diagnosis was first recorded in a medical claim. The pre-COVID diagnosis period ranged from ten to seven months prior to COVID diagnosis, and the post-COVID diagnosis period started two months after the index date and ended five months after the index date, or until January 31, 2021, whichever came first (see Figure 27.1).

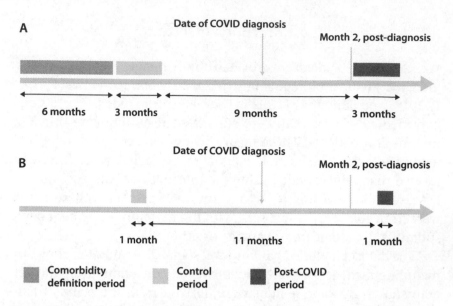

Figure 27.1 Methods for identifying cohorts examined. In A, comorbidities were identified when looking at a six-month period preceding COVID diagnosis; in B, we show that our control period was one year before the post-COVID period.

We identified comorbidities for each patient using ICD-10 codes that were submitted in their medical bills during the six months before the start of the "pre-COVID" control period. To identify potential long-term effects of COVID, we compared ICD-10 diagnostic codes from the pre-COVID period to the post-COVID period.

Further, we examined month-wise prevalence of long-COVID associated sequelae in the post-COVID period by analyzing the ICD-10 diagnostic codes in the third, fourth, and fifth months after index diagnosis.

Finally, we used logistic regression models to examine associations between social determinants of health variables and the probability of a particular long-term effect occurring, where we adjusted for comorbidities and prior health events in the control period. All independent variables used in the model were selected based on chi-square tests. While doing the association tests, the baseline categories for social determinants variables that were used to compare the various sub-populations were: "White" for race, "Completed college" for education, "Greater than $124,999" for income, "Male" for gender, "non-veteran" for veteran status, and "31–40 years" for age. Because we were testing a multiplicity of long-term effects one by one, we generated Bonferroni corrected p-values to ascertain whether associations were statistically significant.

Findings

Our cohort of 1,371,110 patients diagnosed with COVID had a mean age of 55.36 years and was predominantly female (59.44 percent of the cohort was female). Social determinants of health data were available for 43.91 percent of the cohort, with 66 percent of that subset being non-Hispanic White.

We found 36 ICD-10 codes were statistically significantly overrepresented in the post-COVID-diagnosis period when compared to the pre-COVID diagnosis period. In a cross-validation effort, we found that most of those codes were also statistically significantly overrepresented in the post-COVID period when we limited our analysis to those patients who had social determinant data available.

The codes that were overrepresented in the post-COVID diagnosis period included: ongoing pulmonary complications (viral pneumonia—ICD-10 code J12, and acute respiratory distress syndrome—J80), cardiac and thrombotic complications (acute myocarditis—I40, and other venous embolism and thrombosis—I82), diagnoses likely related to COVID treatment (intraoperative and postprocedural complications—J95), and malnutrition (including codes E43, E44, and E46) (see Table 27.1).

In addition, ICD-10 code G93.3 (post-viral fatigue syndrome) was 4.4 times more prevalent in the post-COVID period than pre-COVID. We found one set of co-occurring conditions that were statistically more common in the post-COVID diagnosis period. Other

Table 27.1   ICD-10 Codes That Were Observed in a Significantly Higher Proportion in the Post-COVID Window Compared to the Control Window

ICD-10	Description	Non-SDOH Cohort		SDOH Cohort	
		Control%	Post%	Control%	Post%
A41	Other sepsis	0.667	0.813	0.684	0.761
B49	Unspecified mycosis	0.012	0.019	0.012	0.021
B94	Sequelae of infectious and parasitic diseases	0.002	0.041	0.001	0.040
D84	Other immunodeficiencies	0.036	0.052	0.043	0.058
E43	Severe protein-calorie malnutrition	0.126	0.214	0.131	0.204
E44	Medium/Mild protein-calorie malnutrition	0.158	0.200	0.167	0.201
E46	Unspecified protein-calorie malnutrition	0.148	0.232	0.144	0.224
G72	Unspecified myopathies	0.032	0.107	0.042	0.144
G92	Toxic encephalopathy	0.090	0.112	0.093	0.111
G93	Other disorders of the brain	0.702	0.847	0.702	0.846
I26	Pulmonary embolism	0.206	0.309	0.293	0.392
I40	Acute myocarditis	0.002	0.010	0.002	0.006
I46	Cardiac arrest	0.030	0.099	0.030	0.095
I82	Other venous embolism/ thrombosis	0.419	0.484	0.539	0.574
J12	Viral pneumonia	0.055	0.938	0.055	1.110
J69	Pneumonitis	0.151	0.190	0.128	0.160
J80	Acute respiratory distress syndrome	0.018	0.127	0.019	0.137
J84	Other interstitial pulmonary diseases	0.218	0.276	0.326	0.362
J91	Pleural effusion	0.036	0.049	0.041	0.053
J93	Pneumothorax and air leak	0.036	0.067	0.040	0.070
J95	Intraoperative/postprocedural complications	0.043	0.072	0.040	0.072
J96	Respiratory failure	1.065	1.822	1.178	1.910
K94	Complications of artificial openings of the digestive system	0.085	0.114	0.054	0.093
L63	Alopecia areata	0.029	0.041	0.038	0.050

Table 27.1   *(continued)*

ICD-10	Description	Non-SDOH Cohort		SDOH Cohort	
		Control%	Post%	Control%	Post%
L64	Androgenic alopecia	0.013	0.026	0.018	0.033
L65	Telogen effluvium	0.116	0.354	0.142	0.439
L89	Pressure ulcer	0.335	0.605	0.368	0.674
M30	**Polyarteritis nodosa and related conditions**	**0.005**	**0.013**	**0.004**	**0.003**
O98	**Maternal infectious and parasitic diseases**	**0.057**	**0.079**	**0.041**	**0.045**
R13	Aphagia and dysphagia	1.077	1.249	1.069	1.168
R43	Disturbances of smell and taste	0.026	0.147	0.040	0.153
R57	Shock	0.052	0.095	0.054	0.089
R64	Cachexia	0.032	0.047	0.033	0.045
R65	Systemic inflammation and infection	0.238	0.320	0.256	0.304
R77	Other abnormalities of plasma proteins	0.042	0.077	0.048	0.084
R78	Findings of drugs and other substances, not normally found in blood	0.166	0.207	0.173	0.212

ICD-10 codes that were not significant in the social determinants of health cohort are in bold. *SDOH* means social determinants of health.

Source: Mukherjee S et al., 2022 / Springer Nature / CC BY 1.0

anemias (D64) and essential hypertension (I10) co-occurred more frequently after COVID diagnosis in both the overall and the social determinants cohort. However, over time, several of the conditions seemingly resolved (see Table 27.2).

When we explored the relationship between social determinants of health and these longer-term post-COVID diagnoses, we found that older age was significantly positively associated with most diagnoses and that gender was sometimes positively (L63) and sometimes negatively (A41 and I40) associated with post-COVID diagnoses. Social determinants were generally not associated with higher rates of particular diagnoses in the post-COVID diagnosis period (see Figure 27.2).

Table 27.2　ICD-10 Codes That Were Significantly Overrepresented in Each of Three One-Month Post-COVID Periods

ICD-10	Description	Month 3	Month 4	Month 5
D84	Other immunodeficiencies	No	No	No
L63	Alopecia areata	No	No	No
B49	Unspecified mycosis	Yes	No	No
G92	Toxic encephalopathy	Yes	No	No
I82	Other venous embolism/thrombosis	Yes	No	No
J69	Pneumonitis	Yes	No	No
J91	Pleural effusion	Yes	No	No
K94	Complications of artificial openings of the digestive system	Yes	No	No
M30	Polyarteritis nodosa and related conditions	Yes	No	No
O98	Maternal infectious and parasitic diseases	Yes	No	No
R78	Findings of drugs and other substances, not normally found in blood	Yes	No	No
L64	Androgenic alopecia	No	No	Yes
A41	Other sepsis	Yes	Yes	No
E44	Medium/Mild protein-calorie malnutrition	Yes	Yes	No
G93	Other disorders of the brain	Yes	Yes	No
I40	Acute myocarditis	Yes	Yes	No
J84	Other interstitial pulmonary diseases	Yes	Yes	No
J93	Pneumothorax and air leak	Yes	Yes	No
J95	Intraoperative/postprocedural complications	Yes	Yes	No
R13	Aphagia and dysphagia	Yes	Yes	No
R57	Shock	Yes	Yes	No
R64	Cachexia	Yes	Yes	No
R65	Systemic inflammation and infection	Yes	Yes	No
R77	Other abnormalities of plasma proteins	Yes	No	Yes
B94	Sequelae of infectious and parasitic diseases	Yes	Yes	Yes
E43	Severe protein-calorie malnutrition	Yes	Yes	Yes
E46	Unspecified protein-calorie malnutrition	Yes	Yes	Yes
G72	Unspecified myopathies	Yes	Yes	Yes
I26	Pulmonary embolism	Yes	Yes	Yes

Table 27.2   *(continued)*

ICD-10	Description	Month 3	Month 4	Month 5
I46	Cardiac arrest	Yes	Yes	Yes
J12	Viral pneumonia	Yes	Yes	Yes
J80	Acute respiratory distress syndrome	Yes	Yes	Yes
J96	Respiratory failure	Yes	Yes	Yes
L65	Telogen effluvium	Yes	Yes	Yes
L89	Pressure ulcer	Yes	Yes	Yes
R43	Disturbances of smell and taste	Yes	Yes	Yes

Source: Mukherjee S et al., 2022 / Springer Nature / CC BY 1.0

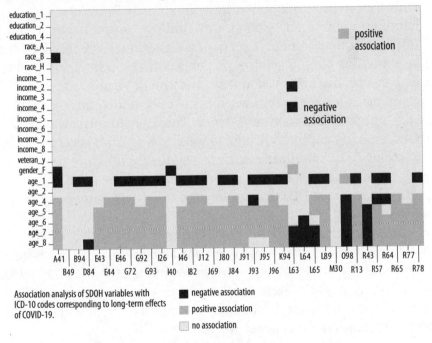

Figure 27.2   Social determinants of health variables that were statistically significantly associated with the long-term post-COVID diagnoses that we found. Age was persistently associated with post-COVID diagnoses; gender, sporadically so; and rarely, other social determinants were (dark grey means positively associated and black means negatively associated with the ICD-10 code listed on the x-axis) (Mukherjee S et al., 2022 / Springer Nature / CC BY 1.0).

Discussion

In this comprehensive study, we analyzed more than 1.37 million patients to explore the long-term health effects of SARS-CoV-2 infection. We sought to address limitations in existing research, such as small sample sizes and lack of comparison groups, by utilizing ICD-10–coded diagnoses from medical encounters.

We found several relationships. First, we found an association between SARS-CoV-2 infection and subsequent malnutrition or wasting. This finding confirms prior research showing that a substantial percentage of COVID patients lost significant body weight post-hospitalization. This finding is particularly important because malnutrition can predispose individuals to respiratory diseases, including pneumonia. Second, our findings supported that, after COVID infection, patients experience higher rates of complications like post-viral fatigue syndrome, persistent respiratory symptoms, myalgia, and disturbances in taste and smell. While some of these symptoms mitigate over time, longer-term studies are needed to determine their ultimate persistence. Third, we found several codes that seemingly captured complications arising from severe COVID infections or hospitalizations, codes capturing pressure ulcers and enterostomy, or instance. These findings suggest that the aftermath of severe COVID extends beyond the direct damage from the virus itself.

Interestingly, we found that commonly reported complications in the literature—such as headaches, anxiety, and sleep disturbances—were not overrepresented in the post-COVID period. This finding likely reflects the limitations of using medical billing data, as opposed to electronic medical record data, in which symptoms are more likely to be recorded.

Finally, while we found that older age was associated with higher persistence of post-COVID symptoms, and age variably was associated with billing codes, we did not find that other social determinants of health variables were associated with long COVID.

Our study has several limitations:

- First, findings are associative and not causal. While our ability to use a pre-COVID period control strengthens the possibility of causality, causality cannot be assumed.
- Second, using administrative billing codes is an imperfect measure of actual disease presence; billing codes do not necessarily capture all symptoms or diagnoses revealed during a patient–provider encounter.
- Third, we studied primarily commercially insured patients; studies of patients with other insurances could generate different results.
- Finally, data on social determinants of health were available for only about 44 percent of the study population; it is unlikely that the patients for whom these data were available were randomly selected. Therefore, findings may not be generalizable to other populations.

Despite these limitations, our work addressed several gaps in the existing literature, provided compelling insights into the association between COVID and a range of subsequent health issues, and demonstrated that artificial intelligence modeling can be used in the evaluation of medical billing data.

What We Learned

We learned several lessons while conducting this study. First, particularly in the healthcare space, we learned how important it is to collaborate not only with organizations that have data (like Change Healthcare), but also with subject matter experts. Physicians have specialized knowledge that ranges from the pathophysiological process to how they bill for services rendered. This information is critical to understanding the context in which information is recorded and what the information really means.

Further, we learned that we need to partner with experts in the proper use of particular study approaches. Data science is not a panacea—we cannot dump data into a model, push a button, and get useful information. We had to manage and process our dataset to be able to derive meaningful insights from it. This included, for instance, using a control period that was one year before the assessment period—such an approach avoids seasonal variation that might have impacted outcomes (for instance, it is much more common for flu to be recorded in the winter than in the summer). While artificial intelligence techniques are useful, they are limited: they must be explainable to be useful.

Finally, we found that objective analysis of datasets can provide evidence that is antithetical to our hypotheses. We anticipated that social determinants of health data would be strongly associated with long COVID diagnoses; we did not find that. When conducting research, is important to maintain objectivity and to accept outcomes, even if they were not the ones expected.

The full article on which this summary is based is:

Mukherjee S, Kshirsagar M, Becker N, Xu Y, Weeks WB, Patel S, Lavista JM, Jackson ML. "Identifying long-term effects of SARS-CoV-2 and their association with social determinants of health in a cohort of over one million COVID-19 survivors." *BMC Public Health* 2022; 22: 2391. doi: 10.1186/s12889-022-14806-1.

Chapter 28
Using Artificial Intelligence to Inform Pancreatic Cyst Management

—*Juan M. Lavista Ferres, Felipe Oviedo, William B. Weeks,*
Elliot Fishman, and Anne Marie Lennon

Executive Summary

Pancreatic cancer is the most lethal cancer, marked by a distressingly low five-year survival rate of just over 12 percent. Over the past decades, while many cancer types have seen advancements in treatment and prognosis, pancreatic cancer continues to be tantamount to a death sentence for many patients.

A proportion of pancreatic cancer cases originate from pancreatic cysts—abnormal masses in the pancreas. While these cysts are detectable and potentially removable, their surgical removal is challenging: while the surgery's complexity and associated risks vary case by case, there is a high mortality rate in certain scenarios. Further, not all pancreatic cysts progress to cancerous states; cysts that are not pre-cancerous require much less aggressive treatment. Given the high prevalence of pancreatic cystic lesions—recent studies show that 17 percent of individuals in their 30s and over 75 percent of those older than 80 have pancreatic cysts—accurately identifying the nature of pancreatic cysts could improve care outcomes, reduce treatment risks, and reduce healthcare costs.

Our study explored the potential of an explainable boosting machine (EBM) learning model. This EBM model, trained on past surgical cases, significantly surpassed clinical guidance in discerning the cyst type. It provides a calibrated probability for each patient, guiding decisions on whether surgery is necessary, if monitoring is required, or if the patient can be safely discharged without the need for follow-up.

Our preliminary results were promising. If our findings are broadly applicable, the implementation of this model could reduce unnecessary surgeries by 59 percent while improving the accuracy of the need for surgical intervention by 7.5 percent. This advancement in predictive modeling stands to transform the clinical approach to pancreatic cysts, potentially saving lives and reducing unnecessary risk exposure through more targeted and effective interventions.

Why Is This Important?

Pancreatic cysts are surprisingly common, especially as we age, with studies showing that over 75 percent of people over 80 may have them. However, not all cysts require intervention: some are benign and harmless, while others can be precursors to pancreatic cancer. Therefore, deciding whether to monitor a cyst, remove it surgically, or simply let it be is a critical and complex decision. In the past, this decision has often been fraught with uncertainty, sometimes leading to unnecessary surgeries or, conversely, missed opportunities for early intervention in high-risk cases.

The challenge lies in the sheer complexity of factors that providers need to consider when evaluating a pancreatic cyst—from a patient's symptoms and medical history to detailed imaging and molecular markers found in cystic fluid. AI models, with their capacity to analyze and make sense of complex, diverse data and clinical features, are proving to be helpful in addressing such complex problems. These models can assist doctors in making more accurate assessments, thereby reducing the chances of both unnecessary procedures and missed diagnoses. One such model, called the Multivariate Organization of Combinatorial Alterations (MOCA), has shown promise in better categorizing these cysts.

Recent advancements in AI can generate models that not only provide predictions but also present explanations that are understandable to doctors. These *glass-box* models offer insights into why a certain management path is recommended, enhancing trust in and understanding of the model's recommendations. Here, we sought to use these newer methods to determine whether they can better guide the right treatment decisions and potentially avoid unnecessary surgeries, which not only pose risks to patients but also strain healthcare resources.

Methods Used

We used a publicly available dataset involving 862 patients with pancreatic cysts that was collected in various international centers. These cases included a mix of non-malignant and malignant cysts. In all cases, the whole pancreas was removed and data included pathological analysis of cystic fluid. We divided this dataset into two equal parts: one for training our AI models and the other for validating them. Our comparison benchmarks included pathological diagnoses, current clinical management approaches, and results from other existing models.

Our AI framework was structured around a two-step decision-making process that used two distinct AI models. These models

were designed to inform the best course of clinical management—be it surgery, monitoring, or discharge—for patients with
a pancreatic cyst. The first model considers information obtained
before collecting cystic fluid for further analysis—itself a potentially avoidable procedure with some morbidity and cost (the left
side of Figure 28.1). At that point in the clinical pathway, the
cyst has been discovered through radiography and so only information on cyst size, location, and number—as well as clinical
and demographic information from patients—is available. The
second model leverages information collected after cystic fluid
analysis (the right side of Figure 28.1). Then, additional information derived from cystic fluid obtained through biopsy is used in
a second model to predict pancreatic cyst type and, therefore, the
suggested clinical pathway.

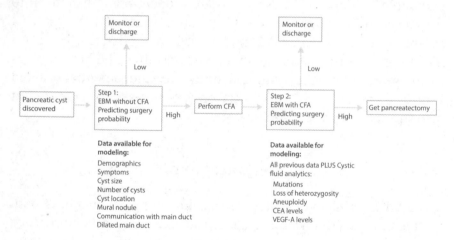

Figure 28.1   Two-step clinical management approach based on an AI model
without cystic fluid analysis (CFA) (left) and a model including results from
CFA (right).

The core of our AI models is based on an advanced machine
learning technique known as explainable boosting machines
(EBMs). EBMs, which are evolved versions of Generalized Additive Models (GAMs), are particularly suited for clinical applications due to their ability to integrate and learn from complex data

while providing clear explanations for their predictions. These models are adept at identifying and quantifying the influence of various factors on the predicted outcomes, ensuring that the predictions are not only accurate but also understandable. A key feature of our EBMs is their capability to provide calibrated probabilities for each outcome, making them highly reliable and clinically relevant.

The final stage of our study involved an evaluation of the accuracy of our AI models. We compared the first model, based solely on clinical data obtained before a cystic fluid biopsy, to established clinical care standards. We used various statistical tools to compare the second model (which included information obtained from the pancreatic cyst fluid analysis) to results generated from the MOCA model.

Findings

Comparing our EBM model to current clinical management practices showed that the EBM model, even without considering cyst fluid analysis (CFA), outperformed current clinical practice in most aspects (see Table 28.1). Our EBM model had higher sensitivity, specificity, and overall accuracy in identifying patients who either require surgery or can be safely monitored. Specifically, the EBM model's accuracy for the clinical decisions of monitoring and surgery were 0.71 and 0.66, respectively, surpassing that of current clinical management (0.62 and 0.58, respectively). However, when identifying individuals with benign cysts suitable for discharge, current clinical management shows a slight edge over the EBM model. The addition of CFA features substantially improved our model's performance with sensitivity increasing from 3 to 46 percent for patients who could be discharged, while maintaining 100 percent specificity (right side of Table 28.1). Additionally, sensitivity increased from 49 to 75 percent for patients requiring monitoring, while specificity for patients requiring surgery increased from 46 percent to 75 percent.

Table 28.1 Comparison of the EBM Model (With and Without CFA) to Recommended Current Clinical Management Guidelines

Model	Current Clinical Management			EBM			EBM with CFA		
	Sensitivity	Specificity	Accuracy	Sensitivity	Specificity	Accuracy	Sensitivity	Specificity	Accuracy
Discharge (n=68)	0.19	0.99	0.86	0.03	0.99	0.84	0.46	1	0.91
Monitoring (n=185)	0.34	0.83	0.62	0.49	0.88	0.71	0.75	0.88	0.82
Surgery (n=168)	0.88	0.38	0.58	0.95	0.46	0.66	0.94	0.75	0.82

We also compared our EBM model with CFA to the MOCA model with CFA (Table 28.2). Using the same cohort for each model, our EBM with CFA model was more sensitive, specific, and accurate than the MOCA model in managing patients requiring monitoring or surgery. The largest improvement was in the sensitivity for monitoring cysts (from 48 to 71 percent) and specificity for surgery (from 59 to 72 percent). However, MOCA slightly outperformed our EBM with CFA model in identifying patients with cysts suitable for discharge (63 percent, compared to 53 percent for the EBM model).

Table 28.2   Comparison of the EBM Model to the MOCA Model, Including CFA Results

Model	MOCA with CFA (n=342)			EBM with CFA (n=342)		
	Sensitivity	Specificity	Accuracy	Sensitivity	Specificity	Accuracy
Discharge (n=51)	0.63	1	0.94	0.53	1	0.93
Monitoring (n=139)	0.48	0.87	0.71	0.71	0.93	0.84
Surgery (n=152)	0.91	0.59	0.73	0.97	0.72	0.83

When compared to standard clinical care, application of the EBM model with CFA in a cohort of patients who underwent surgical resection could potentially have reduced unnecessary surgeries by 59 percent, increased correct surgeries by 7.5 percent, improved identification of patients needing monitoring by 122 percent, and better classified patients safe for discharge by 138 percent.

Discussion

We applied newer AI methods to an existing dataset and found that the models we used performed better than old models and—if widely applied—might provide better diagnostic accuracy and avoid a substantial number of unnecessary surgeries. One of the most appealing aspects of the EBM model we developed is its "explainable" or "glass-box" nature. Unlike other machine learning models, such as deep neural networks, the EBM model provides a clear and transparent explanation of how it arrives at its predictions. This feature is invaluable in a clinical setting, as it allows healthcare professionals to understand and verify that the model's predictions align with clinical reasoning. Additionally, the EBM model does not simply offer binary outcomes: it provides a probability vector for each possible outcome for an individual patient. This offers clinicians and patients a more nuanced understanding of the model's operation and the uncertainty involved in clinical decision-making.

However, our study has several limitations:

- The dataset we used, despite being the largest publicly available one for pancreatic cystic lesions, suffers from a limited sample size, particularly for less common types of cysts.
- Moreover, all patients in the dataset underwent surgical resection, which, while advantageous for using surgical pathology as a benchmark, also means the dataset may not be representative of the general patient population undergoing surveillance. This highlights the need for larger, more diverse datasets that include both patients under surveillance and those undergoing surgical resection.
- Additionally, the explanations provided by our model are predictive rather than causal, indicating that the observed trends could be influenced by unaccounted factors. As AI models evolve and are trained on larger datasets, it will be important to continually assess the relevance and accuracy of their feature importance and align them with clinical judgment.

In conclusion, we developed and evaluated two AI models that used either clinical features alone or in combination with CFA. These models were more accurate in recommending the best clinical management strategy—be it discharge, monitoring, or surgery—than either current clinical management or older AI models.

Our EBM model, in particular, provides a transparent and understandable approach, allowing both doctors and patients to comprehend the basis of clinical management recommendations. Importantly, the use of the EBM model with CFA has the potential to enhance the management of at least 25 percent of patients, illustrating the significant impact AI can have in healthcare.

What We Learned

We learned that AI, particularly EBM models augmented with CFA data, can significantly improve decision-making in the management of pancreatic cysts. Given the high prevalence of pancreatic cysts and their potential to progress into cancer, this is an important contribution. Further, this work demonstrated the potential of integrating AI into clinical decision-making, thereby allowing for a more precise, personalized approach to patient care. Further, the EBM model's ability to provide understandable explanations for its predictions fosters trust and clarity in clinical decision-making.

We also learned about the importance of collaboration in medical research. The publicly available dataset that we used, which included diverse patient profiles, was instrumental in training and validating our AI models. The ability to leverage AI expertise with clinical expertise underscores the significance of pooling resources across institutions to tackle complex medical challenges. By pursuing a collaborative approach, we were able to develop a model that not only performs with higher accuracy than existing clinical practices but also offers a broadly applicable solution to managing pancreatic cysts.

We also learned the potential role of using advanced AI models like EBM to transform healthcare practices. Our study demonstrated that integrating AI into clinical decision-making could lead to more effective, efficient, and personalized patient care. This is especially significant in fields like oncology, where early and accurate diagnosis can improve patient outcomes, but also over-diagnosis and over-treatment can worsen them. This blend of technology and medicine is a promising direction for future healthcare innovations and has the potential to improve care quality while reducing waste and unnecessary risks in medicine.

Importantly, our EBM model's "glass-box" nature offers insights into the *why* behind the model's recommendations, aligning closely with clinical reasoning. We found that such transparency is vital in healthcare, where understanding the rationale behind a decision can be as important as the decision itself. We also learned that larger, more diverse datasets and continuous model evaluation will be needed to keep pace with the rapidly advancing field of AI.

In the future, integrating AI models into clinical practice can result in more precise, personalized care. Developing models that provide a nuanced understanding of optimal clinical care pathways can enrich the doctor–patient relationship and ensure that each patient gets the care and information that is right for them. This is particularly important in conditions like pancreatic cysts, where risks of both unnecessary intervention and misclassification are high. As AI continues to evolve, its potential in guiding and improving healthcare decisions will become valuable, embodying the true spirit of AI for Good.

For Trevor Noah's review of this project and other commentaries, visit: https://aka.ms/AI4GThePrompt.

Chapter 29
NLP-Supported Chatbot for Cigarette Smoking Cessation

—*Jonathan B. Bricker, Brie Sullivan, Marci Strong,*
Anusua Trivedi, Thomas Roca, James Jacoby,
Margarita Santiago-Torres, and Juan M. Lavista Ferres

Executive Summary

Globally, cigarette smoking accounts for 8 million premature deaths and 25 percent of all cancer deaths annually. Despite progress made by government policies, anti-smoking campaigns, and shifting norms, existing public health interventions continue to have very modest treatment engagement and cessation rates. Conversational chatbots are becoming ubiquitous in society. They use natural language processing (NLP)—usually in the form of large language models (LLMs)—to understand user questions and provide conversational responses. Yet whether they are potentially more effective than current standard public health interventions for increasing treatment engagement and helping adults quit smoking has not been examined.

Here we describe the three-year process (2020 to 2023) that lead to the development of a chatbot for smoking cessation capable of answering user's specific clinical questions about quitting smoking. We created the core conversational feature of a chatbot for smoking cessation, called QuitBot, by generating a training bank of 11,000 user questions and clinician answers from linguistic analysis of questions from adults who wanted to quit smoking, call and chat-log transcripts from previous interventions, and chatlog transcripts from the U.S. National Cancer Institute Call Center. We then tested the capabilities of different NLP approaches for answering the questions from our training bank.

Comparing four common NLP approaches—Azure QnA, ParlAI, DialoGPT, and GPT-3—we found that Azure QnA performed well in handling questions present in our predefined question/answer pairs library. On the other hand, our fine-tuned GPT-3 performed better in handling questions beyond the boundaries of our existing library. Adults who smoke (N=14) were recruited to provide feedback on the QuitBot prototype over a period of 14 days. They expressed a preference for structured clinical conversations; however, they noted that the free-form chats required additional fine-tuning to enhance comprehension of the posed questions. We fine-tuned the free-form chat feature by iterating on smoking-context contextualizing parameters of Curie GPT-3, followed by GPT-3.5. After completing the fine-tuning process, we conducted a randomized trial involving a nationwide sample of adults in the United States who wanted to quit smoking, randomizing patients to either QuitBot or the NCI's SmokefreeTXT, which primarily provides one-way preprogrammed texting. Preliminary results from the trial (N=1182) show that QuitBot's engagement exceeds that of typical human clinician-delivered interventions. QuitBot has the potential to improve existing public health cessation interventions—with application to changing multiple health behaviors.

Why Is This Important?

Globally, cigarette smoking accounts for 8 million premature deaths and 25 percent of all cancer deaths annually. Despite progress made by government policies, anti-smoking campaigns, and shifting norms, existing public health interventions continue to have very modest treatment engagement and cessation rates, with a disproportionately low impact on marginalized communities. Marginalized populations, synonymous with vulnerable or disadvantaged groups, are segments of society facing systemic disadvantages and barriers in accessing resources and opportunities. These groups, marked by factors such as racial or ethnic minority status, sexual or gender identity differences, low education and income levels, higher unemployment rates, and increased prevalence of mental illness, encounter discrimination, social exclusion, and limited influence in decision-making processes. The treatment engagement and efficacy challenges are compounded by there being an insufficient number of trained clinicians and significant barriers, such as cost and lack of insurance, hindering access to existing clinician-delivered interventions. Consequently, there is an enormous need for high-impact, cost-effective population-level interventions for smoking cessation.

For the past 20 years, mobile phone–delivered text messaging interventions have been a prominent technology used to address this need. Usually provided to users for free, text messaging interventions provide automated and proactive advice timed according to a quit date and on-demand keywords for obtaining help for common problems (including having cravings, needing motivation, or having just relapsed). Text messaging smoking cessation interventions have high potential reach: 95 percent of U.S. adults own mobile phones and 85 percent own smartphones. Text messaging is the most common activity of mobile phone owners: 90 percent send text messages at least daily. Given their accessibility, each year smoking cessation text messaging interventions are reaching over 300,000 U.S. adults who smoke and 6 million adults who smoke worldwide.

While text messaging has significant population-level reach, these interventions yield very modest quit rates. The largest trial of text messaging for smoking cessation (N=5800), with 95 percent six-month outcome data retention, reported that the biochemically verified overall six-month abstinence rate was a modest 10.7 percent. Meta-analyses show that text messaging interventions have a weighted average 20.2 percent short-term quit rate (e.g., three-month follow-up) that drops to 8.4 percent by a 12-month follow-up. Like all widely available technologies for smoking cessation (e.g., websites and smartphone apps), a major contributor to the modest effectiveness of text messaging is their low user engagement. Thus, the scientific premise of this project was that text messaging, like all widely available technologies for smoking cessation, has modest quit rates driven largely by low engagement.

The challenge with text messaging lies in its rule-based nature, often limited to one-way interactions. Most commonly, users are sent prewritten text messages each day. In instances of two-way interactions, typically initiated by the user (e.g., user texting the word "CRAVE"), the response from the program is a prewritten message from a library of texts—not reflective of how humans communicate in everyday interactions. This communication structure lacks a conversation tailored to the users' unique challenges and barriers to behavior change.

This is a critical shortcoming because a well-documented finding from research on human-delivered treatment is that the therapeutic conversation is a powerful driver of patient engagement. That conversation, which forms a social-emotional bond with the user, has predicted treatment engagement and, in turn, outcomes across a range of treatments and settings.

Fortunately, a new technology provides a therapeutic conversation to address the problem of engagement impacting text messaging and other digital technologies. Advances in machine learning, natural language processing (NLP), and cloud computing are now making it possible to create and widely disseminate *conversational agents* (CAs), which are computer-powered digital coaches designed to form long-term social-emotional connections with users through conversations. CAs can enhance engagement through an informal therapeutic conversational style, with interactions tailored to users' unique barriers to quitting. CAs are designed to be supportive and empathic, offering reflectively listening, personalized responses, and timely advice aligned with the user's individual needs. CAs only require a text response to operate, thereby making them ideal for all individuals who smoke, including those with low technology literacy. Overall, CAs offer a low-cost solution, are accessible at any time, and have the potential for high population level reach.

In this project, we created the core conversational feature of a smoking cessation chatbot, named QuitBot, with the aim of improving engagement and smoking cessation efficacy over and above current standard public health clinical interventions—both in the United States and worldwide. Our project goal was to build a main function of QuitBot that would allow users to ask freeform and open-ended questions about quitting cigarette smoking and for the QuitBot to respond with accurate, concise, professional, and non-repetitive answers.

Methods Used

Development of QuitBot's question and answer (QnA) feature that allows users to ask free-form questions was an iterative, three-step process.

The first step was to develop a knowledge base of QnA pairs focused on the topic of quitting smoking.

- Smoking cessation clinical data sources included the Alexander Street datasets of counseling transcripts, the National Cancer Institute (NCI) Call Center transcripts of smoking cessation coaching conversations, and transcripts of counseling sessions from the Fred Hutch Cancer Center research lab's prior intervention trials.

- The categories of smoking cessation questions spanned a wide range, including medications to aid smoking cessation, the role of vaping e-cigarettes in quitting smoking, medical consequences of smoking, staying motivated to quit smoking, triggers to smoke, barriers to quitting smoking, tips for managing cravings and withdrawal, relapse prevention, and recovery.
- For generating a diversity of QnA sources, the knowledge base was broad, drawn from Alexander Street transcripts of therapy sessions, National Cancer Institute Call Center transcripts of online live chats, Fred Hutch Cancer Center's HABIT lab cessation counseling intervention transcripts, written clinical content from HABIT lab digital interventions for smoking cessation, and manual generation of questions and answers by HABIT lab clinical team members.

We created a sequence-to-sequence (seq2seq) training model and processed cleaned transcripts, generating more than 8,000 QnA pairs specifically focused on the topic of quitting cigarette smoking. Using an iterative process, we generated 2,000 new questions posed by 32 adults interested in quitting cigarette smoking in a Prolific online survey. Additionally, our HABIT lab clinical team members generated answers to those questions. We also generated 1,000 new questions from NCI call transcripts and transcripts related to our lab's intervention research. This iterative process yielded over 11,000 QnA pairs (i.e., 8,000 plus 3,000 new QnA pairs equals 11,000 QnA pairs).

The second step was to use these QnA pairs to train a series of NLP models. The first NLP model deployed was an Azure API customized for the chatbot's six-level chat architecture that included:

- Motivations to quit smoking; triggers to smoke; and frequency of smoking.
- Dispatcher dialogue flow to interpret and route utterances to the correct target, either Azure's 8000 QnA library or a custom AI model.

- QnA-maker-based "Caring" personality chitchat to express empathy and support to the user.
- QnA-based custom "help" to respond to trigger words like suicide.
- Custom transformer-based model designed for handling chit-chat QnA scenarios in dialogues that do not align with any specific intent.
- Custom transformer-based model designed to address smoking-related QnA scenarios in dialogues that do not align with any specific intent.

We finalized and tested four neural network (transformer-based) models: one pre-existing DialoGPT chitchat model, two smoking content-trained DialoGPT models (one trained on our 8,000 QnA pairs, and one trained on NCI chatlogs), and one smoking content-trained ParlAI model.

We then obtained access to OpenAI's GPT-3, which we were able to compare in model performance with our then best-performing model DialoGPT. GPT-3 outperformed our specially trained DialoGPT. Subsequently, to further improve GPT-3 performance, we compared model options: (a) Davinci, (b) Curie, and (c) fine-tuned Curie. We concluded that the fine-tuned Curie model of GPT-3 provided the best performance.

Upon the release of GPT-3.5 (March 2022), we conducted a performance comparison with the fine-tuned GPT-3 Curie model. This evaluation involved batch testing of the questions that were not present in the QnA library, followed by a ranked review of answers. We concluded that GPT-3.5 provided better or comparable answer quality but required additional contextualizing parameters to match fine-tuned performance specifically tailored for smoking-specific content. Consequently, we employed GPT-3.5 to expand the Azure QnA library by generating variations of existing questions and answers. This procedure expanded the Azure QnA library's capacity to match a wider range of user question formulations, providing greater control over the quality of answers delivered by Quit-Bot to users.

Findings

The third step in the development of the QuitBot's QnA feature involved evaluating the results of the NLP models using both automated and manual evaluation methods, as well as user testing from adults who wanted to quit smoking. The automated evaluation employed a scoring system of entropy (pertinence) and PPL (grammaticalness) scores to rate the quality of answers generated by the NLP models. Additionally, we implemented a filtering and scoring system to enhance the QuitBot's ability to communicate when it fails to comprehend a prompt. In such cases, the QuitBot prompts users to be more specific if the confidence score for an answer falls below a certain threshold. The manual evaluation was conducted by trained raters in our HABIT lab who hand-scored the results of the models on measures of answer *accuracy* (Yes or No), *repetitiveness* (Yes or No), and *tone* (Acceptable or Needs Improvement). Answers requiring improvement underwent manual revisions and were included in future iterations of model testing.

The overall results of the automated and manual evaluations revealed that Azure QnA and the fine-tuned Curie model consistently provided the best answers. However, there was a tendency to deliver the same best answers repeatedly, resulting in a monotonous and "robotic" experience for end users. Comparison of NLP model answers to three sample questions are provided in Table 29.1.

Using this feedback, we devised a GPT-3 Ada model that served as a "gatekeeper" for the fine-tuned Curie model's outputs. We initially trained the model with the QnA pairs and scores from our HABIT lab–trained raters. Subsequently, the response from the Curie model had to meet the criteria set by the Ada model for accuracy, repetitiveness, and tone before being presented to the user. However, this layered approach did not yield performance improvements. Consequently, we revisited Step 1, creating additional training datasets to improve model performance. We used Prolific online

Table 29.1   Comparisons of Natural Language Processing Model Answers to Three Sample Questions on Quitting Smoking

---

What is the quickest way to stop smoking?

Davinci	The quickest way to stop smoking is to not start!
Curie	Tapering down is the best way to stop smoking. Quitting smoking is a process. Make a quit plan and notice what triggers you to smoke.
Fine-tuned Curie	Our program was created to give you a plan that will work for you. We start by making a quit plan. Write down what inspires you to quit smoking. Choose a quit date and start cutting back on cigarettes.
GPT 3.5	The quickest way to stop smoking is to quit cold turkey, which means stopping smoking abruptly and without any aids such as nicotine replacement therapy or medication. However, quitting cold turkey can be difficult and the withdrawal symptoms can be challenging. We found that it works best to follow the program steps: make a quit plan and notice what triggers you to smoke. Then use quit smoking medication to help with withdrawal and use our tools to help urges pass as you quit gradually. Either way, it's important to find a method that works for you and stick with it.

I smoke when I am lonely. What should I do?

Davinci	You are addicted to the nicotine in cigarettes. The only way to truly stop smoking is through nicotine replacements or prescription medications.
Curie	It's hard to feel lonely. Notice what thoughts and feelings are there, and try not smoking them away.
Fine-tuned Curie	The first step is to make a quit plan. Write down what inspires you to quit smoking. Choose a quit date and start cutting back on cigarettes. Be aware of what triggers you to smoke.
GPT 3.5	It's hard to feel lonely. Notice what thoughts and feelings are there, and try not smoking them away. Trying being a friend to yourself in that moment and do something that would be nourishing to you.

Aren't e-cigarettes similar to the nicotine inhaler?

Davinci	No, because unlike nicotine inhalers, e-cigarettes are used as simultaneous consumption of nicotine and air.
Curie	No. While e-cigarettes/vaping don't have the harmful contaminants of tobacco smoke, they are not safe.

(continues)

Table 29.1 *(continued)*

Fine-tuned Curie	They appear similar but are actually very different. The content of the nicotine inhaler is regulated by the FDA and when used stays mostly in the throat and mouth. E-cigarettes are less harmful than regular cigarettes; however, they are still addictive and contain noxious chemicals that can damage the heart and blood vessels.
GPT 3.5	Although they may look similar, the content of nicotine inhalers and e-cigarettes is actually very different. The nicotine inhalers are regulated by the FDA and the nicotine content stays mostly in the throat and mouth. The e-cigarettes are not regulated and the nicotine content can vary greatly, sometimes having more nicotine than a cigarette. They can also have other harmful substances besides nicotine. Because it is heated into a mist, the vapor goes into the lungs.

market research recruitment (N=30) to create two surveys that yielded 2,000 new questions related to quitting smoking. Additionally, we generated 1,000 new questions from the NCI call transcripts and transcripts from our lab's intervention research. The revised training dataset comprises 11,000 QnA pairs (8,000 in the prior version plus 3,000 new pairs).

In 2022, adults who smoke (N=14) were recruited to provide feedback on the QuitBot prototype over a period of 14 days. They expressed a preference for the structured clinical conversations; however, they noted that the free-form chats required additional fine-tuning to enhance comprehension of the posed questions. Based on the user feedback, we determined the final organization of the bot architecture, combining two different models (see Figure 29.1):

- Microsoft's Azure QnA maker for handling questions that matched our library of 11,000 QnA pairs. QnA maker uses the Microsoft Language Understanding framework (LUIS) that leverages transformer models for structured questions, answering with a professional personality.

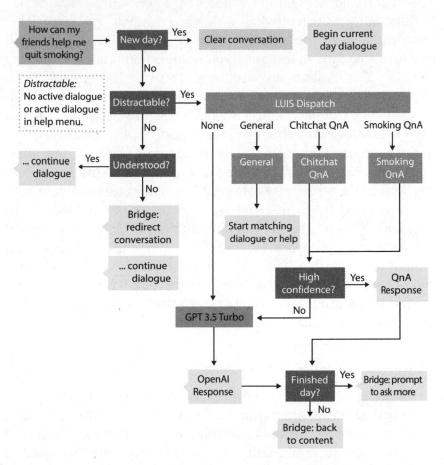

Figure 29.1   An overview of the QuitBot's architecture for handling freeform questions about quitting smoking.

- Fine-tuned GPT-3.5 Turbo model to respond to questions that extend beyond our existing library of QnA pairs. Curie answers with human-like variability, answering smoking and quitting questions like "What are the effects of secondhand smoke on pets?" accurately but with different wording variations each time.

Final Version of QuitBot

The final version of QuitBot features (a) a series of 34 days of two to three-minute structured clinical conversations, guiding participants through distinct stages of quitting smoking and (b) the ability for participants to text any freeform question related to quitting smoking. The structured conversations provide the valuable function of a clear step-by-step program for staying motivated, learning triggers to smoke, setting a quit date, and staying smoke-free. Complementing the structured conversations, the freeform question feature provides the users the freedom to ask their own questions, address unique clinical needs, and follow up on the content provided in the structured conversations. The combination of both structured and freeform conversation features is intended to balance their main strengths and limitations: the guided clinical format offers a guided program on quitting smoking, albeit with limited user question flexibility, while the open-ended format provides freedom but may encounter instances of not fully understanding the user's questions—despite the positive performance of the QnA feature thus far.

Quit Efficacy Randomized Controlled Trial

To test the efficacy of the QuitBot for cigarette smoking cessation, we launched a randomized controlled trial in July 2022. The trial design involved the random assignment of a nationwide sample of 1,520 adults who smoke daily and want to quit, to either QuitBot or the NCI's SmokefreeTXT, which primarily provides one-way pre-programmed texting. Follow-up surveys to assess smoking cessation outcomes were scheduled for each participant at 3-, 6-, and 12-months post-randomization. Currently, 1,182 adults who smoke from all 50 U.S. states have enrolled in the trial, with baseline characteristics indicating a mean age (SD) of 42.0 (9.7), 76 percent female, and 25 percent with minority race/ethnicity backgrounds. In the QuitBot arm, participant engagement metrics revealed that 98 percent have used the bot at least once, mean (SD) number of chatbot openings are 20.2 (33.4), and the number of days from the first to last use averaging 71.7 (66.1). Follow-up cessation outcome survey response rates at 3, 6, and 12 months are currently at 91.4 percent, 96.5 percent, and 91.4 percent, respectively.

Discussion

We created the core conversational feature of a chatbot for smoking cessation, named QuitBot, with a main function that would allow users to ask freeform and open-ended questions about quitting cigarette smoking and for the QuitBot to respond with accurate, concise, professional, and non-repetitive answers. We developed a library of 11,000 QnA pairs on the topic of quitting cigarette smoking. The results of our model testing showed that Microsoft's Azure-based QnA maker could handle any question that matched our library of 11,000 QnA pairs. In contrast, a fine-tuned, contextualized GPT-3.5 could answer questions that extended beyond our library of QnA pairs.

QuitBot has several key limitations that might present a challenge for users who want fast responses to their questions:

- The QuitBot was designed for users to wait until the end of the two to three-minute structured clinical conversations before they can ask freeform questions. This design element was necessary to prevent breaking the logic of each of the structured conversations, and thereby going off on tangents without an ability to return to the structured conversation. We address this design element by asking the user to hold onto their questions until the end of the structured conversation at various times throughout the program. To date, this message appears to have been effective at training the users to wait until the end of the structured conversation to ask freeform questions.
- The second major limitation is the freeform question response time latency when the GPT servers are running at capacity. While the response latency is usually only a few seconds, we

have observed some instances where it can take up to 30 seconds. We are addressing this potential delay by telling the users that it may take a moment to answer their question, so their patience is appreciated.

On the other hand, QuitBot has many strengths that have the potential to advance clinical practice to aid smoking cessation:

- To the best of our knowledge, QuitBot is the first chatbot that allows users to ask freeform and open-ended questions about quitting smoking with answers provided by a vast expert knowledge base. This technical capability has been afforded by LLMs that underlie the state-of-the-art versions of Azure QnA maker and GPT. The result is that users can obtain succinct, accurate, and informative answers to their questions that would otherwise be more difficult to glean and evaluate from Internet searches. The supportive and conversational tone of the messages has the potential to lead to a long-term social-emotional connection. Indeed, the interim trial result of a mean of 72 days from first to last use is longer than we observed in rule-based text messaging interventions for smoking cessation (which typically last about seven days) and longer than typical human clinician-delivered interventions such as telephone quit coaching (which typically last about seven days). Length of intervention engagement is a strong predictor of treatment success, so these initial results on QuitBot's engagement certainly appear promising.
- The second major strength is that the freeform QnA feature is delivered in the context of a comprehensive smoking cessation smartphone app that guides users through each major step of quitting smoking. This program is based on over 15 years of clinical treatment protocols for smoking cessation developed and tested within our research lab.

While we developed and tested QuitBot in the United States for an English-speaking audience, the program could be tailored to other nationalities and languages across the world. As a health behavioral change platform, QuitBot has the potential to be adapted to other behavior changes, including alcohol and drug use, dietary change, and physical activity.

In sum, QuitBot is a research-engineered conversational chatbot showing participant engagement that exceeds typical human clinician-delivered and digital interventions. Trial enrollment and retention have been successful to date, with trial completion and cessation efficacy results expected in June 2025.

What We Learned

QuitBot was developed in the midst of rapid changes in NLP technology, during what is arguably one of the most rapidly transformative periods of AI history (2020 to 2023). Thus, the most important lesson we learned was the value of investing time in continuing to iterate and improve on our freeform QnA feature as new NLP models were continuously being released. Indeed, when we started to develop the freeform QnA feature in 2020, NLP capabilities were primitive by current standards. Despite being based on 345 *million* parameters, we learned that DialoGPT was limited in its ability to determine the intent of our questions. By the time GPT-3.5 was released (based on 175 *billion* parameters), the performance of the freeform QnA feature was far superior, which in turn allowed us to improve on the quality of answers provided by Azure QnA.

The second most important lesson we learned is the challenge of training an NLP model for a specific clinical domain. The popular press has provided ample examples of NLPs like GPT providing very detailed answers to questions on a wide variety of topics. While much has been written about the tendency for NLP models to "hallucinate" (i.e., provide confident-sounding answers that are factually wrong or fabricated), the more common problem we encountered in our development process was in providing a sufficiently large knowledge base for the NLP to answer highly specific questions about a specific clinical domain.

In our experience, off-the-shelf NLPs are like dilettantes: they know a little bit about a lot of topics, but they do not know a lot about a given topic. From this project, we glean that this characteristic holds particularly true when the subject matter requires expertise in clinical experience and familiarity with scientific literature within a specific clinical domain. Addressing this challenge required multiple iterations of building the knowledge base of empirically supported best practices for quitting smoking. The answers need to be accurate and clinically sensitive. We suspect that a similar knowledge-building process will be required for building chatbots in any other clinical domain.

For Trevor Noah's review of this project and other commentaries, visit: https://aka.ms/AI4GThePrompt.

More information on the study that this summary describes is available at: www.clinicaltrials.gov/study/NCT04308759.

Acknowledgments: The authors gratefully acknowledge the National Cancer Institute for providing their Call Center transcripts; Tara Ward at Moby Inc. for providing technical project management; Jessica Harris, Sarah Hwang, Julie Packard, Victoria Sanborn, and Christeine Terry in the Fred Hutch HABIT Lab for supporting the QnA development; Daniella Kim at Halibut Flats for conducting user testing; the research staff at OpenAI for providing access to and technical support for fine-tuning GPT; and the research staff at Microsoft's AI for Good Lab for providing technical expertise in NLP models.

Chapter 30
Mapping Population Movement Using Satellite Imagery

—*Tammy Glazer, Gilles Hacheme, Amy Michaels,*
and Christopher J.L. Murray

Executive Summary

Population estimates are imperative for understanding the potential impact of interventions designed to address sustainability, humanitarian action, and health issues. However, population estimates are just that—estimates, ones often challenged by lack of recent and accurate census data, changing fertility rates, and migration patterns.

Here, we used a multi-step process that combined satellite data (providing information on building density), census data, and household surveys to estimate the number of people per building, as well as deep learning modeling techniques with model-based geostatistics to estimate the number of people living in the Sahel region of Africa, an area experiencing extreme effects of climate change and humanitarian crises.

While our findings are preliminary, we found our population estimates to be accurate and to be replicable in other regions. We also were able to combine the human structure maps we created with environmental data to predict risk and migration in Kenya, finding that humans in Kenya are moving away from areas of heat, rainfall, and days of extreme heat and that ecological niche is highly predictive of malnutrition there.

The methods that we developed show great promise. We learned that collaboration across institutions and the ability to leverage the expertise and data that each institution contributes is critical to addressing the world's problems.

Why Is This Important?

Today, there are more than 8 billion people on the planet—or so we think. According to the United Nations, the global human population reached 8 billion in mid-November 2022 and is expected to increase by nearly 2 billion people over the next 30 years. Population estimates, however, are just that: they represent approximations based on statistical models and available survey data and can vary substantially under different scenarios (see Figure 30.1). Knowing the exact count of people in the world at any given time presents a formidable challenge to demographers due to shifts in birth rates, death rates, and migration patterns. Censuses, which are typically conducted once every ten years, face their own limitations, ranging from non-response to changing enumeration areas. Even the most accurate population maps fail to capture urbanization between census years or to adequately describe vulnerable groups such as undocumented persons or individuals experiencing homelessness.

In an era of unprecedented natural disasters, civil conflict, and climate-induced resettlement, knowing where people live is imperative. Effective public policies and equitable resource allocation hinge on a nuanced understanding of shifting populations, globally, and in near real-time. Recently, there has been an emergence of geospatial products that attempt to infer population density using remote sensing data. Our evaluation of these datasets, however, has found today's available products to be too coarse, outdated, or imprecise for most practical applications. For instance, population maps often place people in uninhabitable areas or uniformly assign people to grid cells with known human structures. Existing population maps lack the spatial coverage, temporal consistency, and update frequency needed by governments and organizations to anticipate populations' needs or deliver essential services.

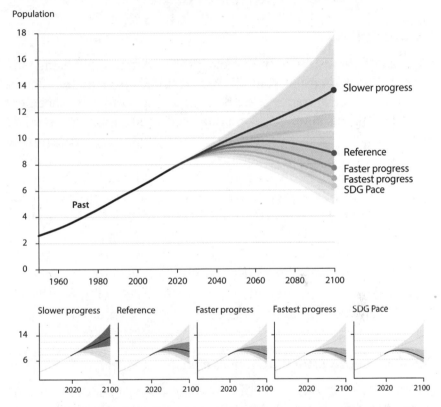

Figure 30.1   Global population projections under different scenarios of female educational attainment and contraceptive need met, 1950–2100. SDG means sustainable development goals.

The Institute for Health Metrics and Evaluation (IHME), Planet, and Microsoft's AI for Good Lab partnered to produce the first accurate, quarterly, 30-meter gridded population density maps derived from high-resolution satellite imagery. Using three-meter Planet-Scope basemaps, we combined deep learning modeling techniques with model-based geostatistics (MBG) to disaggregate populations and distribute people to human structures. The resulting global dataset marked a significant leap forward in temporal population mapping, offering unprecedented insights into human movement for a wide variety of life-saving applications.

Methods Used

Geographic Focus

We began by focusing on the Sahel region of Africa. Increasing temperatures and irregular rainfall have resulted in droughts, floods, and food insecurity across the Sahel, leading to the displacement of over 2 million people and creating a severe humanitarian crisis. Researchers at the United Nations estimate that increased temperatures, desertification, and deforestation have degraded 65 percent of farmable lands in the region. Despite historic migration patterns and resettlement, some countries in the region have not conducted a census in over ten years. These factors make understanding population dynamics in the Sahel of the utmost priority.

With this geographic context in mind, we applied a two-step modeling approach: first, modeling building density using Planet imagery, and then, estimating the number of people per structure using covariates.

Building Density Estimated from Remote Sensing Data

To begin, we estimated building density using a model that took Planet quarterly mosaics as inputs and applied building density— measured as percentage of each 30x30-meter patch covered by buildings—as labels. We used two strategies to generate labels. First, we aligned layers of three-meter resolution Planet imagery sampled across the Sahel with publicly available building footprint polygons. For this step, we combined polygons from the latest Microsoft Building Footprints dataset and Google V3 Open Buildings, totaling over 2.5 billion footprints. As of November 2023, this combined dataset represented the most comprehensive collection of building footprints available, covering 92 percent of Level 0 administrative boundaries. The Microsoft Building Footprints dataset was detected from Bing Maps images captured between 2014 and 2023, including Maxar, Airbus, and IGN France imagery. The Google Open Building dataset was detected in May 2023 imagery from an undisclosed source. As a result, it is important to note that it is often difficult to know exactly which imagery vintage was used to produce building footprints in the dataset.

For each 30x30-meter patch, we computed the percentage of area covered by buildings using the "all touched" algorithm. We began with 4096x4096-pixel scenes provided by Planet and computed the percentage of each 8x8-pixel patch covered by buildings, resulting in matrices of 512x512 pixels. Each pixel had a value between 0 (no buildings) and 1 (all buildings). In Kenya, this method produced 1,698 images, representing combined building density over a nine-year period (see Figure 30.2).

Microsoft Building Footprints Paired with Planet Mosaics

Building footprints   Planet imagery (3)   Align footprints   Building density (30m)

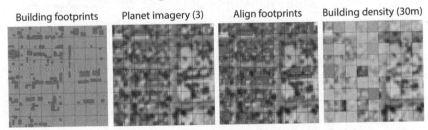

Figure 30.2   Microsoft Building Footprints paired with Planet mosaics.

In addition to this feature and label set, we leveraged an open-source dataset of Planet imagery and building footprints prepared for the SpaceNet 7 Multi-Temporal Urban Development Challenge. This dataset comprises over 40,000 square kilometers of imagery coupled with exhaustive hand-labeled building polygons, totaling over 11 million annotations. Satellite imagery was collected by

Planet's Dove constellation between 2017 and 2020, covering 101 distinct areas of interest (AOIs) with 24 images per scene (one per month). This dataset has the unique advantage of pairing footprints with image timestamps, characterizing change over time.

Given a scene, our goal was to predict coarse building density per 30x30-meter patch. To this end, we began by generating train, validation, and test splits of SpaceNet image AOIs and labels. We then trained a state-of-the-art convolutional neural network (CNN) semantic segmentation model known as U-Net on the input imagery. U-Net was designed in 2015 at the University of Freiburg and was advanced by Microsoft Research Asia to localize abnormalities in biomedical images. This architecture uses an encoder and decoder network to down-sample and up-sample feature maps and has been found to be highly performant on a variety of segmentation tasks.

Our model was pre-trained on the ImageNet dataset, used a ResNeXt-50 32x4d backbone, and had a loss function and performance metric of mean squared error (MSE) (see Figure 30.3). To minimize noise introduced by clouds, haze, and other atmospheric effects, we stacked three images per scene as model input: image at time t, image at time t-1, and label at time t-1. We experimented with hyperparameter tuning, finding that the best model performance used AdamW optimization, a 0.000562 learning rate, and a 0.1 weight decay. Finally, we used a set of test-time augmentations to smooth estimates. All experiments were performed using the PyTorch Lightning deep learning framework in Python, built on the PyTorch library.

Using this global model, we then performed regional fine-tuning. Fine-tuning the model on images from the Sahel paired with "weak" (non-temporal) labels allowed it to learn and adapt to the region's unique geography. To reduce arbitrary spikes in estimates due to variations in image brightness and cloud cover, we experimented with a variety of post-processing steps. For instance, in one experiment, we fit a piecewise step function to each pixel over time (see Figure 30.4). This step allowed us to enforce functional constraints on localized output, such as ensuring that

Building Density Modeling Pipeline

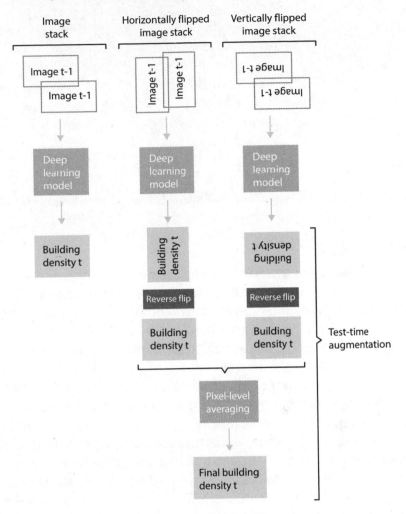

Figure 30.3   Building density modeling pipeline.

building density only fluctuated a fixed number of times within a given time span. Finally, we experimented with using a digital elevation model (DEM) and a land cover map to correct for false positives based on geographic factors, including terrain slope and proximity to water.

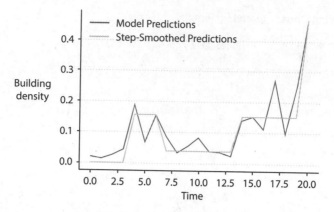

Figure 30.4   Piecewise smoothing of pixel-level building density over time.

Estimating People per Structure

Countries have conducted decennial censuses at different points in time. Depending on the country, these census tabulations are available at different administrative levels. These census tabulations are sometimes available with an associated shapefile that defines the boundaries of the relevant administrative unit. Other sources, such as household surveys with a clearly defined primary sampling unit (PSU) and a full enumeration of households and individuals in the PSU, also provide important information on people per unit area and people per human structure.

Our goal was to estimate the number of people per structure from the available data for a location in a particular year and to use this information to estimate the number of people in each structure in that year. This information could also be used to estimate the population prior to and after the most recent census or household survey. Based on the availability of data from a census or survey at different administrative levels and whether a shapefile at that level has been released, we used one of two methods.

Where disaggregated tabulations were available with information on the land area for the disaggregated administrative unit but no detailed shapefile, we estimated population per kilometer squared at the detailed level. This information was then used with

MBG to estimate a surface of population density for each country. Where time-series data were available, the MBG surface of population density was estimated in time and space. MBG models have been widely used in global health analyses. They use available data, geospatial covariates, and the correlation structure of the data over space and time to generate estimates. IHME has experience using MBG to develop fine-grained estimates of child mortality, HIV prevalence, access to clean water, malnutrition, and other health determinants (see Figure 30.5).

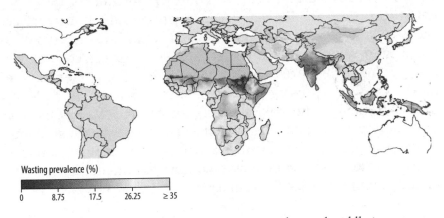

Wasting prevalence (%)

| 0 | 8.75 | 17.5 | 26.25 | ≥35 |

Figure 30.5 Local patterns of childhood wasting in low and middle-income countries, 2000–2017.

Next, the surface of population density was combined with the map of human structures to weigh each human structure by the likely number of people. This weighted quantity was then ranked into the population tabulations available at different administrative levels. In other words, areas with sparse populations and low-density human structures within an administrative level were assigned fewer people than human structures in the same administrative unit where the density surface implies more individuals should be present. Where detailed shapefiles and census tabulations were available at the fourth, fifth, or even sixth administrative levels, we used the data to directly develop an MBG surface of people per structure. As with the number of people per unit area, this MBG surface of people per structure was used with the human structures and was ranked to the overall counts for that unit. These surfaces provided an estimate of the people in human structures in the year of the census or household survey.

To estimate the population before or after a census or household survey, we used the human structures time series developed from satellite imagery. Specifically, we used the finalized surface of people per structure, reflecting both the MBG surface and ranked results from human structures and census tabulations.

This updated surface was based on two components: the original MBG surface and the ranking factors that adjusted this surface such that the number of people in each set of human structures matched the census tabulations at the most disaggregated level. We could estimate this surface backward and forward in time from the most recent census using the covariate relationships in the MBG model and holding the ranking factors constant. In this way, income growth or even climate change and its effect on people per structure could be captured. The time index surface of people per structure was then used with the time indexed map of human structures to directly estimate people living in each pixel.

Findings

As of November 2023, this project remained in progress; therefore, results remain preliminary. Our initial models and experiments, however, exhibited great promise and validated our proposed approach. For an out-of-sample test set of five distinct SpaceNet scenes across the Sahel, we achieved a mean absolute error for building density of 0.039, suggesting that building density estimates have an average error of just 3.9 percent across a variety of urban and rural settings. The following images display Planet imagery and estimates for Tindouf, Algeria, a scene in the SpaceNet test set, with clearly detected urban development between February 2018 and January 2020 (see Figure 30.6).

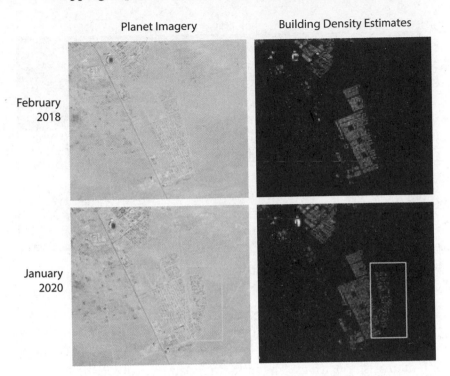

Figure 30.6   Building density estimates in Tindouf, Algeria.

To further validate building density model performance, we produced estimates over an entirely distinct landscape in the Maldives. We selected this location due to its prioritization by the United Nations Early Warnings for All initiative, which aims to ensure that everyone on the planet is protected from hazardous weather, water, or climate events through life-saving early warning systems by the end of 2027. The Maldives is vulnerable to heightened environmental risks due to its unique geography, including frequent and severe storm surges, heatwaves, extreme weather hazards, and sea level rise. While we were unable to quantify model performance without verified temporal building footprints, visual spot checking confirmed accurate estimates in high-growth areas (see Figure 30.7).

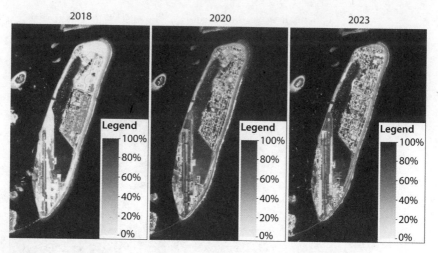

Figure 30.7 Building density growth in the Maldives, 2018–2023.

Overall, we observed a low false negative rate, suggesting that the model could successfully locate human settlements. There were, however, scenarios where our initial model occasionally detected false positives. The model tended to overpredict buildings in mountainous areas and major roadways with a similar brightness to urban centers. The model also tended to detect false positives over clouds, which is expected, as they represent noise in the input imagery. To correct for this in the future, we plan to target locations to impute building density via metadata files called Usable Data Masks (UDMs) that indicate the "usability" of each pixel in an image. Future experiments may include introducing random shadows to simulate cloud cover as a train-time augmentation, using color channel adjustments as a test-time data augmentation, and leveraging model ensembles.

We also combined human structure maps with environmental data to predict risk and migration in Kenya. We examined where people live (see Figure 30.8) and then examined population changes across three dimensions: average annual rainfall, mean annual temperature, and number of days over 30 degrees Celsius. We found

Figure 30.8   Population map in Nairobi, Kenya, 2020. This image represents the distribution of the population across Kenya, zooming in on central Nairobi, which is bordered on its southern edge by Nairobi National Park. Other unoccupied areas include golf courses, the Kenya National Air Force Base, and the Nairobi Arboretum.

very strong patterns that show humans in Kenya are moving away from high-risk combinations of heat, rainfall, and days of extreme heat. In fact, many parts of Kenya are uninhabited and likely will remain uninhabitable unless major interventions such as food aid are provided. The ecological niche is also highly predictive of malnutrition in Kenya: locations with more than 200 days over 30 degrees Celsius experience nearly five times higher rates of wasting. Combining the niche analysis with the Intergovernmental Panel on Climate Change (IPCC) modeling consortium forecasts for various climate scenarios gave an indication of which communities in the future will be living in locations that will either suffer extreme food insecurity or have to move elsewhere (see Figure 30.9).

Discussion

We used a multi-step process that leveraged satellite data, census data, and machine learning to generate population estimates in Kenya and to identify where populations are currently—or at risk of—experiencing severe climate stress.

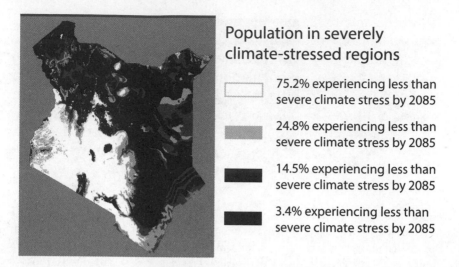

Figure 30.9   Population data in Kenya combined with climate data.

We found several advantages to our methodological approach to measure population movement. Up-to-date, detailed estimates of where people live can be provided with relatively short time lags. In routine conditions, we expect to produce these maps for the world each quarter. In the case of humanitarian crises, estimates can be updated to the most recent satellite imagery.

Additionally, our approach combines information on the presence of human structures with disaggregated census tabulations, allowing us to generate reasonable estimates regardless of the level of detail released by governments. As we obtain updated census tabulations at highly disaggregated levels along with shapefiles clearly defining the boundaries of each area counted in the census, we will be able to continually enhance our results. Survey data can be used to revise and update estimates if PSU boundaries and total population in the PSU are reported. Surveys typically provide information on sample weights, making it possible to generate estimates even when total counts are not explicitly reported at the PSU level.

As more data is added to the dataset, including locations of public facilities such as schools, clinics, hospitals, and water reservoirs, we will be able to develop highly localized risk maps. Other data streams such as mobility data from cell phones in cases where this is available can also be used to characterize where populations move and help indicate when populations have left an area, but human structures remain. Looking ahead, we plan to overlay features from the Global Burden of Disease study that characterize disease with our granular mapping of human populations, to characterize locations at the highest risk.

What We Learned

We learned that knowing where people live, where they came from, and where they are moving is fundamental for informed policy decision-making and the equitable provision of services. From evacuation planning to infectious disease containment, to characterizing the impacts of climate change, it is critical that governments and organizations have access to global, temporal, and high-fidelity population counts.

We also learned about the value of combining multiple datasets and domain experts in addressing critical issues of our day. Census data, while beneficial, often fail to capture the most marginalized, vulnerable populations—the hidden and invisible. By leveraging Planet's satellite data, IHME's expertise in population estimation, and Microsoft's AI for Good Lab's skill in creating and validating machine learning models, we were able to address a complex, persistent problem, the solution to which is foundational to innumerable uses for sustainability, humanitarian aid, and health.

Finally, we learned that this kind of work can be tremendously exciting, inspirational, and generative: we eagerly welcome further applications of these evolving building density and population maps to bridge this critical data gap.

For Trevor Noah's commentary, visit: `www.microsoft.com/en-us/research/video/the-prompt-with-trevor-noah-episode-1-ihme-population-mapping`.

Chapter 31

The Promise of AI and Generative Pre-Trained Transformer Models in Medicine

—*William B. Weeks*

Because this chapter is based on several editorials that discuss how artificial intelligence (AI)–generated generative pre-trained transformer (GPT) large language models can be used in medicine, it has a different structure than earlier chapters. We first describe what these models do and then discuss their potential application in radiology, facilitating self-care management and decision-making, and improving the public's health.

What Are GPT Models and What Do They Do?

The release of OpenAI's ChatGPT in November 2022 brought advanced AI technology to the broader public. Generative pre-trained transformer (GPT) models excel at generating natural, coherent, and grammatically accurate text, thereby significantly advancing the field of artificial intelligence. It has the potential to transform multiple industries, including medicine.

These models are trained on massive amounts of data. Essentially, they scour the data to generate the statistically next most logical and used word, considering coherence, sentence structure, and the prompt used. For instance, if you asked a GPT model to write an essay on domesticated animals, it might start with a sentence beginning, "Domesticated animals include. . ." and then, using algorithms trained on either a specified body of knowledge or the Internet, insert the next most commonly used word in a word series of that construct, in this case, perhaps, "dogs." In subsequent paragraphs, the algorithm might go on to discuss dogs, cats, and fish in more detail.

A number of applications commonly integrated into email or text applications currently serve this function, for instance, by seeing the beginning of your sentence and offering a commonly used phrase that would complete it. These models can be used to write letters or patient care notes, generate draft text for medical research manuscripts, and respond to patient queries about health conditions.

GPT Models in Medicine

GPT models have garnered significant attention in healthcare, not only from the media but also from organizations like the National Academy of Medicine, *The New England Journal of Medicine*, and the World Health Organization. These prestigious medical organizations recognize the potential of artificial intelligence to revolutionize how clinical care is delivered and medicine is organized.

There has been significant research in the medical application of artificial intelligence; however, results comparing its diagnostic abilities to those of human physicians are often inconclusive. GPT models can approach the quality of the diagnostic acumen of world-renowned physicians when examining difficult cases, pass national licensing and board exams, and provide more empathetic, thorough, and accurate responses to patient queries than can physicians assigned the same tasks. In other tasks, the models do not perform as well as physicians. Critical aspects of what promotes better performance of GPT models includes the version of GPT used (newer versions perform better), the materials on which the models are trained (training on specific medical knowledge as opposed to the Internet may achieve better performance for specific medical queries), and the comparison group used (models may perform better when compared to less trained as opposed to more highly trained providers).

The last point is critically important when one considers the documented variability in the quality of healthcare services that currently exists; it begs the question: to what level of professionals should GPT model output be compared? In the United States and developed countries, the reality is that not all doctors have the same level of performance, there are no real indicators of quality of care that are generally integrated into a patient's choice of providers, and an average patient has access to an average provider. In low and middle-income countries, care quality likely varies more. For about half of the world's population, care access is severely limited.

So, one might argue that GPT model performance should be compared to the average provider to whom an individual might have access and not to the top two or three performers in the world. If GPT models can improve care—say, from the 50th percentile (which is what one might expect the average patient to experience) to the 75th percentile, wouldn't that improve care quality for most patients?

And, recall that these models are not designed to replace providers, but to help them make the next best decision in care pathways. Medicine is a rapidly evolving field—every year, about 3 million scientific articles are published, and that number is growing by 4 percent a year. It is impossible for healthcare providers to keep up. GPT—which can be trained on the most recent scientific literature—can help providers and patients integrate current findings into treatment decisions.

GPT models are not panaceas. Just like the other AI models discussed in the book, they are limited by the quality of the data on which they are trained: if there are biases in the underlying data inputs, there will likely be biases in model outputs. Models should be deployed responsibly and ethically. The limitations of the models must be recognized: they can sometimes "fabricate" answers, which is to say that in their eagerness to complete the sentence or paragraph, the models might generate content that is not factually based.

Nonetheless, GPT models have the potential to be used to help providers, policymakers, and patients make more informed care decisions. In the following sections, we provide examples of how GPT might do so in three areas.

Radiology

GPT models can revolutionize various aspects of radiology practice, including report generation, patient and referrer communication, provision of decision support, and data analysis. While some are concerned that these models may replace radiology labor, historically, technology has been a net job creator in the radiology field. While some roles, like radiology reporting, may be streamlined, new opportunities will arise.

As has been shown elsewhere in the Health section, AI can be used to identify on which areas of a radiological exam (from a CT scan to an MRI) a radiologist should focus their attention. Radiologists spend most of their time reviewing normal exams; fatigue can impair their performance. Further, radiology is a scarce medical specialty. Artificial intelligence has the potential to indirectly expand the radiology workforce by first sorting radiological exams into those that need a radiologist's review and those that do not. Even if algorithms were selected to reduce the number of false negatives (exams identified as not being abnormal and therefore requiring additional review, when, indeed, they are abnormal and require additional review by a radiologist) perhaps half of radiologists' time spent reviewing normal exams could be made available. Further, by focusing radiologists' reviews of exams on areas that were highly likely to have pathology, radiologists might be able to put more of their effort into examining those areas carefully, instead of spending time searching for them. Reducing the amount of time that radiologists require to review a typical exam can massively expand the radiology workforce and, thereby, reduce per-capita costs of care, improve care access, and improve both the provider experience (radiologists might get more intellectual stimulation reviewing problematic and challenging parts of exams than normal films) and patient experience (patients might get results back quicker and receive reports that use more patient-friendly language).

The future of artificial intelligence in radiology could be amplified by integrating multi-modal artificial intelligence, which integrates various data types like images, text, and speech. By facilitating the use of multiple datasets, such integration can revolutionize how—and the speed with which—medical diagnoses are made and treatments are delivered. Further, integration of GPT models might revolutionize how radiologists communicate with patients. Currently, communication is through a third party: a healthcare provider (perhaps a surgeon or a primary care provider) orders a radiological exam, the radiologist reads the exam and generates a report, the report is sent to the provider who ordered the exam, and the report is posted to the patient's chart. Normally, the provider who ordered the exam will review the results with the patient. Integration of GPT models might allow radiologists to generate more easily accessible reports that are easier for patients to understand.

The role of AI in radiology is growing rapidly, offering both benefits and posing new challenges. Issues of healthcare inconsistency, documented by projects like the Dartmouth Atlas project (www .dartmouthatlas.org), show that there is ample room for improvement in the medical field; diagnostic errors currently contribute to a considerable number of deaths in the United States each year. Given these inconsistencies, GPT-generated assistance in radiological interpretation could be an effective supplement, particularly in integrating the latest medical findings and guidelines directly into clinical workflows in a way that strengthens doctor–patient relationships rather than replacing them.

Patient Self-Care Management and Informed Decision-Making

GPT models have not only demonstrated the remarkable capabilities of computing power, but they have also brought that potential to the masses. For decades, most exploration of AI models was limited to researchers and experts in the field. However, with GPT models' ability to engage users through natural language, the general population now has access to a wealth of medical information.

While we have already suggested that these models should supplement, and not replace, providers, the reality is that most care currently provided is self-care management that occurs outside of clinical settings. Over the past 100 years, due to advancements in medical technology and public health measures like sanitation and clean water, healthcare has transformed from focusing mostly on short-term diagnosis and treatment of acute conditions—like trauma or an infection—to focusing on the long-term management of chronic illnesses, like diabetes, atherosclerosis, and hypertension.

While overseen by medical professionals and guided by evidence, the management of these chronic diseases largely falls to patients. Patients need to remember to take their medications, adjust their insulin doses based on their blood glucose levels, and manage their diets and exercise patterns to reduce the long-term sequelae of their conditions. They do this on a daily basis, without contacting their providers.

But, as mentioned, new information regarding the effectiveness of particular interventions is reported daily. For example, in the past year, studies on the minimum number of daily steps, the weekly required minutes in intense exercise, and the content and pattern of caloric intake required to reduce obesity and control diabetes have been published with sometimes dramatically different findings than have previously been reported. Patients may see their providers only once or twice a year, and then only for 15 minutes or so each time—it would be challenging for them to get the most up-to-date, high-quality information during those encounters.

GPT models provide patients the same kind of access to the latest information that healthcare providers have traditionally had. Importantly, these models can convey that information in a more conversational style; they are able to expand on details about which patients are curious and allow patients to repeatedly query them, without having a time limit and in less technical ways that patients might better understand.

And, perhaps even more revolutionarily, a search for medical information no longer requires knowledge of medical terminology: patients can engage with GPT models using their own words and in their own language. GPT models have the potential to address the medical literacy gap that often interferes with adherence to guideline-recommended care.

Importantly, GPT models might also be able to provide objective evidence about treatment options for patients. This is especially true with preference-sensitive care conditions, which are common conditions that have two or more reasonable treatment options. For example, a patient with knee osteoarthritis might reasonably choose to pursue either a course of medical management that includes physical therapy and taking anti-inflammatory medications or get a knee replacement, based on their own preferences. When GPT models are integrated in a multi-modal way to evaluate large datasets that include patient-reported outcome measures obtained from patients who have pursued one of those pathways, patients might get reasonable answers to a question like, "Given my age, gender, pain level, and activity level, in five years, what are my likely pain and activity-level outcomes if I pursue medical management as opposed to knee replacement to address my knee osteoarthritis?" Such information might guide a patient to decide whether to get a knee replacement. If the patient decides to do so, a second question, "Which provider in my area has the best knee replacement outcomes for people like me?" could guide them to the best provider from whom to obtain a knee replacement.

Use of GPT in helping patients determine whether and where to obtain care for preference-sensitive conditions would revolutionize healthcare delivery. Patients would be in control of their medical fates; they could make informed decisions based on their own experiences with their medical disorders and their own values; and they could self-direct to providers who are most likely to give them the best outcomes. All of this patient-centric and patient-driven care would empower patients, improve patients' experiences and care outcomes, and reduce per-capita healthcare costs, by avoiding unnecessary interventions, reducing complications, and reducing unnecessary long-term condition management.

Public Health

AI's most transformative potential may lie in its ability to improve the public's health, particularly in regions with limited access to medical services. Currently, nearly 4 billion people worldwide have limited access to healthcare, and when they obtain care, it might not be high-quality care. Artificial intelligence could serve as an invaluable tool for improving both the quality and accessibility of healthcare in these areas. GPT models' abilities to integrate the latest research findings into medical practice in real time could substantially shorten the estimated 17-year gap between scientific discoveries and their application in routine clinical care. This could be particularly beneficial for people in low and middle-income countries (LMICs).

In LMICs, where access to specialty care is limited but broadband and mobile connectivity are increasingly available, AI and GPT models can be especially impactful. These models can empower community health workers with diagnostic tools and provide the general population with reliable medical information. For instance, AI-enhanced community health worker programs are already making strides in diagnosing conditions like diabetic retinopathy, chronic otitis media, and leprosy, thus optimizing the use of limited healthcare resources.

The application of artificial intelligence to public health is not restricted to clinical care: it has applications in addressing social determinants of health, humanitarian aid, and sustainability. In effect, AI can be employed to tackle the root causes of global health inequities. To realize this vision, there must be a focus on ethical considerations, including patient safety, transparent algorithms, and equitable access.

Critically important in using AI and GPT models to improve public health, in both developed and in low and middle-income countries, is ensuring that policymakers are part of that effort. Policymakers and community leaders can represent the interests of the public: they know what local people prioritize and want. Without local representatives leading the development and application of AI and integrated GPT models in the pursuit of improvement of public health, interventions will not be effective. The models must be used, not just theorized.

As part of an effort to improve public health in cities, Microsoft's AI for Good program has partnered with the Novartis Foundation to explore how data on the social determinants of health can be used to model the prevalence of healthcare conditions, like diabetes and atherosclerotic heart disease, that could be reduced with interventions in the social determinants of health arena. For example, reducing particulate matter in the air (generated from smog and car emissions) can reduce not only short-term measures (like emergency room visits for asthma) but also the development of chronic conditions (like hypertension and cardiovascular disease). Policymakers might reasonably seek to take measures to reduce car emissions and anticipate a "return on investment" to the health of the population in reduced incidence of hypertension. This type of cutting-edge application of AI models, which can also guide patients on exercise and diet regimens designed to reduce the incidence of chronic conditions, can improve public health.

And the improvement of public health, itself, has long-term dividends. Not only does a healthy public reduce demands on the healthcare system, it also reduces disability rates (thereby reducing governmental disability payment costs), improves the health of the labor force (thereby improving productivity and expanding the workforce, which increase tax revenues), and potentially helps citizens get better jobs (thereby increasing discretionary income, improving quality of life, expanding gross domestic product, and increasing tax revenues).

Conclusion

The development and deployment of AI and GPT models hold immense promise for advancing healthcare globally. While still evolving, these models have the potential to augment clinical care, improve patient empowerment and decision-making, and boost health equity and measures of population health. AI and GPT models can fill current gaps in healthcare access, diagnostics, and resource allocation. As efforts to train more healthcare workers are underway—a process that could take decades—these models can serve as an effective interim solution, elevating public health standards in both high and low-income countries while integrating with and improving how healthcare is delivered in the future.

The rate of technological change in healthcare is accelerating, and AI and GPT models are at the forefront of this transformation. The technology has moved from the realm of theoretical to practical, and its applications in fields like radiology, patient empowerment, and public health are being explored. While there are limitations to the technology, the rapid pace of improvement suggests a promising future. Particularly if clinicians actively guide its incorporation into medical practice, solutions can easily be used by patients to address the questions that they have. Policymakers and community leaders will be integral to the development of successful solutions designed to improve population health.

The full articles on which this summary is partially based are:

Weeks WB, Taliesin B, Lavista JM. Using artificial intelligence to advance public health. *International Journal of Public Health* 2023; 68:1606716. doi: 10.3389/ijph.2023.1606716.

Lavista JM, Weeks WB, Chu LC, Rowe SP, Fishman EK. "Beyond chatting: the opportunities and challenges of ChatGPT in medicine and radiology." *Diagnostic and Interventional Imaging* 2023; 104(6): 263-264. doi: 10.1016/j.diii.2023.02.006.

Fishman EK Weeks WB, Lavista JM, Chu LC. "Watching innovation in real time: the story of ChatGPT and radiology." *Canadian Association of Radiologists' Journal* 2023; May 3; 8465371231174817. doi: 10.1177/08465371231174817.

More information on the Novartis Foundation's AI for Healthy Cities project is available at: www.novartisfoundation.org/transforming-population-health/ai4healthycities.

Part V

Summary, Looking Forward, and Additional Resources

I n the final two chapters, we provide an epilogue that summarizes the overall learnings from the work presented in the previous chapters.

During its short life, the Lab has been extremely productive. We sought to use artificial intelligence and machine learning techniques to address some of the world's biggest problems, and we have done so.

To be sure, much more work needs to be done. To facilitate readers doing that work, we provide a brief list of additional resources. The URLs for these resources will be updated over time on the AI for Good and AI for Health websites.

Thank you for reading the book. The world has some big problems. The only way to solve these problems is to convene multidisciplinary subject matter experts from multiple sectors to collaborate in addressing these problems using the latest proven technologies.

We provided a sampling of such efforts in the book. We anticipate that our readers will generate many more.

Epilogue
Getting Good
at AI for Good

—The AI for Good Lab

A I for Good (AI4G) projects focus on developing AI-based solutions to advance goals in areas such as sustainability, health, humanitarian aid, and social justice. Through over 100 AI4G projects in the last five years, we have gained insights from successful strategies and, crucially, we have learned from mistakes. The most significant lesson that we have learned in this process is the importance of collaborating with partner organizations that have expertise in the relevant domain and experience in working toward specific goals in sustainability, humanitarian action, and health. This epilogue focuses on learnings from these experiences, covering different aspects of collaborations with partners, including communication, data, modeling, and impact. We also address the unique challenges of AI4G projects compared to machine learning projects in academic and corporate settings and outline strategies for successfully undertaking these projects. Finally, we distill 11 key takeaways to guide AI4G projects in general.

Communication

In the realm of AI4G projects, effective communication between data scientists and partner organizations, which are typically domain experts, is crucial. Here, we provide three areas of insight that data scientists can use to enhance this relationship for the success of AI4G projects.

Setting Realistic Expectations for AI

Partner organizations often have inflated expectations about AI capabilities, influenced by media hype. It is important that data scientists set realistic expectations early in the project. This involves educating partners about the capabilities and limitations of AI, the necessity for quality training data, and reframing project goals to align with what is achievable with current AI technology. For instance, in the Nature Dependent Tourism project (described in Chapter 5), a natural language processing model's scope was adjusted from extracting nuanced author intent to multi-label topic classification, leading to a successful outcome.

Confronting Technical Limitations

Data scientists should make partner organizations aware of specific challenges in building AI models, like overfitting, model bias, generalization issues, and data privacy concerns. For example, while mapping glacial lakes (described in Chapter 12), a model trained on only the latest high-resolution satellite images will have model bias issues. Historical imaging data can be used as an additional channel in the model, but such a model will overfit to the past data due to its abundance. Timely transfer of this relevant knowledge is key to navigating these technical limitations and exploring alternative solutions.

Project Scoping and Implementation

Setting accurate goals is important in AI4G projects, wherein data scientists must engage in detailed discussions with partner organizations to understand the project goals and constraints. This involves considering factors like data and resource availability, technical expertise, deployment support, privacy concerns, and the need for novel machine learning techniques. Additionally, integrating the partner organization's domain knowledge about features and evaluation metrics into the modeling process is vital for the project's success.

Data

In AI4G initiatives, the data collection process significantly influences the success of projects, often more than in commercial or academic AI endeavors. These initiatives frequently use datasets collected by partner organizations for specific application problems, which might not align with requirements for building generalizable models. Other data challenges in AI4G projects involve issues of dataset suitability, label subjectivity, and the need for thoughtful data splitting to ensure model generalizability. Addressing these challenges requires a nuanced understanding of the data's context.

Adapting to Previously Collected Datasets

In projects such as wildlife bioacoustics detection (described in Chapter 6), partner organizations might have collected data on a limited set of animals or data with varying audio quality for their ecological research. Therefore, a supervised machine learning model trained on one quality of audio datasets might not generalize to audio datasets of a different quality, limiting the applicability of the model. This discrepancy arises because the primary goal of partner organizations is to solve an application problem, not to create a dataset optimized for machine learning models. This is a sharp contrast to enterprise applications, where data is specifically curated for machine learning tasks and a rigorous procedure has been set up for data collection.

Additionally, AI4G projects often involve sensitive data, necessitating adherence to stringent ethical and legal standards. This complexity makes data usage and publication of the analysis more challenging, as was the case in the Broadband Connectivity project (described in Chapter 19, "Broadband Connectivity"), where broadband coverage percentages were reported at the ZIP Code level and the protection of data from individual households was essential. Specialized privacy-preserving methods and synthetic data generation become crucial yet bring their own set of challenges, such as vulnerability to membership inference attacks.

Moreover, AI4G projects may face limitations in the amount of available data that have subjective data annotation where there is semantic ambiguity of labels depending on the context. For instance, labeling uncommon features in satellite imagery, such as poultry barns (described in Chapter 10, "Mapping Poultry Operations at Scale") or solar farms (described in Chapter 11, "Identifying Solar Energy Locations in India"), can be costly and labor-intensive, limiting the available labels. Further, open datasets, while valuable, often suffer from significant curation issues and misleading predictions, and they can lack efficient query infrastructure.

Creating Training and Test Sets with the Application Scenario in Mind

Poor choices of training, validation, and test set splits can result in an estimated model performance that does not reflect performance when deployed. This is especially relevant in humanitarian aid and conservation applications where models are expected to generalize well spatially and/or temporally.

For example, data splits for building damage assessment should be done across diverse disaster scenarios like tornados, flooding, tsunamis, and earthquakes since images from the same disaster scenario appearing in both training and validation/test splits will give a falsely optimistic performance. Similarly, with marine mammal sound detection, data splits should be done across underwater noise variations, wildfire risk prediction must account for the stochastic nature of events, and medical imaging projects should consider hospital-specific features, not just the medical conditions being screened.

Modeling

AI4G models are developed with domain-specific motivations and limitations in mind. Consequently, models developed for mainstream machine learning fields, such as natural language processing or computer vision, require cautious adaptation and deployment to the specific domain. Furthermore, the process of model development is motivated first by application requirements instead of pure novelty or state-of-the-art performance.

Incorporating Domain Expertise

Domain expertise from partner organizations can help in model development, as domain experts often have decades of experience and accumulated knowledge in defining and solving related problems.

Effective AI4G models often require a deep understanding of the domain to select the relevant data and engineer features that truly matter. We see this in the analysis of the long-term effects of COVID (described in Chapter 27, "Long-Term Effects of COVID-19"), where the partner organization suggested a self-control study design and the specific time windows pre- and post-COVID diagnosis that should be compared.

Partner organizations also can provide domain-specific knowledge, which is useful in the choice of the model components most suited to the AI4G problem, as well as inductive biases and loss function, which in turn will significantly enhance model performance. For instance, to assess the risk of natural hazards in India (described in Chapter 15), "Dwelling Type Classification", the statistical model component that performed risk scoring was informed by SEEDS, a disaster preparedness and response organization.

Importantly, domain experts can leverage the outputs of interpretable models for broader insights, as seen in food security analysis in Malawi (described in Chapter 17), where model outputs helped identify spatial and seasonal patterns.

Model Development with Resource Constraints

Resource constraints play a significant role in AI4G modeling. AI4G models often need to be cost-effective. For example, a convolutional neural network used for creating a land cover map requires a balance between computational cost and performance. Further, models may need to operate in remote or resource-constrained environments, like applications that help visually impaired individuals through optimized deep learning architectures (described in Chapter 18, "BankNote-Net: Open Dataset for Assistive Universal Currency Recognition").

Finally, it is important to consider the carbon footprint of models developed in AI4G efforts. One of the AI4G focus areas is sustainability, and Microsoft has committed to becoming carbon negative by 2030. Sophisticated computing techniques can consume substantial energy resources and models can be optimized to minimize that consumption. Sustainability must be considered in all AI4G projects.

Evaluation and Metrics

AI4G projects require careful consideration of evaluation metrics since common machine learning metrics like precision, recall, and mean squared error may not always align with domain-specific needs.

Therefore, it is important to use domain-specific metrics in model evaluation. These metrics—such as the Dice Similarity Coefficient in lesion detection from prostate cancer images (described in Chapter 25, "Automated Segmentation of Prostate Cancer Metastases") or Fréchet distance for measuring the performance of glacial lake mapping models (described in Chapter 12)—can provide insights beyond standard machine learning metrics, capturing nuances relevant to the specific domain.

In addition, fully understanding data used is important in model evaluation. Metrics computed from imperfect data can lead to inaccuracies in the conclusions derived from the results. Therefore, acknowledging these limitations is crucial in considering generalizability.

Humans in the Loop

The role of humans in AI4G is indispensable. Many AI4G applications, such as medical diagnostics, require human interpretation and decision-making, emphasizing the need for models that complement human expertise.

While ongoing data collection and user-supplied labels allow models to be improved over time, the so-called "data flywheel" effect, the one-off nature of AI4G projects precludes this common way of improving model performance.

However, an active learning approach allows for direct engagement of partner organizations in the modeling process, making human feedback a part of the model training and refinement, as seen in applications like species identification in satellite imaging, exemplified in work wherein annotators were shown satellite images most likely to contain whales, as general satellite data would be far too difficult to annotate since whales are only present in a fraction of the satellite images (described in Chapter 7, "Using Satellites to Monitor Whales from Space").

Impact

AI4G projects present unique challenges when it comes to evaluating success. Unlike conventional business ventures, which rely on clear metrics like revenue and user engagement, AI4G initiatives must gauge their effectiveness based on their impact on a partner organization's mission. The path to success in AI4G involves not only technological development but also the critical steps of deployment, adoption, and impact assessment.

Uphill Path to Deployment and Adoption

AI4G ventures diverge from typical research focused on novel techniques or theoretical exploration. They require not just the development of models but also their deployment and, crucially, their adoption by partner organizations and related communities. This "last mile" of bringing the technology into practical use is often the most challenging. Deployment can take various forms:

- **Onetime scoring:** This involves a single use of the AI model to analyze data for a partner organization's analysis and publication. For instance, our work on building damage assessment with Turkey's Ministry of Interior Disaster and Emergency Management culminated in a report with estimates of the number of buildings damaged in four cities (described in Chapter 16, "Damage Assessment Following the 2023 Earthquake in Turkey").
- **Real-time application programming interface (API):** This form offers ongoing model access for applications such as determining a patient's risk of having leprosy (described in Chapter 24, "Detecting Leprosy in Vulnerable Populations") or identifying retinopathy of prematurity (described in Chapter 26, "Screening Premature Infants for Retinopathy of Prematurity in Low- Resource Settings"). In addition, the model from our work on banknote recognition (described in Chapter 18) has been incorporated into the latest version of Microsoft's Seeing AI application.
- **Batch processing:** This entails automated or user-triggered processing of large data volumes for regular analysis, like classifying dwelling types (described in Chapter 15).

Real-time APIs incur ongoing costs and maintenance, whereas batch processing can leverage cost-effective cloud computing. Understanding the partner organization's needs is critical to deployment, adoption, and true impact. While deploying machine learning models on edge devices is gaining popularity, especially in low-connectivity areas, trade-offs in model performance due to compression techniques like quantization need to be clearly communicated.

Adoption presents a more complex challenge, as it largely lies outside the technical team's control. Taking input from human–computer interaction experts is helpful in identifying how machine learning metrics translate into time saved in the partner organization's workflows, an indicator that may promote adoption. We have also found that open sourcing the model development code builds trust in the model and results in community engagement.

Measuring Impact

In AI4G, success metrics diverge from conventional machine learning projects. While model evaluation metrics (like an F1 score or the ROC-AUC, described in Chapter 3, "Commonly Used Processes and Terms") are important, they serve more as a basis for discussions about a model's capabilities. The key performance indicators for AI4G projects are often outcomes that are several steps removed from model outputs. Understanding a partner organization's key performance indicators during the project's scoping phase is critical for ensuring adoption.

We rely on domain experts from partner organizations to define the positive impact of a project. AI approaches typically help partner organizations in two ways: uncovering insights from large datasets and enhancing domain experts' workflows. It is essential to collaborate with partner organizations to track both the immediate and long-term impacts of AI4G projects on their missions.

In our work with the Netherlands Red Cross on post-disaster building damage assessment (described in Chapter 14), the partner organization indicated that runtime and speed of the model were as important as accuracy, which resulted in reshaping the focus of the work. Likewise, in working with the American Red Cross (ARC) on Hawaiian wildfires, we found that in addition to the time-to-providing-assistance, the geographic area that they could cover with our model's outputs (as compared to their earlier "boots on the ground" approach) was an important part of defining the impact of the AI model.

Typical partner organizations are non-governmental organizations that lack a traditional business model: helping partner organizations grow their technical capabilities can be more valuable than providing funding for resources. Maintaining post-project relationships with partner organizations helps in understanding the long-term impact of the work and feeds into a larger loop for problem-solving.

Conclusion

Microsoft's philanthropic AI for Good Lab has engaged with numerous partner organizations to apply artificial intelligence to solve some of the world's most pressing problems. In those partnerships, we have learned to work with partners more efficiently and effectively. We hope that readers can use what we have learned to accelerate employment and deployment of AI models.

Key Takeaways

These eleven key takeaways that we have learned may help readers use what we have learned:

- Educating partner organizations about AI's limits and opportunities is a core part of an AI4G project; potentially unrealistic expectations for AI can often be reframed into achievable goals designed to streamline the partner organization's workflows.
- To ensure we develop solutions that are practically useful, project scoping needs to be part of an ongoing dialogue with the partner organization.
- Datasets in AI4G projects may not be immediately useful for creating models. When creating models with such data, it is important to understand the associated metadata, collection process, and any security or privacy concerns.
- In several important domains, labels suffer from subjective annotation. Such situations should be identified early to avoid introducing inconsistencies in the modeling pipeline.
- Carefully consider how to split the data into training and test sets so that the model's ability to generalize to unseen inputs is measured.
- Endeavor to incorporate the partner organization's domain expertise in model development, when possible, through methods such as feature selection and engineering, model choice, and model regularization.

- Carefully consider a project's constraints during deployment before settling on a modeling approach.
- Check whether domain-specific metrics can be incorporated during training and validation of models and determine which machine learning metrics are relevant to solving the problem at hand.
- AI4G projects require humans in the loop to some extent. Active learning pipelines can enable partner organizations to engage with the modeling process directly during a project.
- Maintaining deployed models requires long-term engineering resource commitments. Focusing on time saved by the partner organization instead of pure machine learning metrics helps organizations adopt the technology.
- Domain experts in partner organizations should define mission-related impacts. When quantification of direct model impact is needed, work with the partner organization to identify opportunities to quantify both immediate and long-term project impact.

The full article on which this summary is based is:

Kshirsagar M, Robinson C, Yang S, Gholami S, Klyuzhin I, Mukherjee S, Nasir M, Ortiz A, Oviedo F, Tanner D, Trivedi A, Xu Y, Zhong M, Dilkina B, Dodhia R, Lavista JM. "Becoming Good at AI for Good." Available at `arxiv.org/pdf/2104.11757`.

AI and Satellites: Critical Tools to Help Us with Planetary Emergencies

—Will Marshall and Andrew Zolli

The early 21st century is a strangely incongruous moment for life on Earth. On the one hand, ours is a time of extreme, self-induced planetary-scale risks. On the other hand, we're living through a second Renaissance—an unprecedented flowering of human knowledge, capability, and tool-making.

In our unquenchable lust for resources, for movement, and for convenience, and in our sheer fecundity, we have transformed almost every corner of the land, the air, the oceans, and the web of life that spans them.

For example, we have terraformed the lands and forests, converting a third of them for agriculture and animal pasture. Once human beings roamed a hostile world, full of predators red in tooth and claw. Now, by weight, a mind-boggling 96 percent of all mammalian life on Earth is made up of human beings and our livestock—with just the remaining 4 percent composed of wildlife.

We have warmed the atmosphere and acidified the oceans, making life harder, and stranger, for the life that remains, including our own. A climate-changed world, filled with extremes of water (droughts and floods) and heat (heatwaves, wildfires, and ever-more powerful typhoons), promises to make life more unpredictable in most places and potentially unbearable in others. While all human beings are at risk from climate change, not all of us are *equally* at risk. Some of those least responsible for our changing climate are the most vulnerable to the suffering and disruptions that could ensue—like food insecurity, forced migration, destruction of property, and loss of livelihoods.

Fortunately, this difficult story is not the only one we are living through. While we may be living through early days of the *Sixth Extinction*—the sixth time in the recorded history of life that biodiversity nearly collapsed on our planet—it's *also* true that we're living through a second Renaissance—an unprecedented flowering of human knowledge, capability, and tool-making. In such a circumstance, we have ethical—as well as wholly self-interested—reasons for aligning the latter with the former.

One of the most powerful and promising of these tools comes from the combination of artificial intelligence and data from Earth-observing satellites. Artificial satellites have been observing our planet since shortly after the times of Sputnik. Typically, the images they produced were rare, expensive, and available almost entirely to specialized scientists and technical analysts working in obscure corners of government and academia. But recent innovations have meant that quality, resolution, geographic reach, timeliness, and broad availability of satellite data has undergone a revolution. Today, a new generation of satellites from Planet Labs PBC (or just "Planet"), for example, images of the entire landmass (surface) of the Earth, every day, in high resolution, makes the data widely available.

When analyzed with the tools of artificial intelligence, the data these satellites produce allow us to detect, understand, and act on change as never before, in near real time, and in places and in ways that would be impossible otherwise. Together, AI and satellite data hold a tantalizing promise: to help us build a guidance system for human civilization, and to help us make more informed and faster decisions, reducing our ecological impacts and human suffering in a volatile world.

Buckminster Fuller made the analogy that the Earth is our spaceship. We all sit on it, billions of astronauts, hurtling around the sun. And like any spaceship, we need to take care of it or risk dying. We need to stop it spinning out of control, ensure we have enough oxygen, and so on. But that starts with measuring how that spacecraft is doing. As the saying goes, "You can't manage what you don't measure." How, we may anticipate our grandchildren asking, did we manage the Earth before we sensed and analyzed it daily? Not well, it turns out! But with these tools we are in a position to do so. In short, we have the tools for a Mission Control of the spaceship Earth.

Amazing Things in the Amazon

All this is no longer hypothetical. Planet helps 64 nations with daily imagery to prevent deforestation. Consider what the combination of satellites and AI means for the Amazon rainforest. Take the Amazon as an example. It is one of the most ecologically important places on Earth, containing an estimated three million species, and storing more than 150 billion metric tons of carbon, making it vital to both climate and biodiversity. It's also important for *human* diversity. Forty-seven million people call the Amazon home, including more than 400 different indigenous groups, comprising more than two million people.

And yet, the Amazon is under constant threat from humanity's industrial appetites. Rivers are illegally mined for gold, polluting their waters and riverbanks with mercury and cyanide. Forests are illegally felled to make way for agriculture and the cultivation of livestock. In the process, the formerly forested land is transformed from a carbon *sink* to a carbon *source*—exacerbating the climate emergency for every living being.

Protecting the Amazon from these kinds of incursions is daunting, given its sheer size. The Amazon is about 70 percent larger than the U.S. state of Texas or one and a half times larger than the EU—far too vast to monitor with people or drones. Yet satellites from Planet allow us to image the entirety of the Amazon, every day, down to a resolution of a few meters. Taken together, these satellite images contain a visual record of every act of illegal mining, deforestation, and development that occurs, everywhere in Amazonia.

Of course, the sheer volume of these images means inspecting them with human eyes would be impossible. To make the images *actionable* requires additional capabilities that are only available through artificial intelligence. Using the same supervised machine learning techniques that are used to discriminate between a picture of a dog and a cat, an algorithm can be trained to detect the difference between a forested area and a recently deforested or degraded one. The "haystack" of gigabytes of daily satellite imagery can then be compared, day to day, to find the "needle" that we care about —signs of recent deforestation. *AI is like a massive magnet to find the needles!*

Even better, these same algorithms have now been trained to look for signs of *impending* deforestation *before* it occurs, not just after the fact. That's because, to clear an area deep in the jungle, the first thing a deforester must do is create an illegal road, in order to bring in the heavy equipment required to take out the trees. These roads are visible in the satellite imagery, and we can find them using the same AI-driven search techniques.

Amazing things happen when you make these kinds of capabilities available to the institutions charged with addressing the problem. In Brazil, tools powered by AI and Planet's satellite imagery were made available to the unit of the Brazilian Federal Police charged with countering illegal deforestation. This tool automatically detected recent signs associated with deforestation and generated automated reports. In their first year, in the course of more than 100 raids conducted with the support of this tool, the Federal Police destroyed more than 1,000 machines responsible for deforestation in the field and collected the equivalent of more than $2 billion U.S.

in fines. Helped in part by these techniques, the Brazilian govern-ment in 2023 announced that rates of deforestation had dropped 66 percent, year-on-year—a huge win for people and the forests.

Quick Help Saving Lives in Disaster Response

A similar example is found in the combined use of satellite imagery and AI to rapidly assess the impacts of natural disasters and speed humanitarian aid where and when it's needed most. Here, again, the fact that satellites image every place on Earth the day *before* a disaster occurs is critical to assessing the damage that occurs.

For example, on August 8, 2023, intense wildfires broke out on the U.S. Hawaiian island of Maui. Strong winds whipped the fires into a tsunami of flame, quickly turning the buildings to ash and tragically causing the deaths of 100 people in the coastal town of Lahaina.

The day *before* that horrific event, Planet's Earth-observing sat-ellites had imaged the entirety of Lahaina, as they had done every day since the middle of 2017, and as they would again the following day, in the middle of the wildfire disaster.

This before-and-after imagery, taken of the same place just one day apart, was essential to an AI-powered analysis produced by the team at the Microsoft AI for Good Lab, which deployed a machine-learning algorithm to automatically analyze the satellite imagery, looking for before-and-after differences, and classifying the level of damage to every building in the community—all in a matter of minutes.

This information was then quickly delivered to the American Red Cross, which used it to target its response to the fires, targeting its efforts to those areas that needed it most and helping speed the evacuation of thousands of Lahaina residents who'd been affected. As Kasie Richards, senior director of Situational Awareness and Decision Support at the American Red Cross told *Forbes*, "The vol-ume of information that can be synthesized would typically take us several days to process. But this model has allowed us to operate in a more condensed period."

Both of these examples demonstrate the benefits of a developing field, which we might call "planetary AI." It arises from the collective efforts of many organizations to capture, categorize, assess, and alert human beings to the state of the planet, in real time. It allows us to create new kinds of feedback loops, rushing scarce resources, such as environmental law enforcement or humanitarian aid workers, to the places where they can have the most impact.

Planetary AI begins with the collection of countless new data feeds from sensors on the ground, in people's pockets, in the air, and in space. These large streams of raw, unstructured data are then harmonized, correlated, and assessed, typically with machine learning techniques, to extract spatial indicators of the world's most critical phenomena —a mapping of things like water, carbon, biodiversity, agriculture, human population, and infrastructure, down to a resolution of a few meters.

When laid atop one another, these AI analyses reveal how risk is distributed—often unevenly—in a given place. They can show us who and what might be exposed to various risks and hazards, such as floods, food insecurity, and novel diseases. Those same satellites can then monitor those places for the first signs of change, alerting us when action is urgently needed.

In so doing, these technologies invite us into a different relationship with the Earth, and with our fellow inhabitants. Together, AI and satellite data make the invisible visible and the visible actionable. And that which is actionable today, eventually becomes that for which we are responsible tomorrow.

Additional Resources

—Lucia Ronchi Darre

We began this book by defining artificial intelligence as a machine's ability to learn. So, it is only fair that in closing this book, we offer our human readers the same opportunity to learn by directing them to additional resources.

When it comes to learning more about AI and its potential for positive real-world impact, a beginner-friendly starting point is the AI for Good Specialization[1] developed by DeepLearning. AI in partnership with our research lab. This specialization comprises three courses that explore how AI can address challenges in critical areas like public health, climate change, and disaster management. These courses provide a step-by-step framework for developing AI projects, present real-world case studies, and offer ample opportunities for practicing data analysis and AI modeling. They also delve into the limitations, concerns, and ethical questions surrounding AI—equally important, if not more so, than its potential for good.

Our readers might find this course particularly relevant as it instructs on common AI tools—such as topic modeling, computer vision, time series, and neural networks—applied to problem spaces akin to those discussed in this book. For instance, in the AI and Disaster Management course, readers can construct an image classification pipeline for damage assessment after a natural disaster, like the projects detailed in Chapters 14, "Post-Disaster Building Damage Assessment," and 16, "Damage Assessment Following the 2023 Earthquake in Turkey," of this book.

To get a quick glimpse of what this specialization is about, these two videos available on YouTube might help:

- #8 AI for Good Specialization [Course 1, Week 1, Lesson 2]:[2] An introduction to Microsoft AI for Good Lab, by Juan M. Lavista Ferres
- #10 AI for Good Specialization [Course 1, Week 1, Lesson 3]:[3] AI for Anomaly detection in breast cancer, by Felipe Oviedo

For a more comprehensive study of the spectrum of AI tools available, the Machine Learning Specialization[4] developed by Stanford University and DeepLearning.AI is a classic among AI online courses. It starts by introducing traditional supervised learning models such as linear regression, progresses to advanced algorithms like neural networks, and culminates in unsupervised learning, recommenders, and reinforcement learning. This beginner-friendly specialization also allows for hands-on modeling.

For those particularly interested in the AI models applied throughout this book, an intriguing learning path to pursue is the DeepLearning Specialization,[5] also offered by DeepLearning.AI. This intermediate-level specialization consists of five courses, requiring a bit more commitment and some prior knowledge. It commences by establishing foundational concepts around neural networks and concludes with advanced topics, such as the application of convolutional neural networks for object detection.

For readers preferring the tangible experience of books, several foundational texts offer comprehensive insights into AI and data science:

- *Introduction to Statistical Learning,* by Daniela Witten, Gareth M. James, Trevor Hastie, and Robert Tibshirani
- *Hands-on Machine Learning,* by Aurélien Géron
- *Deep Learning with Python,* by François Chollet
- *Deep Learning,* by Ian Goodfellow
- *The Book of Why,* by Dana Mackenzie and Judea Pearl
- *A Student's Guide to Bayesian Statistics,* by Ben Lambert
- *Trustworthy Online Controlled Experiments: A Practical Guide to A/B Testing,* by Ron Kohavi, Ya Xu, and Diane Tang
- *The Art of Insight: How Great Visualization Designers Think,* by Alberto Cairo
- *Data Analysis for Business, Economics, and Policy,* by Gábor Békés and Gábor Kézdi

These books, each in their own way, provide valuable knowledge and will serve readers as worthy companions in their AI and data science journey.

Given the limited space in this book's pages, the projects we included here are only a curated selection. Thus, for readers genuinely interested in exploring more about the problem spaces the AI for Good Lab engages with, the best avenue is our Microsoft site.[6] Here, readers can delve deeper into our lab's projects and impact, access all our publications, replicate our code, and download our datasets.

For instance, in Chapter 10, "Mapping Poultry Operations at Scale," we discussed our Mapping Poultry Operations project. All the data and code necessary to replicate our work can be found in the "Poultry Barn Mapping" GitHub repository[7] listed under Downloads. Similarly, for the dataset resulting from the Broadband Connectivity project detailed in Chapter 19, "Broadband Connectivity," readers can visit the GitHub repository called "U.S. Broadband Usage Percentages Dataset"[8] under the same Downloads section.

Another interesting section on our Microsoft website that might spark readers' curiosity is "The Prompt,"[9] a series hosted by Trevor Noah, Microsoft's Chief Questions Officer, who explores how AI can help address urgent global issues. Each episode features a new prompt and a guest who discusses how they are using AI to solve problems in various domains. The first two episodes are:

- Episode 1: Mapping the world's forgotten populations at the IHME,[10] which references the project discussed in Chapter 30, "Mapping Population Movement Using Satellite Imagery"
- Episode 2: How is AI protecting vulnerable communities?,[11] which references the project discussed in Chapter 15, "Dwelling Type Classification"

For Trevor Noah's other commentaries, visit: `https://aka.ms/AI4GThePrompt`.

For those particularly interested in our health initiatives, we have a dedicated AI for Health site.[12] Both this one and our broader AI for Good website are great overviews of our work and are continuously updated for the reader.

Finally, impactful change often springs from collaborative efforts, which is why it is so important to partner with experts and NGOs entrenched in specific problem spaces. Platforms like the Worldwide NGO Directory[13] and `Idealist.org`[14] host a plethora of NGOs dedicated to addressing diverse challenges. Engaging with these organizations not only offers deeper insights but also cultivates opportunities for collective action.

As we draw the final lines of this chapter, we extend an open invitation to our readers—an invitation to embrace the resources shared within these pages and turn knowledge into action. The door to making a difference with AI swings wide open—it's time to step through and craft a future where technology and compassion intersect for the greater good.

Endnotes

1. `www.deeplearning.ai/courses/ai-for-good`
2. `https://aka.ms/AAnu89y`
3. `https://aka.ms/AAnv2hr`
4. `www.deeplearning.ai/courses/machine-learning-specialization`
5. `www.deeplearning.ai/courses/deep-learning-specialization`

6. www.microsoft.com/en-us/research/group/ai-for-good-research-lab/overview

7. https://github.com/microsoft/poultry-cafos

8. https://github.com/microsoft/USBroadbandUsagePercentages

9. www.microsoft.com/en-us/research/group/ai-for-good-research-lab/the-prompt

10. www.microsoft.com/en-us/research/video/the-prompt-with-trevor-noah-episode-1-ihme-population-mapping

11. www.microsoft.com/en-us/research/video/the-prompt-with-trevor-noah-episode-2-how-is-ai-protecting-vulnerable-communities

12. www.microsoft.com/en-us/ai/ai-for-health

13. www.wango.org

14. www.idealist.org

Acknowledgments

T he studies summarized in this book resulted from collaborative efforts. Here, we acknowledge our current and former lab members and partners for their efforts in the summarized and other work.

Montserrat Acosta-Morel	The Nature Conservancy
Elizabeth Adamson	Novartis Foundation
Joshua Allen	Microsoft Corporation
Daniel Andriantsimba	Catholic Relief Services
Val Anthony	Tripadvisor
Nicholas Becker	Microsoft AI for Good Lab (former)
François Bénard	BC Cancer
Fred B. Bercovitch	University of the Free State
Avleen S. Bijral	Microsoft Corporation
Cameron Birge	Microsoft Philanthropies
Kris Bock	Azure FastTrack Engineering
Jo Ivey Boufford	New York University School of Global Public Health

Christoph J. Brabec	Helmholtz-Institute Erlangen-Nürnberg
Ji Eun Chang	New York University School of Global Public Health
Yu-Chia Chen	University of Washington
Aneesh Chopra	CareJourney
Linda C. Chu	Johns Hopkins University
Aaron D. Cole	University of California, Santa Cruz
Sherry Constantine	The Nature Conservancy
Soham Deshmukh	Microsoft Corporation
Paulo Duarte	American Red Cross
Benjamin Elizalde	Microsoft Corporation
Susana Patiño Espinosa	Business Data Evolution
John Fisher III	Massachusetts Institute of Technology
Sumedh Ranjan Ghatage	Gramener
Ritwik Gupta	Berkeley Artificial Intelligence Research Lab
Brandon Haigood	The Carter Center
Giselle Hall	The Nature Conservancy
Sara Harsini	BC Cancer
David Hayden	Massachusetts Institute of Technology
Carlos Felipe Peñaranda Henao	Clínica Oftalmológica Peñaranda
Thomas Heumeuller	Helmholtz-Institute Erlangen-Nürnberg
Alejandro Sánchez Hoil	Asociación para evitar la ceguera en México IAP
Michael L. Jackson	Kaiser Permanente
Anusheel Kamle	Catholic Relief Services
Kate Keator	The Carter Center
Justin Kitzes	University of Pittsburgh
Ivan Klyuzhin	University of British Columbia
Carlos Andrés Valdés Lara	Clínica de Alta Especialidad Visual
Kate Longley-Wood	The Nature Conservancy
Hemant Malhotra	Microsoft Corporation

Sundeep Reddy Mallu	Gramener
Jacopo Margutti	510, an initiative of the Netherlands Red Cross
Valerie Pietsch McNulty	The Nature Conservancy
Shrestha Mohanty	Microsoft Corporation
Jennifer Morris	The Nature Conservancy
Richa Naik	Massachusetts Institute of Technology
Barry A. Nickel	University of California, Santa Cruz
José Pagán	New York University School of Global Public Health
Pavitraa Parthasarathy	Microsoft Corporation
Shwetak Patel	University of Washington
Brenda Natalia Peña	Centro integral de salud visual Daponte
Jose Dario Perea Ospina	Universidad ICESI
Chris Perry	University of Queensland
Kris Pitcher	American Red Cross
Erick Pound	Defense Innovation Unit
Arman Rahmim	BC Cancer Research Institute
Sumanth Ratna	Yale University
Kasie Richards	American Red Cross
Barbra Richardson	University of Washington
Melissa Rosa	Planet Labs
Steven P. Rowe	Johns Hopkins University
Raymond Sacks	University of Sydney
Gabriela Saidman	Red RoP de la Provincia de Buenos Aires
Ria Sankar	Microsoft AI for Good Lab (former)
Steven R. Schill	The Nature Conservancy
Peter W. Schuhmann	University of North Carolina, Wilmington
Tina Sederholm	Microsoft AI for Good Lab (former)
Eugene Seleznev	Microsoft Seeing AI
Carlos Serafin	Business Data Evolution
Narinder Singh	University of Sydney

Arfon Smith	GitHub
Peter Speyer	Novartis Foundation
Brian Taliesin	PATH
Weiyushi Tian	New York University
John Torres	Microsoft Corporation
Carlos F. Uribe	University of British Columbia
Avirishu Verma	Microsoft Corporation
Srinivas Vinnakota	Microsoft Corporation
Huaming Wang	Microsoft Corporation
Kevin Weil	Planet Labs
Jim Weinstein	Microsoft Research
Kevin White	Microsoft AI for Good Lab
Hansong Xue	National University of Singapore
Juan Salvador Mármol Yahya	Business Data Evolution
Siyu Yang	Microsoft AI for Good Lab (former)
Shun Zhang	Microsoft AI for Good Lab (former)
Yongkang Zhang	Weill Cornell Medical College

Additionally, we deeply appreciate the invaluable contributions of the Microsoft AI for Good Lab team and internal Microsoft collaborators, enabling this book's production and supporting our collaborative endeavors.

Nicole Adams	Tom Burt
Paul Arden	Andres Hernandez Celis
Mariana Pereyra Azcunaga	Rachel Chernaskey
Ginny Badanes	Sina Chhen
Javier Delgado Barbaro	Brent Christofferson
Katie Bates	Brent Colburn
Kate Behncken	Jean-Philippe Courtois
Karen Bergin	Natasha Crampton
Julie Brill	David Cuddy
Carol Ann Browne	Burton Davis
Candace Lowry Bryant	Luisa Vargas Daza

Marcelo Duarte
Sylvie Duchamp
Alonso Guevara Fernández
Pedro Costa Galiana
Jaime Galviz
Dhiya Gerber
Ursula Hardy
Laura Hoffman
Hillary Holmer
Michele Horn
Eric Horvitz
Fred Humphries
Teresa Hutson
Diogo Ide
Robert Ivanschitz
John Kahan
Dean Kain
Minji Kim
Leoreina Lacuin
Shannon Larson
Jenny Lay-Flurrie
Simon Liepold
Lupina Loperena
Amy Luers
Naria Santa Lucia
Jennifer Lyons
Mario Madden
Adrianna Mangion
Luana Marotti
Melina Martinez

Matthew Masterson
Scott McCullers
Divya Michael
Anna Moran
Melanie Nakagawa
Hossein Nowbar
Gerry Petrella
Alexandre Pinho
Ivana Pontet
Brian Rain
Katie Recken
Andres Rengifo
Aimee Riordan
Vickie Robinson
Joaquin Rivero Rodriguez
Catherine Romero
Fabian Salamo
Santiago Salcido
Mohammadreza Salmanpour-
    paeenafrakati
Chris Sharrock
Brad Smith
Justin Spelhaug
Aaron Thiese
Jéhu Torres
Kweku Ulzen
Liz Wan
Clint Watts
Ming Zhong

The book couldn't have been completed without you. Thanks!

Juan and Bill

About the Editors

Juan M. Lavista Ferres is Microsoft Chief Data Scientist, Vice President, and Director of the AI for Good Lab at Microsoft. He leads a team of data scientists and researchers who specialize in artificial intelligence, machine learning, and statistical modeling, contributing to Microsoft's AI for Good initiatives. These projects cover areas such as sustainability, humanitarian action, accessibility, and health.

Juan co-founded the lab in 2018. Since its inception, he and his team have undertaken over 200 projects worldwide, ranging from enhancing the detection of pancreatic cancer to assisting organizations after natural disasters. Collaborating with prominent organizations such as the United Nations, American Red Cross, The Nature Conservancy Group, PATH, Seattle Children's Hospital, Harvard University, Stanford University, and Johns Hopkins University, they have consistently been at the forefront of using AI for the betterment of humanity.

In just five years, the AI for Good Lab has gained global renown, with branches in Redmond, New York, and Nairobi. The lab's contributions have been published in top academic journals and conference literature, including *Nature Communications, Lancet, Blood, and JAMA Ophthalmology*. The lab's work has also been featured in prominent media outlets such as *The New York Times, The Washington Post, The Wall Street Journal, CNN, The Economist,* and over 100 other news platforms worldwide.

Juan joined Microsoft in 2009 to work on the Microsoft Experimentation Platform (EXP). There, he designed and executed randomized controlled experiments for various Microsoft groups. He was also a pivotal member of the Bing Data Mining team, leading a unit that applied machine learning, statistical modeling, and online experimentation on a vast scale while also providing data services for Bing. He played a significant role in shaping the data science discipline within Microsoft and serves as the editor of the *Microsoft Journal of Applied Research* (MSJAR).

Before joining Microsoft, Juan held the position of CTO and was a co-founder of `alerts.com`. He also spent six years in Washington with the InterAmerican Development Bank, using data science to assess the efficacy of programs aimed at reducing poverty and inequality in Latin America and the Caribbean.

Juan holds two computer science degrees from the Catholic University in Uruguay, a graduate degree in data mining and machine learning from Johns Hopkins University, and a PhD with a focus on AI in healthcare from Vrije Universiteit in Amsterdam. He lives in Kirkland, WA, with his wife and three children. Passionate about education, Juan teaches computer science at Global Idea Elementary School. He has lectured at prestigious institutions like Harvard, Stanford, Johns Hopkins, Berkeley, and Cornell and has spoken in numerous countries, including Canada, Switzerland, Argentina, Colombia, Costa Rica, and Uruguay. Additionally, Juan has been a featured TEDx speaker.

William B. Weeks is a physician–economist who leads Microsoft's philanthropic AI for Health efforts within the AI for Good Lab. There, he conducts research in concert with not-for-profit organizations and academic centers designed to improve health and health outcomes, applying artificial intelligence techniques to address three broad areas: computer vision, public health, and large language modeling. The AI for Health program has partnered with grantees on projects designed to accelerate medical research, build research capabilities, increase global health insights, and address health inequities.

Dr. Weeks obtained his MD from the University of Texas Medical Branch, his PhD in economics from Aix-Marseille University, and his MBA from Columbia University. At Dartmouth, Dr. Weeks completed a residency in general psychiatry and addiction psychiatry and is board certified in both; his clinical career has spanned running a PTSD Clinical Team, developing an Evaluation and Brief Treatment PTSD Unit, and treating patients with substance use disorders.

Most of Dr. Weeks's career has been focused on research. Dr. Weeks has published a book and over 250 peer-reviewed manuscripts examining economic and business aspects of healthcare services utilization and delivery, physicians' return on educational investment, healthcare delivery science, social determinants of health, population health, and healthcare value. Dr. Weeks has been honored with the 2009 National Rural Health Association Outstanding Researcher Award, the 2016 Jerome F. McAndrews award for excellence in research from the National Chiropractic Medical Insurance Corporation Group, the 2016 Fulbright-Tocqueville Distinguished Chair at Aix-Marseille University, and a 2020–23 Fulbright Specialist Award.

Dr. Weeks's research has been funded by the Centers for Medicare and Medicaid Innovation, the National Institutes of Health, the Commonwealth Fund, the National Chiropractic Medical Insurance Corporation Group, the Department of Veterans Affairs, the Agency for Health Research and Quality, the Fulbright Commission, L'Institut d'Études Avancées d'Aix-Marseille Université, Bupa, AXA, and Sanitas Mayores. Dr. Weeks also serves as the medical director for Bing.

Dr. Weeks has six children and, at the moment, four grandchildren. He currently lives in New York City.

About the Authors

Microsoft's AI for Good Lab

Lucia Ronchi Darre holds an Industrial Engineering degree from Instituto Tecnológico de Buenos Aires and a Master of Science in Applied Data Science from the University of Chicago. She is an Applied Data Scientist at Microsoft's AI for Good Lab, where she harnesses diverse data science methodologies to address social and environmental challenges.

Rahul Dodhia obtained a Bachelor of Arts degree in Mathematics (summa cum laude) from Brandeis University and earned his PhD in Psychology from Columbia University using artificial intelligence to examine human memory and decision-making models. Rahul is deputy director of Microsoft's AI for Good Lab, where he leads a team of AI researchers addressing global challenges in sustainability, humanitarian action, health issues, and climate adaptation in the Global South. Prior to his current role, he led machine learning teams at several organizations, including eBay, Amazon, and Expedia. He also served at the NASA Ames Research Center, where he applied foundational research on human memory to address safety concerns in general aviation and space flight.

Will Fein obtained a Bachelor of Arts degree in English with a minor in Mathematical and Computational Sciences from Stanford University and a Master's degree in Business Analytics from the Massachusetts Institute of Technology. He is a data and applied scientist at Microsoft's AI for Good Lab. His work focuses on tracking and combating the spread of misinformation and propaganda on the Internet using AI tools. At Microsoft, he collaborates closely with interdisciplinary groups from Microsoft's Threat Intelligence and Corporate Social Responsibility teams. Having studied both quantitative techniques and communication, he is passionate about conveying complex technical concepts to a wide manner of audiences.

Simone Fobi obtained a Bachelor of Science degree from Oregon State University and a Master of Science degree from Stanford University, both in environmental engineering; she obtained her PhD in mechanical engineering from Columbia University. She is a research scientist at Microsoft's AI for Good Lab. Her research focuses on applying computer vision techniques and geospatial machine learning to remote sensed imagery in order to support post-disaster and infrastructure mapping and to address climate change problems. Her research interests include self-supervised learning, domain adaptation approaches with local differentiation, and learning in low data regimes. Simone also serves as the data lead for Climate Change AI, a non-profit organization catalyzing impactful work at the intersection of climate change and machine learning.

Shahrzad Gholami earned her PhD in computer science from the University of Southern California. She is a research scientist at Microsoft's AI for Good Lab. Her research interests include using artificial intelligence and machine learning to address global societal and environmental issues in the areas of environmental sustainability, humanitarian efforts, and healthcare innovations. In her role at Microsoft, she collaborates with interdisciplinary teams to drive forward research projects aimed at creating positive societal impact.

Tammy Glazer holds a Master of Science in Computational Analysis and Public Policy from the University of Chicago and a Bachelor of Arts in Politics from Princeton University; she has completed a Princeton-in-Asia Fellowship in Bangkok, Thailand. Tammy is a Senior Applied Data Scientist with Microsoft's AI for Good Lab, where she uses predictive analytics, computer vision, and deep learning techniques to ensure community resilience. Her research interests include using geospatial machine learning techniques to address climate change and respond to humanitarian crises, as well as bringing best practices in machine learning and crowdsourcing to mission-driven organizations.

Amrita Gupta obtained her PhD in Computational Science and Engineering from the Georgia Institute of Technology. She is a researcher and data scientist at the Microsoft AI for Good Lab. Her work centers on co-developing machine learning and computational models with decision-makers and practitioners in biodiversity conservation and sustainability. Amrita's research interests include methods that facilitate the effective use of limited data and resources, such as: transfer learning to train models with limited labeled data; active learning to identify the most informative data samples for training models; out-of-distribution generalization to maximize the utility of models trained on localized datasets; and mathematical optimization to help managers and practitioners make systematic and informed decisions about the allocation of resources.

Gilles Hacheme earned his PhD in econometrics and machine learning from Aix-Marseille University, where he focused on applying machine learning to economics, using econometric tools to make black box models more interpretable, and using online data to answer economic questions. He is a Research Scientist at Microsoft's AI for Good Lab, where he uses computer vision, remote sensing, and statistics to address societal issues such as food security, climate change, and disaster response. He is an active member of the Masakhane NLP research community, where he works on breaking language barriers in Africa. He also co-founded Ai4Innov, a non-profit organization where he works on adapting and building AI technologies to tackle societal challenges in Africa.

Allen Kim obtained a Bachelor of Arts degree in architecture and a Bachelor of Science degree in construction management from the University of Washington. He is the senior director of data analytics and visualization with Microsoft's AI for Good Lab. His interests include bringing the AI for Good Lab's learnings to light via "data stories" developed for a broad audience and illustrated using sophisticated data visualization tools. He has a particular interest in making complex data easier to grasp to increase understanding and catalyze others to uncover hidden insights.

Meghana Kshirsagar holds a PhD in computer science from Carnegie Mellon University where her graduate studies were supported by the Richard King Mellon Foundation's fellowship for Life Sciences. Prior to joining Microsoft, she completed her postdoctoral studies at Memorial Sloan Kettering Cancer Center. She is a research scientist in the AI for Good Lab at Microsoft where her work spans from exploring the intricacies of proteins and their structures at the micro-level to addressing broader issues of population health and equity at the macro-level. She previously worked in the machine learning group at IBM Research and at Yahoo! Labs.

Lucas A. Meyer obtained his MBA and his MSc in Finance from the University of Washington. He is a principal research scientist at Microsoft's AI for Good Lab. His research is focused on fraud and misconduct. His current work in the Lab focuses on building large language model applications to combat disinformation and aid sustainability and AI literacy efforts. Prior to joining the AI for Good Lab, he worked at Microsoft Treasury, creating models that used natural language processing to improve the forecast of Microsoft's cash positions and to detect irregular transaction patterns.

Zhongqi Miao obtained a Bachelor's degree in environmental engineering from Southeast University, China, and a Master's degree in ecology from Colorado State University. He obtained his PhD from UC Berkeley, specializing in computer vision and deep learning applications, particularly in camera trap recognition. He is an applied research scientist at Microsoft's AI for Good Lab, where he focuses on incorporating artificial intelligence into environmental science and ecology domains. Dr. Miao obtains wildlife recognition data from diverse sources such as ground-based imagery, bioacoustics, and aerial imagery from planes, drones, and satellites. Motivated by real-world challenges, he seeks to address complex issues like long-tail distribution, multi-domain applications, human-in-the-loop interactions, and the deployment efficiency of large foundation models.

Amy Michaels obtained a PhD in English from the University of Washington. She is principal product manager at Microsoft's AI for Good Lab where her focus is using the potential of artificial intelligence for positive social impact. Amy's expertise in technology spans machine learning, propensity modeling, and digital customer acquisition and engagement. Beyond Microsoft, she has held leadership roles in engineering, product management, and marketing at Amazon, T-Mobile, and Meredith Corporation.

Amit Misra obtained a Bachelor of Science in physics from Case Western Reserve University and a PhD in astronomy and astrobiology from the University of Washington. He is a principal data and applied scientist at Microsoft's AI for Good Lab. During his PhD, he worked on building computational models of exoplanet atmospheres and spectra. During his industry experience, he has worked across a variety of data science and machine learning disciplines, including causal inference, non-convex optimization, and large language models. His current work focuses on building large language model applications, leveraging Microsoft data to help non-profits and governments, and improving flood risk models.

Sumit Mukherjee obtained a PhD in Electrical and Computer Engineering from the University of Washington. He is a staff machine learning scientist at insitro where he develops machine learning–derived disease-relevant traits from clinical data and tools to evaluate the utility of such traits for drug discovery. Previously, as a senior applied scientist at Microsoft's AI for Good Lab, he developed novel tools for privacy-preserving data sharing in healthcare and worked with large-scale medical claims data to study the long-term effects of COVID-19.

Md Nasir obtained his Bachelor degree in engineering from Jadavpur University and his PhD in electrical engineering from the University of Southern California. He is a senior applied research scientist with Microsoft's AI for Good Lab. He works on various machine learning problems that seek to have a positive impact on the environment and society by applying computer vision and natural language processing applications to health, conservation, and emergency management problems.

Anthony Ortiz obtained a Bachelor of Science degree in telematics engineering from the Pontificia Universidad Católica Madre y Maestra, Santiago de los Caballeros, Dominican Republic, and a PhD in computer science from the University of Texas at El Paso. He is a research scientist with Microsoft's AI for Good Lab. His research interests include tackling large-scale problems in medical imaging, remote sensing, machine learning, and computer vision. He has a particular interest in using artificial intelligence to solve societal problems.

Felipe Oviedo obtained a Bachelor of Science degree in engineering at the Universidad San Francisco de Quito and completed a PhD at the Massachusetts Institute of Technology examining the intersection of computer science and material science. He is a senior research scientist with Microsoft's AI for Good Lab. Prior to joining Microsoft, he was an intern at CERN. His research interests lie at the intersection of science and medicine and machine learning, including sustainability, medical imaging, and physics-informed machine learning.

Mayana Pereira obtained Bachelor of Science and Master of Science degrees in electrical engineering from the University of Brasilia, Brazil. She is a research scientist at Microsoft's AI for Good Lab. Her research focuses on the intersection of digital safety, security, trust, artificial intelligence, and privacy-preserving machine learning and synthetic data. She is a collaborator with OpenDP, an open-source project for the differential privacy community that seeks to develop general-purpose tools for differential privacy.

Caleb Robinson obtained a Bachelor of Science in computer and information science from the University of Mississippi and a PhD in computer science from the Georgia Institute of Technology. He is a research scientist at Microsoft's AI for Good Lab, where he co-leads the Geospatial Machine Learning Center. His research interests include self-supervised learning, domain adaptation, and few-shot learning methods for use with remotely sensed data. He applies these techniques to help solve large-scale problems in disaster response, sustainability, and conservation. He is particularly interested in democratizing methods for extracting insights from huge amounts of satellite imagery, so that anyone can help solve the pressing problems that face our society.

Thomas Roca holds a PhD in Development Economics from Bordeaux University and an MSc in Economics from University Paris I Pantheon-Sorbonne. He is a senior applied data scientist with Microsoft's AI for Good Lab where he works in natural language processing and computer vision. In his previous role at Microsoft, Thomas worked with LinkedIn's Economic Graph team. Before joining Microsoft, Thomas was a researcher and statistician at the *Agence Française de Développement* (AFD) – France's Bilateral Cooperation Bank. Thomas also spent time at the United Nations in New York contributing to UNDP's 2010 and 2015 Human Development Reports.

Anthony Cintron Roman earned his Bachelor of Science degree in computer science and his MBA with a specialty in the management of information systems at the Inter American University of Puerto Rico. He is currently the director of data architecture with the AI for Good Lab at Microsoft, where he works with a team of data engineers, data scientists, and researchers in machine learning and data science projects across Microsoft AI for Good efforts. He specializes in cloud solution architecture and open innovation.

Saqib Shaikh obtained a Bachelor of Science in Computer Science from the University of Essex and a Master's of Science in Artificial Intelligence from the University of Sussex. At Microsoft, he founded and leads the Seeing AI lab, blending emerging technologies such as artificial intelligence and augmented reality with natural user experiences to empower people, like himself, who are blind. The Seeing AI mobile app is a visual assistant which enables someone who is blind to hold up their phone and hear more about the things in their surroundings. Saqib is driven by the power of technological innovations to positively transform people's lives, as he knows from his personal experience; he is an advocate for accessibility and inclusion.

Girmaw Abebe Tadesse received his PhD at Queen Mary University of London, under the Erasmus Mundus Double Doctorate Program in Interactive and Cognitive Environments and was a postdoctoral ML researcher for healthcare at the University of Oxford. He is a Principal Research Scientist and Manager at Microsoft's AI for Good Lab where he leads the Africa team in developing AI solutions for critical challenges in agriculture, healthcare, and biodiversity. His research focuses on developing impactful and trustworthy AI solutions with active collaboration with domain experts across non-profits, governmental, and academic institutions.

Darren Tanner completed his doctoral work at the University of Washington in linguistics and his postdoctoral work at the Pennsylvania State University in cognitive psychology and neuroscience. He was subsequently on the faculties of Linguistics, Psychology, and Neuroscience at the University of Illinois, where his work focused on the cognitive and neural systems supporting language learning and language use. He is a senior applied research scientist at Microsoft's AI for Good Lab. There, his research focuses largely on public health, with a strong interest in using advanced statistical modeling and artificial intelligence tools to help build actionable insights that can improve health outcomes across populations.

Jane Wang obtained a Bachelor's degree in Finance from Zhejiang Gongshang University, a Master of Science degree in Information Management from the University of Washington, and a Master of Science degree in Accounting and Finance from the University of Exeter. She is a senior data scientist at Microsoft's AI for Good Lab. Her current focus is on digital safety, security, trust, and artificial intelligence, with a keen interest in unraveling and articulating insightful narratives from complex datasets.

Yixi Xu received her Bachelor's degree in applied mathematics from the University of Science and Technology of China and her PhD in statistics from Purdue University. She is a research scientist at Microsoft's AI for Good Lab. Her research interests focus on harnessing artificial intelligence and machine learning to address pressing societal issues as applied to medical imaging, computer vision, and privacy.

Akram Zaytar received a Master of Science degree and a PhD in computer science from Université Abdelmalek Essaâdi. He is a Senior Applied Research Scientist at Microsoft's AI for Good Research Lab where he specializes in employing satellite imagery, computer vision, and data science to address critical environmental challenges like climate change and food security. Prior to Microsoft, he conducted postdoctoral research at IBM Research, focusing on geospatial machine learning and applied research. His research interests include geospatial machine learning, deep neural networks, and self/weakly supervised learning.

Collaborators

Ann Aerts is Head of the Novartis Foundation, an organization committed to transform the health of low-income populations by leveraging the power of data, digital technology, and artificial intelligence to reimagine health and care around the world. Ann holds a degree in Medicine, a Master's in Public Health from the University of Leuven, Belgium, and a degree in Tropical Medicine from the Institute of Tropical Medicine in Antwerp, Belgium. Passionate about improving population health through data, digital and AI, Ann chairs the Broadband Commission for Sustainable Development Working Group on Digital and AI in Health and is a member of the Philips Foundation Board. Dr. Aerts was named one of the top 50 innovators in 2020 by the World Summit AI community.

Monica Bond is a wildlife biologist and CFO and co-founder of the Wild Nature Institute as well as a postdoctoral research associate at the University of Zurich. She obtained her PhD in Ecology at the University of Zurich. Her research is focused on population ecology, habitat selection, and social behavior of wildlife. She has conducted field research on gray-tailed voles, Western Burrowing Owls, Spotted Owls, Black-backed Woodpeckers, arboreal salamanders, northern elephant seals, Hawaiian monk seals, eastern white-bearded wildebeests, and Masai giraffes. Monica has published more than 50 peer-reviewed scientific journal articles and book chapters, and she is co-editor of the book "Tarangire: Human–Wildlife Co-existence in a Fragmented Ecosystem." She has also authored several children's books about African wildlife.

Jonathan B. Bricker is a Full Professor of Public Health at the Fred Hutchinson Cancer Research Center and Affiliate Professor and member of the graduate faculty in Psychology at the University of Washington in Seattle, Washington. A licensed clinical psychologist, he received his PhD in Clinical Psychology from the University of Washington. Dr. Bricker is an expert in the field of health behavior change interventions and is founder and leader of the Health and Behavioral Innovations in Technology (HABIT) Research Group. The HABIT research group focuses on developing and testing innovative theory-based behavioral interventions for tobacco cessation and weight loss, especially those delivered in widely disseminable technology platforms. Currently, he serves as Senior Editor of the journal Addiction, the highest-impact substance abuse journal.

Tonio Buonassisi obtained his BS in Applied Physics from University of Notre Dame and his PhD in Applied Science & Technology from UC Berkeley. He is a Professor of Mechanical Engineering at the Massachusetts Institute of Technology (MIT). He is pioneering the application of artificial intelligence to develop new materials for societally beneficial applications. His research in solar photovoltaics and technoeconomic analysis assisted technology developments has been used in dozens of companies, earning him a US Presidential Early Career Award for Scientists and Engineers (PECASE), a National Science Foundation CAREER Award, and a Google Faculty Award. He directs the Accelerated Materials Lab for Sustainability at MIT, and he has served as founding director for the Accelerated Materials Development for Manufacturing Programme in Singapore.

James Campbell is the Chief of Party for Catholic Relief Systems' Rapid Feedback Monitoring System Project in the Malawi Country Program. Prior to this, James was the Monitoring, Evaluation, Accountability, and Learning Regional Technical Advisor for CRS' Southern Africa Regional Office, where he spearheaded the initial development, piloting, and refinement of measurement indicators for resilience analysis, provided leadership to strengthen organizational, staff, and partner capacity to design and implement effective monitoring and evaluation systems. James has worked in the aerospace industry as a systems engineer and as an applied researcher with a focus on contemporary public health and biomedical issues in developing countries. He holds a master's degree in Biostatistics from the University of Massachusetts, Amherst.

Elliot K. Fishman is Professor of Radiology, Surgery, Urology, and Oncology at Johns Hopkins School of Medicine. He received his MD from the University of Maryland and completed his residency training and fellowship at Johns Hopkins Hospital. Dr. Fishman's clinical and research interests have focused on advanced medical imaging with specific emphasis on CT, 3-dimensional imaging and artificial intelligence. He serves as the principal investigator of the Felix Project for Early Detection of Pancreatic Cancer, focused on deep learning in medical imaging. He has been a leader in 3D software development for the past three decades and has worked closely with industry including Pixar, Apple, Microsoft, GE Healthcare, and Siemens.

Kim Goetz works at the National Oceanic and Atmospheric Administration (NOAA) Alaska Fisheries Science Center, Marine Mammal Laboratory in Seattle, Washington, where she focuses on the ecology, movement, distribution, and abundance of cetaceans. Prior to NOAA, Kim completed her PhD at the University of Santa Cruz where she studied the movement and foraging behavior of Weddell seals in the western Ross Sea, Antarctica. Her research interests include spatial ecology, marine mammal and seabird conservation, movement and behavior of animals, and science communication.

Kevin T. Greene is an Associate Research Scholar in the Empirical Studies of Conflict project at Princeton University. He previously served as a postdoctoral fellow in the Computer Science Department at Dartmouth College. His research focuses on the role of information communication technologies in international and domestic politics. He earned a PhD in Political Science from the University of Pittsburgh, an MA in Political Science from Michigan State University, and a BA in Political Science and BS in Economics from UNC Charlotte.

Al-Rahim Habib is a registrar specializing in Otolaryngology, Head and Neck Surgery and a PhD candidate at the University of Sydney. Dr. Habib is exploring the role of artificial intelligence to triage ear disease in rural and remote areas of Australia for aboriginal and Torres Strait Islander people. Research support has been provided by the Passe and Williams Memorial Foundation, Microsoft's AI for Humanitarian Action grant, and the Avant Mutual Early Career Research Grant. Dr. Habib is a graduate from the Faculty of Health

Sciences at Simon Fraser University, School of Population and Public Health at the University of British Columbia, and the Sydney Medical School at the University of Sydney.

Daniel E. Ho is the William Benjamin Scott and Luna M. Scott Professor of Law, Professor of Political Science, Professor of Computer Science (by courtesy), Senior Fellow at Stanford's Institute for Human-Centered Artificial Intelligence, Senior Fellow at the Stanford Institute for Economic Policy Research, and Director of the Regulation, Evaluation, and Governance Lab (RegLab) at Stanford University. He received his JD from Yale Law School and PhD from Harvard University and clerked for Judge Stephen F. Williams on the U.S. Court of Appeals, District of Columbia Circuit. Dr. Ho serves on the National Artificial Intelligence Advisory Commission, advising the White House on artificial intelligence, as senior advisor on Responsible AI at the U.S. Department of Labor, and as a public member of the Administrative Conference of the United States.

James Jacoby earned his Bachelor's of Science in computing and software systems at University of Washington. He is co-founder and Chief Technology Officer at Moby, an agency specializing in digital solutions. He is an experienced technical architect with over 20 years of expertise in web, mobile apps, gaming, commerce, big data, and AI. Known for his ability to grasp the big picture while attending to details, his approach revolves around the fusion of technology, design, and practicality. A leader at heart, he excels in steering teams through complex problems and fostering collaboration across disciplines.

Christin Khan is a marine mammal scientist at the National Oceanic and Atmospheric Administration (NOAA) Northeast Fisheries Science Center in Woods Hole, MA. Dedicated to making a positive impact in the world, she is a passionate conservationist and AI enthusiast with a deep commitment to protecting North Atlantic right whales. Her work focuses on leveraging cutting-edge technology and extensive partnerships to drive real-world change in the field of marine conservation. Currently she is focused on creating an operational system to detect whales with VHR satellite imagery and solving the geolocation challenges around the development of on-demand fishing.

Joseph Kiesecker is Lead Scientist for The Nature Conservancy, the world's largest environmental organization. He obtained his PhD in ecology, conservation biology, and animal behavior at Oregon State University. He is a recognized scientific leader in energy siting and mitigation and his work has changed the way governments and industry respond to environmental impacts from development. He has also been at the forefront of recognizing that as we transition to renewable energy, we must advance smarter approaches for development and the environment, so that meeting climate goals does not come at the expense of human development or healthy lands and waters. He documents these approaches in a recent book *Energy Sprawl Solutions: Balancing Global Development and Conservation*. He has published over 200 articles on topics ranging from climate change to the effectiveness of conservation strategies. Prior to joining the Conservancy, he was a professor at Penn State University and has also held faculty appointments at Yale University and the University of Wyoming.

Erwin Knippenberg is an economist at the World Bank in the poverty and equity global practice. He specializes in food security and social protection, the impact of climate change on the poor, use of big data and machine learning. He previously worked at a startup, using machine learning and data science to inform policy decisions in food security, public health, and climate resilience. Erwin has a PhD in Applied Economics from Cornell University, where he wrote his dissertation on resilience and food security in the context of climate change. Erwin also has an MSc in Economics for Development from Oxford and a joint BS/MA from Georgetown University's School of Foreign Service.

Derek Lee is a quantitative wildlife biologist and CEO of the Wild Nature Institute who has expertise in conservation demography and population ecology. He obtained his PhD in Biological Sciences,

Ecology, and Evolutionary Biology at Dartmouth College. Derek is also an Associate Research Professor at Pennsylvania State University. He received a Fulbright Fellowship to study African ungulates, and his current research investigates Masai giraffes and other large mammal populations within a human-impacted landscape in Tanzania. Derek has published more than 60 peer-reviewed scientific journal articles and book chapters, and he is co-editor of the book, *Tarangire: Human–Wildlife Co-existence in a Fragmented Ecosystem*.

Anne Marie Lennon obtained her medical degree from the Royal College of Surgeons in Ireland, and her PhD from University College Dublin. She completed a gastroenterology fellowship in the United Kingdom, and an advanced endoscopy fellowship at Johns Hopkins Hospital. She is a Professor of Medicine, Surgery, Radiology, and Oncology at the Johns Hopkins University School of Medicine. Dr. Lennon's clinical and research interests are focused on pre-cancerous lesions of the pancreas, early cancer detection and prevention.

Will Marshall obtained a PhD in Physics from the University of Oxford and a Master's in Physics with Space Science and Technology from the University of Leicester. He was also a Postdoctoral Fellow at George Washington University and Harvard. Will is Chairman, Co-Founder & CEO of Planet. Will is a scientist-turned-entrepreneur with extensive experience building and leading teams in the technology space. Prior to Planet, Will was a Scientist at NASA/USRA where he helped formulate the Small Spacecraft Office at NASA Ames Research Center, worked as a systems engineer on lunar orbiter mission "LADEE" and a member of the science team for the lunar impactor mission "LCROSS", served as Co-Principal Investigator on PhoneSat, and was the technical lead on research projects in space debris remediation. Will was recognized as a Young Global Leader by the World Economic Forum and serves on the board of the Open Lunar Foundation.

Maria Ana Martinez-Castellanos is a Professor of Pediatric Retinology, of the Retina Service at the Association to Prevent Blindness

in Mexico APEC, Hospital "Luis Sanchez Bulnes" from the National
Autonomous University of Mexico (UNAM). There, she directs a
private pediatric retina clinic that is orientated for both surgical and
medical diseases of the retina in the pediatric population in Toluca,
Mexico and runs the retinopathy of prematurity prevention pro-
gram at five different hospitals in Mexico City and Toluca, Mexico.
Dr. Martinez-Castellanos received her MD from the Autonomous
University of the State of Mexico UAEM in Toluca, Mexico. After
completing her Ophthalmology residency at the Central Military
Hospital of the University of the Mexican Army and Air Force
UDEFA, she went on to a fellowship in Vitreoretinal Surgery at the
Association to Prevent Blindness in Mexico APEC, Hospital "Luis
Sanchez Bulnes" and UNAM. She is a Mexican board-certified
ophthalmologist whose clinical practice involves the surgical and
medical management of adult and pediatric vitreoretinal disease;
her primary research interests focus on the pathogenesis and management of retinopathy of prematurity.

Mir Matin is an experienced researcher and manager with over
30 years of experience in geospatial information services. He currently works at the United Nations University Institute for Water
Environment and Health. Matin's previous roles include positions
at the International Centre for Integrated Mountain Development
in Nepal, the International Water Management Institute in Sri
Lanka, and the Center for Environmental and Geographic Information Services in Bangladesh. His expertise encompasses a broad
range of areas including water resources, hydroclimatic disaster
risk reduction, agriculture, food security, ecosystems, and climate
services. Mr. Matin holds an MS in Research in Glaciology degree
and a BSc in environmental science, both from Kathmandu University as well as a PhD in Forestry and Environmental Management from the University of New Brunswick. Prior to working in
ICIMOD, he worked for the Cryosphere Monitoring Project (CMP)
at Kathmandu University as a Research Associate.

Guillermo Monteoliva is an ophthalmologist who specializes in pediatric ophthalmology and treatment of retinopathy of

prematurity. He is on the staff at Hospital Italiano de Buenos Aires where he focuses on telemedicine and prevention of blindness. He received his MD from Universidad Nacional de La Plata, a Master's degree in tele-ophthalmology from Universidad Católica de Salta, and a Master's degree in Health Information from Instituto Universitario Hospital Italiano.

Christopher J.L. Murray is Chair of Health Metrics Sciences at the University of Washington and Director of the Institute for Health Metrics and Evaluation (IHME). His career has focused on improving population health worldwide through better evidence. A physician and health economist, his work has led to the development of innovative methods to strengthen health measurement, analyze the performance of health systems, understand the drivers of health, and produce forecasts of the future state of health. Dr. Murray also leads the Global Burden of Disease (GBD) collaboration, a systematic effort to quantify the comparative magnitude of health loss due to diseases, injuries, and risk factors by age, sex, and geography over time. The GBD is now a network of 10,600 scientists and decision-makers from 162 countries who together generate annually updated estimates. He is an elected member of the National Academy of Medicine (NAM) and the 2018 co-recipient of the John Dirks Canada Gairdner Global Health Award. Dr. Murray holds Bachelor of Arts and Science degrees from Harvard University, a DPhil in International Health Economics from Oxford University, and a medical degree from Harvard Medical School.

Kris Sankaran is an Assistant Professor with the Department of Statistics, University of Wisconsin-Madison and a Discovery Fellow with the Wisconsin Institute for Discovery. His group applies representation learning and interactive computing techniques to support ecological and biological problem-solving. He received a PhD degree in Statistics from Stanford University in 2018 where he investigated techniques for microbiome data integration and modeling. He was a postdoctoral researcher with the Mila-Quebec AI Institute, where he focused on the use of remote sensing to support societal response to climate change.

Margarita Santiago-Torres studied Human Biology at the University of Puerto Rico and obtained a PhD in Nutritional Sciences from the University of Wisconsin-Madison. She then completed an NCI-funded postdoctoral fellowship at Fred Hutch before transitioning into a Staff Scientist position. Currently, she is a Senior Staff Scientist in the HABIT lab at the Fred Hutch Cancer Center where her research focuses on the development, implementation, and dissemination of lifestyle behavioral interventions that are scalable and culturally appropriate among underserved populations.

Michael Scholtens is the Manager of Data and Analytics for The Carter Center facilitating data-driven programs across the Center's governance and public health projects. He has worked on projects addressing digital threats to democracy and conflict resolution in 15 countries and has a research interest in the monetization of misinformation online. He holds a Master's degree in analytics from Georgia Institute of Technology and a Master's degree in international relations of the Middle East with Arabic from The University of Edinburgh.

Jacob Shapiro is Professor of Politics and International Affairs at Princeton University. He co-founded and directs the Empirical Studies of Conflict Project, a multi-university consortium that studies politically motivated violence in countries around the world. His research focuses on conflict, development, security, and the information environment. He earned a PhD in Political Science and MA in Economics at Stanford University and a BA in Political Science at the University of Michigan. He is a veteran of the United States Navy.

Anshu Sharma has a background in urban planning obtained from the School of Planning and Architecture, New Delhi, and a PhD in global environmental studies from Kyoto University, Japan. In 1994 he co-founded the non-profit agency SEEDS (Sustainable Environment and Ecological Development Society), which is a global leader in disaster management. He is an expert on post-disaster reconstruction programs and pre-disaster educational activities and a co-founder of STS Global, a techno-environment catalyst that enables end-to-end humanitarian interventions at scale and makes them accessible to the last-mile citizen. Dr. Sharma has worked as a senior consultant and advisor on disaster management to various UN agencies, the World Bank, Asian Development Bank, International Red Cross, and international NGOs.

Tenzing Chogyal Sherpa is ethnic Sherpa and is the grandson of the last surviving member of the 1953 British Mount Everest expedition team. Now he works as a cryosphere analyst at ICIMOD. He has a MRes in glaciology and a BSc in environmental science from Kathmandu University. His research interests focus on understanding the dynamics of glaciers in the HKH region and their evolution with the changing climate. He is also very keen on understanding how these changes would impact people living in mountain regions, specifically in the context of glacial hazards.

Finu Shrestha is a Remote Sensing and Geo-information Analyst at ICIMOD in Nepal. She has 14 years of experience working on cryosphere research in Hindu Kush Himalaya and glacial-associated hazards such as glacial lake outburst floods (GLOFs) in High Mountain Asia. She holds an MSc in Hydrology and Meteorology from Tribhuvan University, Nepal. She has numerous publications, technical reports, training manuals, and peer-reviewed papers to her credit.

Mark Spalding obtained an MA in Zoology and PhD in Biogeography from the University of Cambridge. He is a Senior Scientist for The Nature Conservancy and an Honorary Research Fellow at the University of Cambridge. For the last 15 years his work has focused on understanding, modeling, and mapping the value of nature to people. This work has included the development of recreation and tourism values, where Mark pioneered global approaches, drawing on a combination of big data and expert knowledge to understand the value of coral reefs and mangrove forests, with ongoing work addressing recreational fishing.

Marci Hepner Strong obtained a Bachelor of Science in applied and computational mathematics with an emphasis in machine learning from Brigham Young University. She is currently a data scientist on the update platform team within Windows where she optimizes the update experience to promote user adoption and productivity. In addition to her research in medical computer vision, she has collaborated with the AI for Health team since 2020 on a variety of natural language processing projects that have empowered others to take charge of their health.

Brie Sullivan received her Master's Degree in Cognitive Psychology from Pennsylvania State University and her Project Management Professional certification from the Project Management Institute. She is the Project Manager for the HABIT Group where she manages the group's research administration, operating procedures, and randomized clinical trial development and execution.

Anusua Trivedi received her Master's of Science in Computer Science from the University of Utah. She is Senior Director of Applied AI at Flipkart US R&D. Anusua leads the charge in spearheading GenAI products and enhancing chatbot capabilities using advanced ML, deep learning, and generative AI algorithms. In her previous role as a data science leader at Microsoft, she helped grow the impactful AI for Good initiative, positioning Microsoft as a leader in the AI space.

Kevin Xu is a Senior Software Engineer at GitHub. At GitHub, he focuses on projects related to building trust through transparency, contributing his skills in data analysis/visualization, full stack engineering, and legal research. He holds a Juris Doctor from Berkeley Law and a Bachelor of Science in Biology from UC San Diego. Previously, he served as a Clinical Supervising Attorney at Berkeley Law.

Andrew Zolli received a BA in Cognitive and Computer Science at Vassar College, and did graduate studies in foresight at the University of Houston. Andrew is Chief Impact Officer at Planet. With more than 20 years' experience working at the intersection of technology, social, and ecological change, he previously served as the

Executive Director and Curator of PopTech, a network of scientists, humanitarians, technologists, designers, innovators, corporate, and governmental leaders who together explored the social and environmental impacts of technology. Andrew is the author of the critically-acclaimed book *Resilience: Why Things Bounce Back.* He has advised a wide array of governments, NGOs, foundations, startups, and corporations on their sustainability and social impact programs. Andrew also serves on the global Board of Directors of Human Rights Watch.

Microsoft AI For Good Lab, July 2023 (Pedro Costa Galiana).

Index